FIRST YEAR FOUNDATIONS FOR TOTAL SUCCESS

D1299616

Co-edited by

Melissa Grant
Michelle Relyea

Long Island University

KENDALL/HUNT PUBLISHING COMPANY
4050 Westmark Drive   Dubuque, Iowa 52002

Interior Photos by Katie Countryman

Copyright © 2006 by Kendall/Hunt Publishing Company

ISBN 13: 978-0-7575-3210-8
ISBN 10: 0-7575-3210

Printed in the United States of America
10 9 8 7 6 5 4 3 2 1

CONTENTS

May 9, 2006

Welcome to the Brooklyn Campus of Long Island University! We are confident that you made the right decision in choosing to become students of our campus community.

The mission of the Freshman Program is to provide all new students with a solid foundation for *academic, professional,* and *social success.* Through credit bearing courses, special events, workshops, publications, and peer mentoring, the Freshman Program offers new students personal support and guidance in developing abilities, identifying talents, exploring academic and professional opportunities, and forming meaningful relationships. It is the goal of the Freshman Program to help all new students acclimate to university life and ensure that they become an integral part of the LIU Brooklyn Campus.

Our freshman seminar course, Orientation Seminar 1, is designed with this mission and these goals in mind. Each workshop in this course aims to help you attain success in all of your endeavors. Your Orientation Seminar instructor's role is not only to support your achievements during class time, but also to be your personal mentor during your entire first year of college.

It is our hope that this book will provide you and your classmates with the information, incentive, and inspiration you need to begin your LIU years on a strong note. By choosing LIU Brooklyn, you've already taken the most important step. Now get ready to achieve your goals and make your dreams a reality!

Melissa Grant
Freshman Program, Associate Director
Academic & Instructional Resources
Long Island University
Brooklyn Campus

Michelle Relyea
Dean
Academic and Instructional Resources
Long Island University
Brooklyn Campus

CHAPTER 1
Understanding Motivation

Chapter Focus

Read to answer these key questions:

- What do I want from college?
- What is the value of a college education?
- How do I choose my major and career?
- How can I motivate myself to be successful?
- How can I begin habits that lead to success?
- How is persistence a key to success?

Most students attend college with dreams of making their lives better. Some students are there to explore interests and possibilities, and others have more defined career goals.

Being successful in college and attaining your dreams begins with motivation. It provides the energy or drive to find your direction and to reach your goals. Without motivation, it is difficult to accomplish anything.

Not everyone is successful in college. As a freshman in college, I attended an orientation in which I was told to look at the student to the left and the student to the right of me. The speaker said that one of us would not make it through the freshman year. I remember telling myself that the speaker must have been talking about one of the other two students and not me. That was the beginning of my motivation to be successful in college. Unfortunately about one-third of college students drop out in the first year. Forty percent of students who start college do not finish their degree. Having a good understanding of your reasons for attending college, your career goals, and how to motivate yourself will help you to reach your dreams.

◼ What Do I Want from College?

Succeeding in college requires time and effort. You will have to give up some of your time spent on leisure activities and working. You will give up some time spent with your friends and families. Making sacrifices and working hard is easier if you know what you want to achieve through your efforts. One of the first steps in motivating yourself to be successful in college is to have a clear and specific understanding of your reasons for attending college. Are you attending college as a way to obtain a satisfying career? Is financial security one of your goals? Will you feel more satisfied if you are living up to your potential? What are your hopes and dreams, and how will college help you to achieve your goals?

When you are having difficulties or doubts about your ability to finish your college education, remember your hopes and dreams and your plans for the future. It is a good idea to write these ideas down, think about them, and revise them from time to time. Complete the exercise "What Do I Want from College?" located at the end of this chapter.

◼ What Is the Value of a College Education?

Many college students say that getting a satisfying job that pays well and achieving financial security are important reasons for attending college. By going to college you can get a job that pays more per hour. You can work fewer hours to earn a living and have more time for leisure activities. You can spend your time at work doing something that you like to do. A report issued by the Census Bureau in 2002 listed the following education and income statistics for all races and both genders throughout the United States.[1] Lifetime income assumes that a person works forty years before retirement.

[1.] U.S. Census Bureau, "The Big Payoff: Educational Attainment and Synthetic Estimates of Work-Life Earnings," July 2002, retrieved from http://www.census.gov

Average Earnings Based on Education Level		
Education	**Yearly Income**	**Lifetime Income**
High school graduate	$30,400	$1,226,575
Some college, no degree	$36,800	$1,494,989
Associate degree	$38,200	$1,563,702
Bachelor's degree	$52,200	$2,140,864
Master's degree	$62,300	$2,463,059
Professional degree	$109,600	$4,411,542

Notice that income rises with the educational level. A person with a bachelor's degree earns almost twice as much as a high school graduate. Of course these are average figures across the nation. Some individuals earn higher or lower salaries. People have assumed that you would certainly be rich if you were a millionaire. College won't make you an instant millionaire, but over a lifetime you earn over a million and a half dollars by having an associate's degree. People fantasize about winning the lottery. The reality is that the probability of winning the lottery is very low. In the long run, you have a better chance of improving your financial status by going to college.

Let's do some further comparisons. A high school graduate earns an average of $1,226,575 over a lifetime. A college graduate with a bachelor's degree earns $2,140,864 over a lifetime. A college graduate earns $914,289 more than a high school graduate does over a lifetime. So how much is a college degree worth? It is worth $914,289 over a lifetime. Would you go to college if someone offered to pay you $914,289? Here are some more interesting figures we can derive from the table above:

Completing one college course is worth $22,857.
($914,289 divided by 40 courses in a bachelor's degree)

Going to class for one hour is worth $476.
($22,857 divided by 48 hours in a semester class)

Would you take a college class if someone offered to pay you $22,857? Would you go to class today for one hour if someone offered to pay you $476? Of course, if this sounds too good to be true, remember that you will receive these "payments" over a working lifetime of forty years.

Money is only one of the values of going to college. Can you think of other reasons to attend college? Here are some less tangible reasons . . .

- College helps you to develop your potential.
- College opens the door to many satisfying careers.
- College prepares you to be an informed citizen and fully participate in the democratic process.
- College increases your understanding and widens your view of the world.
- College allows you to participate in a conversation with the great minds of all times and places. For example, reading the work of Plato is like having a conversation with that famous philosopher. You can continue great conversations with your faculty and fellow students.
- College helps to increase your confidence, self-esteem, and self-respect.

■ Choosing a Major and Career

Having a definite major and career choice is a good motivation for completing your college education. It is difficult to put in the work necessary to be successful if you do not have a clear picture of your future career; however, three out of four college students are undecided about their major. Depending on the college, 30 to 75 percent of a graduating class will change their major two or more times.[2] Unclear or indefinite career goals are some of the most significant factors that identify students at risk of dropping out of college.[3] Students often drop out or extend their stay in college because they are uncertain about their major or want to change their major. Choosing an appropriate college major is one of the most difficult and important decisions that college students can make.

How do people choose a career? There are many complex factors that go into your career choice. This course will help you to become aware of these factors and to think critically about them in order to make a good choice about your career. Some of the factors involved in choosing a career include

Heredity. You inherit genes from your parents that play a role in shaping who you are.

Intelligence. Every person has a unique mixture of talents and skills. You can work to develop these skills.

Experience. Your experiences can either build your self-confidence or cause you to doubt your abilities.

Environment. What careers have you observed in your environment? Maybe your father was a doctor and you grew up familiar with careers in medicine. Your parents may have encouraged you to choose a particular career. You may want to learn about other possibilities.

Social roles. Maybe you learned that men are engineers and women are teachers because your father is an engineer and your mother is a teacher. It is important to think critically about traditional roles so that your choices are not limited.

Learning. What you have learned will play a part in your career decision. You may need to learn new behaviors and establish new habits. How you learn (your learning style) influences career choice.

Relationships. We sometimes choose careers to enhance relationships. For example, you may choose a career that gives you time to spend with your family or with people who are important to you.

Stress. Our ability to cope with stress plays a part in career choice. Some enjoy challenges; others value peace of mind.

Health. Good health increases career options and enjoyment of life.

Personality. Your personality is a major factor influencing which career you might enjoy.

Values. What you value determines which career you will find satisfying.

Culture. Your culture has an influence on which careers you value.

---

[2] W. Lewallen, "The Impact of Being Undecided on College Persistence," *Journal of College Student Development 34* (1993): 103–12.

[3] Marsha Fralick, "College Success: A Study of Positive and Negative Attrition," *Community College Review 20* (1993): 29–36.

Factors in Career Choice[4]

Traditions. Traditions often guide career choice.

Beliefs. Your beliefs about yourself and the world determine your behavior and career choice.

Interests. If you choose a career that matches your interests, you can find satisfaction in your career.

How can you choose the major that is best for you? The best way is to first understand yourself; become aware of your personality traits, interests, preferred lifestyle, values, gifts, and talents. The next step is to do career research to determine the career that best matches your personal characteristics. Next, plan your education to prepare for your career. Here are some questions to answer to help you understand yourself and what career and major would be best for you.

To learn about yourself, explore these areas:

- **What is my personality type?** Psychologists have studied personality types and career choice. Assessing your personality type will give you some general ideas about careers that will give you satisfaction.
- **What are my interests?** Knowing about your interests is important in choosing a satisfying career.
- **What kind of lifestyle do I prefer?** Think about how you want to balance work, leisure, and family.
- **What are my values?** Knowing what you value (what is most important to you) will help you make good decisions about your life.
- **What are my gifts and talents?** Identifying your special abilities will help you to find a career that matches your talents.

---

[4] Ideas from Lina Rocha, Personal Development Instructor, Cuyamaca College, El Cajon, CA.

To learn about career possibilities, research the following:

- **What career matches my personality, interests, aptitudes, and values?** Learn how to do career research to find the best career for you. Find a career that has a good outlook for the future.
- **How can I plan my education to get the career I want?** Once you have identified your area of interest, consult your college catalog or advisor to make an educational plan that matches your career goals.

By following the above steps, you can find the major that is best for you and minimize the time you spend in college.

■ How to Be Motivated

There are many ways to be motivated.

- You can **apply the principles of learning** and use positive reinforcement as a motivation to establish desirable behaviors.
- You can **improve your concentration** and motivation for studying by managing your external and internal distractions.
- You can be motivated by internal or external factors called **intrinsic or extrinsic motivation**.
- You can become aware of your **locus of control**, or where you place the responsibility for control over your life. If you are in control, you are more likely to be motivated to succeed.
- You can join a club, organization, or athletic team. **Affiliation motivation** involves taking part in school activities that increase your motivation to stay in college.
- **Achievement** and competition are motivating to some students.

Let's examine each type of motivation in more detail and see if some of these ideas can be useful to you.

Applying the Principles of Learning

Psychologists believe that much of our behavior is learned. Understanding these principles of learning can give you some powerful tools for changing your own behavior. We frequently learn through a process called **operant conditioning**. A simple definition of operant conditioning is that behavior is increased or decreased depending on the consequences of the behavior. For example, if you sit in a particular seat in the classroom (your behavior) and a friendly person to whom you enjoy talking sits next to you (consequence), you are more likely to sit in that same seat again (the behavior is increased). If you study for the test and receive an A, you will be more likely to study in the future. In operant conditioning, the consequences of a behavior lead to a change in the probability of its occurrence. We are always affected by the consequences of our behavior and are constantly in the process of learning.

If the consequences of your behavior are positive, you are positively reinforced as in our examples above. You are more likely to continue the behavior. If the consequences of your behavior are negative, that behavior is less likely to occur. If you sit next to a person who is bothersome, you will probably try to avoid the situation by finding a different seat next time. If you receive a traffic ticket and have to pay a large fine, you are less likely to repeat the offense.

You can use **positive reinforcement** on yourself to manage your own behavior. If you want to increase your studying behavior, follow it by a positive consequence or a reward. Think about what is rewarding to you (watching TV, playing sports, enjoying your favorite music). You could study (your behavior) and then watch a TV program (the positive reinforcement). The timing of your reward is important. To be effective, it must immediately follow the behavior. If you watch TV and then study, you may not get around to studying. If you watch the TV program tomorrow or next week, it is not a strong reinforcement because it is not an immediate reward.

Be careful about the kinds of rewards you use so that you do not get into habits that are detrimental to your health. If you use food as a reward for studying, you may increase your studying behavior, but you may also gain a few pounds. Using alcohol or drugs as a reward can start an addiction. Buying yourself a reward can ruin your budget. Good rewards do not involve too many calories, cost too much money, or involve alcohol or drugs.

To understand positive reinforcement, it is interesting to think about certain behaviors that your pets have and try to figure out how they were rewarded to learn that behavior. I have a cat that loves getting attention and being petted. When I would come home, the cat would meet me in the driveway looking for attention. The cat would roll over (behavior) and I would pet the cat (positive reinforcement). Now when I come home, the cat meets me in the driveway and rolls over a dozen times. People walk by and wonder how the cat learned to do that trick.

You can also use a negative consequence to decrease a behavior. If you touch a hot stove and get burned, you quickly learn not to do it again. You could decide to miss your favorite television program if you do not complete your studying. However, this is not fun and you may feel deprived. You might even rebel and watch your favorite TV show anyway. See if you can find a way to use positive reinforcement (a reward) for increasing a behavior that is beneficial to you rather than using a negative consequence.

When we are young, our attitudes toward education are largely shaped by positive or negative reinforcement. My parents always praised me for being a good reader, so I became a good reader. Maybe a teacher embarrassed you because of your math skills and you learned to be anxious about math. Think about areas of your education in which you excel, and see if you can recall someone praising or otherwise reinforcing that behavior. If you are a good athlete, did someone praise your athletic ability when you were younger? How was it rewarded? If you are not good at math, what were some early messages about your math performance? These early messages have a powerful influence on later behavior. You may need to put in some effort to learn new and more beneficial behaviors.

As a college student, you can use a reward as a powerful motivator. Praise yourself and think positively about your achievements in college even if the achievements come in small steps.

Improving Your Concentration

Have you ever watched lion tamers concentrate? If their attention wanders, they are likely to become the lion's dinner. Skilled athletes, musicians, and artists don't have any trouble concentrating. They are motivated to concentrate. Think about a time when you were totally focused on what you were doing. You were motivated to continue. You can improve your concentration and motivation for studying by managing your external and internal distractions.

Manage your external environment. Your environment will either help you to study or distract you from studying. We are all creatures of habit. If you try to study in front of the TV, you will watch TV because that is what you are accustomed to doing in front of the TV. If you study in bed, you will fall asleep because your body associates the bed with sleeping. If you study in the kitchen, you will eat. Find an environment that minimizes distractions. One idea is to study in the library. In the library, there are many cues that tell you to study. There are books and learning resources and other people studying. It will be easier to concentrate in that environment.

You may be able to set up a learning environment in your home. Find a place where you can place a desk or table, your computer, and your materials for learning. When you are in this place, use it for learning and studying only. When you are studying, focus on studying. Make it a habit to study in this place. When you are relaxing, go somewhere else and focus on relaxing.

Because of past experiences and learning, our environment has a powerful influence on our behavior. Choose the right environment for what you are doing. Don't confuse yourself by trying to study in front of the TV! Don't ruin your enjoyment of TV by trying to study while watching it. When you are relaxing, focus on relaxing and don't worry about studying. When you are studying, focus on studying and don't get distracted thinking about relaxing.

Manage your internal distractions. Many of our distractions come from within ourselves. Here are some techniques for managing these internal distractions:

1. **Be here now.**
   Choose where you will place your attention. If you are in a lecture and you begin to think about eating cookies, notice that you are thinking about cookies and bring your attention back to the lecture. You can tell yourself, "Be here now." If you try to force yourself not to think about cookies, you will think about them even more. Just notice when your attention has drifted away and choose to bring it gently back to where you want it. This will take some practice since attention tends to wander often.

2. **The spider technique.**
   If you hold a tuning fork to a spider web, the web vibrates and the spider senses that it has caught a tasty morsel and goes seeking the food. After awhile, the spider discovers that there is no food and learns to ignore the vibrations caused by the tuning fork. When you are sitting in the library studying and someone walks in talking and laughing, you can choose to pay attention either to the distraction or to studying. Decide to continue to pay attention to studying.

3. **Set up a worry time.**
   Many times worries interfere with concentration. Some people have been successful in setting up a worry time. Here's how it works:

   ■ Set a specific time each day for worrying.

   ■ When worries distract you from your studies, remind yourself that you have set aside time for worrying.

   ■ Tell yourself, "Be here now."

   ■ Keep your worry appointment.

   ■ During your worry time, try to find some solutions or take some steps to resolve the things that cause you to worry.

4. **Use the checkmark technique.**
   When you find yourself distracted from a lecture or from studying, place a checkmark on a piece of paper and refocus your attention on the task at hand. You will find that your checkmarks decrease over time.

5. **Increase your activity.**
   Take a break. Stretch and move. Read and listen actively by asking questions about the material and answering them as you read or listen.

6. **Find an incentive or reward.**
   Tell yourself that when you finish, you will do something enjoyable.

7. **Change topics.**
   Changing study topics may help you to concentrate and avoid fatigue.

Intrinsic or Extrinsic Motivation

Intrinsic motivation comes from within. It means that you do an activity because you enjoy it or find personal meaning in it. With intrinsic motivation, the nature of the activity itself or the consequences of the activity motivate you. For example, let's say that I am interested in learning to play the piano. I am motivated to practice playing the piano because I like the sound of the piano and feel very satisfied when I can play music that I enjoy. I practice because I like to practice, not because I have to practice. When I get tired or frustrated, I work through it or put it aside and come back to it because I want to learn to play the piano well.

You can be intrinsically motivated to continue in college because you enjoy learning and find the college experience satisfying. Look for ways to enjoy college and to find some personal satisfaction in it. If you enjoy college, it becomes easier to do the work required to be successful. Think about what you say to yourself about college. If you are saying negative things such as, "I don't want to be here," it will be difficult to continue.

Extrinsic motivation comes as a result of an external reward from someone else. Examples of extrinsic rewards are certificates, bonuses, money, praise, and recognition. Taking the piano example again, let's say that I want my child to play the piano. The child does not know if he or she would like to play the piano. I give the child a reward for practicing the piano. I could pay the child for practicing or give praise for doing a good job. There are two possible outcomes of the extrinsic reward. After awhile, the child may gain skills and confidence and come to enjoy playing the piano. The extrinsic reward is no longer necessary because the child is now intrinsically motivated. Or the child may decide that he or she does not like to play the piano. The extrinsic reward is no longer effective in motivating the child to play the piano.

You can use extrinsic rewards to motivate yourself to be successful in college. Remind yourself of the payoff for getting a college degree: earning more money, having a satisfying career, being able to purchase a car and a house. Extrinsic rewards can be a first step in motivating yourself to attend college. With experience and achievement, you may come to like going to college and may become intrinsically motivated to continue your college education.

If you use intrinsic motivation to achieve your goal, you will be happier and more successful. If you do something like playing the piano because you enjoy it, you are more likely to spend the time necessary to practice to achieve your goal. If you view college as something that you enjoy and as valuable to you, it is easier to spend the time to do the required studying. When you get tired or frustrated, tell yourself that you are doing a good job (praise yourself) and think of the positive reasons that you want to get a college education.

Locus of Control

Being aware of the concept of locus of control is another way of understanding motivation. The word *locus* means place. Locus of control is where you place the responsibility for control over your life. In other words, who is in charge? If you place the responsibility on yourself and believe that you have control over your life, you have internal locus of control. If you place the responsibility on others and think that luck or fate determines your future, you have external locus of control. Some people use internal or external locus of control in combination or favor one type in certain situations. If you favor an internal locus of control, you believe that to a great extent your actions determine your future. Studies have shown that students who use an internal locus of control are likely to have higher achievement in college.[5] In summary, here are the characteristics of students with internal and external locus of control.

Students with an internal locus of control

- believe that they are in control of their lives.
- understand that grades are directly related to the amount of study invested.
- are self-motivated.
- learn from their mistakes by figuring out what went wrong and how to fix the problem.
- think positively and try to make the best of each situation.
- rely on themselves to find something interesting in the class and learn the material.

Students with an external locus of control

- believe that their lives are largely a result of luck, fate, or chance.
- think that teachers give grades rather than students earn grades.
- rely on external motivation from teachers or others.
- look for someone to blame when they make a mistake.
- think negatively and believe they are victims of circumstance.
- rely on the teacher to make the class interesting and to teach the material.

Affiliation

Human beings are social creatures who generally feel the need to be part of a group. This tendency is called affiliation motivation. People like to be part of a community, family, organization, or culture. You can apply this motivation technique in college by participating in student activities on campus. Join an athletic team, participate in a club, or join the student government. In this way you will feel like you are part of a group and will have a sense of belonging. College is more than going to class; it is participating in social activities, making new friends, and sharing new ideas. Twenty years after you graduate from college, you are more likely to remember the conversations held with college friends than the detailed content of classes. College provides the opportunity to become part of a new group and to start lifelong friendships.

Achievement

Some students are motivated by achievement. Individuals who are achievement motivated have a need for success in school, sports, careers, and other competitive situations. These individuals enjoy getting recognition for their success. They are often known as the best student, the outstanding athlete, or the employee of the year. These persons are attracted to careers that provide rewards for individual achievement, such as sales, law, architecture, engineering, and business. They work hard in order to enjoy the rewards of their efforts. In college, some students work very hard to achieve high grades and then take pride in their accomplishments. One disadvantage of using this type of moti-

---

[5] M. J. Findlay and H. M. Cooper, "Locus of Control and Academic Achievement: A Literature Review," *Journal of Personality and Social Psychology* 44 (1983): 419–27.

vation is that it can lead to excess stress. These students often need to remember to balance their time between work, school, family, and leisure so that they do not become too stressed by the need to achieve.

Success Is a Habit

We establish habits by taking small actions each day. Through repetition, these individual actions become habits. I once visited the Golden Gate Bridge in San Francisco and saw a cross section of the cable used to support the bridge. It was made of small metal strands twisted with other strands. Then the cables were twisted together to make a stronger cable. Habits are a lot like cables. We start with one small action and each successive action makes the habit stronger. Have you ever stopped to think that success can be a habit? We all have learned patterns of behavior that either help us to be successful or that interfere with our success. With some effort and some basic understanding of behavior modification, you can choose to establish some new behaviors that lead to success or to get rid of behaviors that interfere with it.

Ways to Change a Habit

You can establish new habits that lead to your success. Once a habit is established, it can become a pattern of behavior that you do not need to think about very much. For example, new students often need to get into the habit of studying. Here is an outline of steps that can be helpful to establish new behaviors.

1. **State the problem.**
   What are your roadblocks or obstacles? What new habit would you like to start? What bad habit would you like to change? Be truthful about it. This is sometimes the most difficult step.

2. **Count the behavior.**
   How often do you do this behavior? For example, if you are trying to stop smoking, it is helpful to count the number of cigarettes you smoke each day. If you are trying to improve your diet, write down everything that you eat each day. If you are trying to establish a pattern of studying, write down how much time you spend studying each day. Sometimes just getting an awareness of your habit is enough to begin to make some changes.

3. **Change one small behavior at a time.**
   If you think about climbing a mountain, the task can seem overwhelming. However, you can take the first step. If you can change one small behavior, you can gain the confidence to change another. For example, a goal to have a better diet is broad and vague. A good way to make it small is to say, "I plan to eat more fruits and vegetables each day." State the behavior you would like to change. Make it small.

4. **State in a positive way the behavior you wish to establish.**
   For example, instead of the negative statement "I will not eat junk food," change it to "I plan to eat fruits and vegetables each day."

5. **Picture in your mind the actions you might take.**
   For example: I see myself in the grocery store buying fruits and vegetables. I see myself packing these fruits and vegetables in my lunch. I see myself putting these foods in a place where I will notice them.

6. **Practice the behavior for ten days.**

   The first three days are the most difficult. If you fail, don't give up. Just realize that you are human and keep trying for ten days. Think positively that you can be successful. Write a journal or note on your calendar about what you have accomplished each day.

7. **Find a reward for your behavior.**

   Remember that we tend to repeat behaviors that are positively reinforced. Find rewards that do not involve too many calories, don't cost too much money, and don't involve alcohol or drugs. Also, rewards are most effective if they directly follow the behavior you wish to reinforce.

■ Keys to Success: Persistence

There is an old saying that persistence will get you almost anything eventually. This saying applies to your success in college. The first two to six weeks of college are a critical time in which many students drop out. Realize that college is a new experience and that you will face new challenges and growth experiences. Make plans to persist, especially in the first few weeks. Get to know a college counselor or advisor. These professionals can help you to get started in the right classes and answer any questions you might have. It is important to make a connection with a counselor or faculty member so that you feel comfortable in college and have the resources to obtain needed help. Plan to enroll on time so that you do not have to register late. It is crucial to attend the first class. In the first class, the professor explains the class requirements and expectations and sets the tone for the class. You may even get dropped from the class if you are not there on the first day. Get into the habit of studying right away. Make studying a habit that you start immediately at the beginning of the semester or quarter. If you can make it through the first six weeks, it is likely that you can finish the semester and complete your college education.

It has been said that 90 percent of success is just showing up. Any faculty member will tell you that the number one reason for students dropping out of college is lack of attendance. They know that when students miss three classes in a row, they are not likely to return. Even very capable students who miss class may find that they are lost when they come back. Many students are simply afraid to return. Classes such as math and foreign languages are sequential, and it is very difficult to make up work after an absence. One of the most important ways you can be successful is to make a habit of consistently showing up for class.

You will also need commitment to be successful. Commitment is a promise to yourself to follow through with something. In athletics, it is not necessarily the one with the best physical skills that makes the best athlete. Commitment and practice make a great athlete. Commitment means doing whatever is necessary to succeed. Like the good athlete, make a commitment to accomplishing your goals. Spend the time necessary to be successful in your studies.

When you face difficulties, persistence and commitment are especially important. History is full of famous people who contributed to society through persistence and commitment. Consider these facts about Abraham Lincoln, for example.

- Failed in business at age 21.
- Was defeated in a legislative race at age 22.
- Failed again in business at age 24.
- Overcame the death of his sweetheart at age 26.

- Had a nervous breakdown at age 27.
- Lost a congressional race at age 34.
- Lost a congressional race at age 36.
- Lost a senatorial race at age 45.
- Failed in an effort to become Vice-President at age 47.
- Lost a senatorial race at age 49.
- Was elected President of the United States at age 52.[6]

You will face difficulties along the way in any worthwhile venture. The successful person keeps on trying. There are some precautions about persistence, however. Make sure that the goal you are trying to reach is attainable and valuable to you. As you learn more about yourself, you may want to change your goals. Also, persistence can be misguided if it involves other people. For example, if you decide that you want to marry someone and this someone does not want to marry you, it is better to focus your energy and attention on a different goal.

One of the best ways to be persistent is to accomplish your goals one step at a time. If you look at a mountain, it may seem too high to climb, but you can do it one step at a time. Araceli Segarra became the first Spanish woman to climb Mount Everest. At 29,028 feet, Mount Everest is the highest mountain in the world. It is so high that you need an oxygen tank to breathe at the top. So how did Araceli climb the mountain? She says that it took strength and concentration. She put one foot in front of the other. When she was near the top of the mountain, she was more tired than she had ever been in her life. She told herself that she would take ten more steps. When she took ten steps she said, "I'm OK. I made it." Then she took ten more steps until she reached the top of the mountain.

The goal of getting a college education may seem like a mountain that is difficult to climb. Break it into smaller steps that you can accomplish. See your college counselor or advisor, register for classes, attend the first class, read the first chapter, do the first assignment, and you will be on the road to your success. Then continue to break tasks into small, achievable steps and continue from one step to the next. And remember, persistence will get you almost anything eventually.

---

[6] Anthony Robbins, *Unlimited Power* (New York: Ballantine Books, 1986), 73.

What Do I Want from College?

Read the following list and place a checkmark next to your reasons for attending college. Think about why you are attending college and add your own personal reasons to the list.

_____ 1. To have financial security

_____ 2. To find a satisfying career

_____ 3. To explore possibilities provided by college

_____ 4. To expand my options

_____ 5. To become an educated person

_____ 6. To figure out what I want to do with my life

_____ 7. To develop my potential

_____ 8. To become a role model for my children

_____ 9. To make my parents happy

_____ 10. To respect myself

_____ 11. To feel good about myself

_____ 12. To see if I can do it

_____ 13. To meet interesting people

_____ 14. To have something to do and prevent boredom

_____ 15. To become the best I can be

_____ 16. To have better job opportunities

_____ 17. To have no regrets later on

_____ 18. To prepare for a good job or profession

_____ 19. To have job security

_____ 20. To gain confidence in myself

_____ 21. To get a degree

_____ 22. To gain a greater understanding of the world

_____ 23. To have fun

_____ 24. To understand myself

_____ 25. To learn how to think

_____ 26. To enjoy what I do for a living

_____ 27. To reach my potential

_____ 28. Because my parents want me to get a degree

_____ 29. For my own personal satisfaction

_____ 30. To make a difference in other people's lives

_____ 31. To have a position of power

_____ 32. To have respect

_____ 33. To have prestige

_____ 34. To have time and money for travel

_____ 35. To acquire knowledge

_____ 36. _____

_____ 37. _____

What are your top six reasons for attending college? If you are tempted to give up on your college education, read this list and think about the reasons you have listed below.

1. _____   4. _____

2. _____   5. _____

3. _____   6. _____

■ Measure Your Success

You will be asked to do a self-assessment on factors leading to success in college at the beginning and at the end of this course. The following is a pretest to get an idea about your success skills at the present time. Think about these statements and be honest in your answers.

Read each description of a skill needed for college success. Use the following scale to rate yourself in each area. Write your rating on the line next to each statement.

> 5   I am very confident of my skills in this area.
>
> 4   I have good skills in this area.
>
> 3   I can get by.
>
> 2   My skills are a little weak.
>
> 1   I need help in this area to be successful.

_____ 1. I am motivated to be successful in college. I know my reasons for attending college and can use motivation techniques to accomplish my goals.

_____ 2. I can remember what I have studied. I am familiar with memory techniques and can apply them to learning many different kinds of materials.

_____ 3. I am a good reader. I read quickly, have good comprehension, and can remember what I have read.

_____ 4. I am familiar with my learning style and know how I learn best. I am confident in my ability to learn.

_____ 5. I know my personality type and how it relates to my career choice.

_____ 6. I know my highest interests and can choose a career that matches my interests.

_____ 7. I know what is most important to me and can make a list of these values.

_____ 8. I can make a list of my gifts and talents and match them to a career.

_____ 9. I have a mental picture of my ideal lifestyle.

_____ 10. I have a definite major in mind and know that it matches my personality, interests, aptitudes, and values.

_____ 11. I have a list of my lifetime goals.

_____ 12. I can manage my time to accomplish the goals I have set for myself.

_____ 13. I know how to prepare for tests and I am a good test taker.

_____ 14. I have good communication skills.

_____ 15. I am in good mental and physical health.

_____ 16. I know how to manage stress.

_____ 17. I am good at money management and know how to pay for college.

_____ 18. I am open-minded and have an appreciation for many different kinds of people.

_____ 19. I am a good writer and feel confident that I can write a good term paper.

_____ 20. I am familiar with how to do career research and how to find out which careers have a good outlook for the future.

_____ Total Points

If you scored

90–100	You are very confident of your skills for success in college. Maybe you do not need this class?
80–89	You have good skills for success in college. You can always improve.
70–79	You have average skills for success in college. You will definitely benefit from taking this class.
Below 70	You need some help to survive college. You are in the right place to begin.

■ Motivation

1. Think of some rewards that you can give yourself to increase your motivation for studying. Remember that good rewards do not have too many calories, don't cost too much money, and don't involve alcohol or drugs.

2. Look at the list of your reasons for going to college. Which are intrinsic motivators (you do them because you want to)?

3. Looking at your reasons for attending college, which of your reasons are extrinsic motivators (you do them because someone else wants you to do them or you do them to obtain a reward)?

■ Internal or External Locus of Control

Decide whether the statement represents an internal or external locus of control and put a checkmark in the appropriate column.

Internal   External

_____   _____   1. Much of what happens to us is due to fate, chance, or luck.

_____   _____   2. Grades depend on how much work you put into it.

_____   _____   3. If I do badly on the test, it is usually because the teacher is unfair.

_____   _____   4. If I do badly on the test, it is because I didn't study or didn't understand the material.

_____   _____   5. I often get blamed for things that are not my fault.

_____   _____   6. I try to make the best of the situation.

_____   _____   7. It is impossible to get a good grade if you have a bad instructor.

_____   _____   8. I can be successful through hard work.

_____   _____   9. If the teacher is not there telling me what to do, I have a hard time doing my work.

_____   _____   10. I can motivate myself to study.

_____   _____   11. If the teacher is boring, I probably won't do well in class.

_____   _____   12. I can find something interesting about each class.

_____   _____   13. When bad things are going to happen, there is not much you can do about it.

_____   _____   14. I create my own destiny.

_____   _____   15. Teachers should motivate the students to study.

_____   _____   16. I have a lot of choice about what happens in my life.

As you probably noticed, the even-numbered statements represent internal locus of control. The odd-numbered statements represent external locus of control. Remember that students with an internal locus of control have a greater chance of success in college. It is important to see yourself as responsible for your own success and achievement and to believe that with effort you can achieve your goals.

Name: _____ Date: _____

■ Behaviors Leading to Success

Part 1. Think of some behaviors or actions that lead to success for you. Think about success in your personal life, in college, and on the job. What activities help you achieve your goals? For example, you might be successful when you get enough rest, write down assignments, and show up to work on time. Think positively about what works well for you and list ten behaviors here.

I am successful when I

1. _____

2. _____

3. _____

4. _____

5. _____

6. _____

7. _____

8. _____

9. _____

10. _____

Part 2. It is more difficult to think about behaviors that lead to failure. These are actions that interfere with your success. Again consider school, work, and personal life. For example, you might observe that you are not successful when you do not eat right, study at the last minute, and are tired at work. List ten behaviors that interfere with your success.

I am not successful when I:

1. _____

2. _____

3. _____

4. _____

5. _____

6. _____

7. _____

8. _____

9. _____

10. _____

Part 3. Look at the two lists above and choose two behaviors you would like to change or establish as a good habit. List them below.

I would like to

1. _____

2. _____

Use the following exercise on how to change a habit to begin working on one of these behaviors.

◼ How to Change a Habit

1. First, state the problem. What are your roadblocks or obstacles? Be truthful about it. This is sometimes difficult to do. Describe the problem or behavior you want to change (or the new habit you would like to begin).

   _____

   _____

   _____

2. Count the behavior. How often do you do this behavior? For example, if you are trying to stop smoking, it is helpful to count the number of cigarettes you smoke each day. If you are trying to improve your diet, write down everything that you eat each day. If you are trying to establish a pattern of studying, write down how much time you spend studying each day. Sometimes just becoming aware of your habit is enough to begin to make some changes. How can you count this behavior?

   _____

   _____

3. Choose one small behavior at a time. If you can change one small behavior, you can gain the confidence to change another. For example, a goal like having a better diet is broad and vague. A good way to make it small is to say, "I plan to eat more fruits and vegetables each day." Look at your habit in the first step above. Break it down into a smaller part that you can accomplish easily.

   _____

   _____

4. State in a positive way the behavior you wish to establish. For example, instead of saying, "I will not eat junk food," say, "I plan to eat fruits and vegetables each day." If necessary, rewrite your goal in a positive way.

   _____

   _____

5. Picture in your mind the actions you might take to accomplish your goal. For example: I see myself in the grocery store buying fruits and vegetables. I see myself packing these fruits and vegetables in my lunch. I see myself putting these foods in a place where I will notice them. Record the actions you plan to take.

   _____

   _____

6. What reward will you use to reinforce the behavior? Rewards are most effective if they directly follow the behavior you wish to reinforce. List your rewards.

_____

_____

7. Practice the behavior for *ten days*. The first three days are the most difficult. If you fail, don't give up. Just realize that you are human and keep trying for ten days. Think positively that you can be successful. Use the space below or a separate sheet of paper to count how many times you did the behavior each day and what happened. Were you successful?

Day 1: _____

_____

_____

Day 2: _____

_____

_____

Day 3: _____

_____

_____

Day 4: _____

_____

_____

Day 5: _____

_____

_____

Day 6: _____

_____

_____

Day 7: _____

_____

_____

Day 8: _____

_____

_____

Day 9: _____

_____

_____

Day 10: _____

_____

_____

How did this project work for you?

CHAPTER 2

Campus Culture
What Is Expected of College Students Today?

Instructor Expectations

Your individual instructor's expectations are contained in his/her course syllabus. You should get one for every course. The syllabus is your contract with that instructor. It should tell you the course objectives, the name(s) of the textbook(s), grading policies, special requirements, and give you a schedule of assignments. Most instructors distribute the syllabus during the first class period. That's why it's so important to be there for the first class. Some of the information given at that time will not be repeated later, but you will be held accountable for knowing it. Instructors expect you to keep track of your syllabus and follow the schedule, even it they never mention it again. The minimum expectations of most instructors are that you attend class on a regular basis, participate in class discussions and activities, complete your assignments on time, and take tests and examinations when they are given.

In college classes you will be held to much higher standards than you were in high school. You will be expected to study more and devote more time to doing homework. The typical rule is that you should spend at least two hours studying outside of class for every hour you spend in class. Often you are required to do more extensive readings of textbooks and/or supplemental readings. In most courses a portion of your grade is based on writing assignments. These can range from journals or short papers to longer essays or even extensive term papers involving research. Many instructors ask that your work be typewritten, and always expect that it will be clean, neat, and well organized. Non-compliance could lower your grade. Late work may not be accepted at all. In college you are responsible for your learning. No one will remind you to complete your assignments or do your homework. If you miss too many classes you may be dropped for non-attendance.

■ Student Expectations

When you thought about what you expected college to be like, did you consider the ways in which it is different from high school? Depending on your high school experience, college may be similar or it may be very different. Take a moment and brainstorm (generate ideas) a list of all the ways college may be different for you. We started with some examples.

- ■ Tuition is charged
- ■ You buy your own books
- ■ You choose your school
- ■ Each program has its own requirements

_____

_____

_____

_____

■ Student Concerns about Starting College

Starting college can cause a certain amount of fear or apprehension. If you were not a strong student in high school you may be nervous about your study skills and your ability to do college level work. Other people worry about relationships and personal problems that will arise. Going to school requires a definite time commitment for attending classes and studying. Significant others may not understand that you are going to be busier than you were before. Child care arrangements and employment schedules may be more complicated than ever. There will be financial considerations, especially if you are not working.

■ Student Rights

As college students and adults you have certain rights that go beyond those of high school students. In high school many of the decisions were made for you. Now that you are taking total responsibility for your education you are also entitled to know your rights.

A. You have the right to be treated with dignity and respect by your fellow students and all college employees.

That means everyone from the president of the college to the campus police; from your instructors to the bookstore clerks and cafeteria workers.

B. You have the right to receive a quality education.

Many colleges are even going so far as to issue educational guarantees. For example, if you get an academic degree (Associate of Arts or Associate of Science) from a community college, it will transfer to the public universities in your state. If you get a vocational degree (Associate in Applied Science) you should have the skills to get a job in your field.

C. You have the right to pursue your education in an environment that is safe and conducive to learning.

Usually the campus has a security or police department to insure that students, their cars, and their belongings are safe. While they cannot promise that nothing will ever get stolen from your car, or that your book bag will remain untouched if you leave it in the cafeteria for two hours, they are routinely patrolling the parking lots and buildings on campus. Many departments have security cameras that allow an officer to monitor all of the parking lots and building entrances at once. Other duties of the campus police include parking, traffic regulations, vehicle stickers, fire safety, escort services, as well as crime prevention. Many security offices also assist students by presenting crime awareness programs, and publishing the campus crime statistics. You have a right to know the amount and nature of crimes that are committed on campus.

An environment that is conducive to learning is one that is free of sexual harassment or any other behavior that is unwelcome, degrading, destructive, and unnecessary. Most schools do have written policies regarding sexual harassment stating what is and is not acceptable behavior, and the disciplinary action for what is not acceptable. Everyone must be made aware of these policies, which are usually in the college catalog and student handbook. Be sure that your behavior is appropriate, and do not allow someone else to violate acceptable standards.

D. You have the right to your own opinion.

Although others in the class or on campus may not share your views, you have all of the constitutional rights to freedom of speech and expression. Remember, though, this does not give you the right to monopolize class time voicing your opinion.

E. You have the right to have your privacy respected.

The Family Educational Rights and Privacy Act (FERPA) is a federal law that gives you the right to know what is contained in your school records. It also protects the privacy of your records. Without your permission the college cannot give out information about your schedule, grades, academic standing, test scores, and such, even to your parents or spouse. That is the reason you must request in writing when you want your transcripts or placement test scores sent to another school. The college is allowed to issue directory information (name, address, etc.), but many schools today will not even release that information, especially over the phone. If you do not wish information about yourself given out, you can request that the college not provide this directory information to anyone.

F. You have the right to appeal instructor-initiated withdrawals.

G. You have the right to seek guidance.

The college offers academic advisors in every major to assist students with educational planning. Advisors can also help locate internships or job opportunities in their field. Even if you are a part-time student and were not assigned an advisor, you can request one. The counselors in the counseling office are another source of advice on educational and career planning. They can also help with limited personal issues.

H. You have the right to express concern or dissatisfaction with any situation that impedes your pursuit of education.

Find out what the grievance procedures are on your campus. Follow through until your problem is resolved. Remember, there are levels of authority in any institution. Usually the best results are obtained when you follow the chain of command.

I. You have the right to withdraw from any course until the withdrawal deadline date.

J. You have the right to a final course review if you feel the instructor's final grade for the course has not been fair.

Contact the instructor first to see if you can solve the problem at that level. If not, go to the department chairperson. Follow the procedure outlined in your catalog or handbook.

■ Student Responsibilities

One reason some students do not do well in college is they do not fully understand their responsibilities. Although many students enjoy the increased freedoms of being in college, they seem to forget that with increased freedom comes responsibilities.

In college there is definitely a shift or transferring of responsibility to the student as an adult in charge of his/her own life.

A. It is your responsibility to recognize and respect the rights of other students.

Talk softly in study areas or near classes that are in session. Be quiet in the library, and return your books when they are due. Don't damage books that others will need to use. If you are able bodied be sure to give priority use of the designated elevators and rest rooms to persons with disabilities. They don't have the option of using the stairs or other facilities.

B. It is your responsibility to treat others with dignity and respect.

In class discussions listen to what others have to say and don't make fun of someone else's remarks. Respect your instructors and fellow students. Don't disrupt the class by chatting with the person next to you during the lecture. It is also disruptive to the instructor and the rest of the class when students "pack-up" 10 to 15 minutes before the end of the period. It is obvious they think there won't be anything of importance said. Some even put their coats on and sit on the edge of their chairs, ready to bolt out of the room the second class is dismissed. This behavior is rude, but it is also self-defeating because the end of the period is when the instructor gives instructions for an assignment, reviews hints for the test, or provides other helpful information.

C. You are responsible for your behavior on campus.

Be responsible to clean up your own mess, don't litter, smoke only in the designated areas, don't steal from others, obey the laws for driving and parking, act in a mature, adult manner in classrooms, student lounge areas, and hallways.

D. It is your responsibility to ask when you do not understand something or when you need help.

For example, if you need special services or tutoring, it is up to you to contact the appropriate department or program. You should make appointments to see your advisor for registration or academic planning. Don't wait for someone else to call you first. You may never get what you need.

E. It is your responsibility to attend and participate in class.

The attendance policy will vary with each course and each instructor. Many college students believe they can make their own decisions about whether or not to attend class. This is always a bad idea. Some instructors may allow you to miss class occasionally for good reason, but think about all that you are going to miss by not being there. A large percentage of the material you will be required to know from the class comes from the lecture. If you know in advance that you cannot attend or if you are ill and must miss a class, notify the instructor. Do whatever you can to make up the work. Submit any assignments due that day.

F. If the instructor is late for class it is your responsibility to wait at least 10 to 15 minutes before you leave.

Everyone has emergencies and anyone can be tied up in traffic, so it is only common courtesy to wait. Should the instructor come after you have left, you will be responsible for the missed material.

G. It is your responsibility to do your homework assignments and turn them in on time.

You are also responsible to be aware of what the assignments are, in other words, to read the syllabus.

H. It is your responsibility to read class materials.

Students must read materials in order to be prepared to ask and answer questions, participate in discussions, and to offer comments in class.

I. It is your responsibility to be an active learner.

This is your education. You have to take the initiative to learn, even if the instructor is boring, unfair, not cool, doesn't like you, etc. Failing a course because you don't like the instructor hurts only yourself. Regardless of who the teacher is, it is your responsibility to do the assignments and go to class prepared to learn.

J. It is your responsibility to be aware of college policies and procedures and the chain of command.

When you have a problem to resolve, it is most effective to follow through with the person who has the authority to implement the solution.

K. Some policies that are a must to know:

1. Course prerequisites. These are found in your college catalog.

2. Payment policies and deadline dates. This information is usually listed on the registration information, or on your bill and on your schedule.

3. Course withdrawal procedures and deadline dates. These are described in the catalog and handbook.

4. Instructor requirements, including attendance policies. You will find this in the course syllabus.

5. Academic, Financial, and Veterans' Standards of Progress. See the college catalog and/or get this info from the financial aid and veterans offices.

6. Major/graduation requirements. These are in the college catalog.

7. Appeals processes. Once again, the catalog is the place to look for this.

L. You are responsible for knowing the information in the Student Code of Conduct and for managing your behavior accordingly.

M. It is your responsibility as a student to try to understand another person's perspectives.

Just as you have the right to speak your mind, you have the responsibility to allow others to do the same. Everyone will not think the same way on any given issue. One of the purposes of education is to get you to think with an open mind, to evaluate what you see and hear, and to develop and use logic and reasoning skills.

N. It is your responsibility to provide thoughtful feedback to instructors on evaluations.

Fill out the course evaluation as honestly and thoroughly as you can whenever you are asked to do so. Add written comments. Even your instructors will value your opinion if you are constructive in your critique. They may improve their teaching techniques to benefit future students.

O. It is your responsibility NOT to develop bad habits.

Students should not talk during class, chew gum, eat, or drink noisily, be late for class, create a disturbance, sleep during class, cut classes, be unprepared, not pay attention, or be apathetic.

P. It is your responsibility as well as your right to participate in student activities.

If you want to make things better, get involved. If you don't like the speakers or entertainment offered on campus, volunteer to be on next year's selection committee. Joining student government, the newspaper staff, or any variety of campus clubs will give you valuable leadership experience as well as an opportunity to make the college better for other students like yourself.

Q. You are responsible for checking your progress with your instructors.

You may be given a midterm report, but it is usually not required by the college. It is up to the students to keep track of grades received on assignments, tests, and quizzes. For an accurate report, make an appointment to meet with the teacher in his/her office to see how you are doing.

R. It is your responsibility to evaluate your time commitments and manage your schedule accordingly.

Everyone has things they must do. It is up to you, however, not to schedule doctor, dentist, or other appointments that will conflict with your class time. You will also need to plan for homework and study time in addition to the hours you spend in class. The more roles you have, the more difficult this will be. But, it is not the instructor's fault if you wait to do an assignment until the night before it is due, have an emergency arise and can't get the assignment done on time.

S. It is your responsibility to accept the consequences if you do not do what you should.

Instructor Rights

Since there are two parties in the teacher/learner relationship, we thought it would be appropriate to acquaint you with the rights and responsibilities of your instructors. The status given to faculty may vary from campus to campus, and full time teachers may have more influence than part timers, but overall they have some basic assumptions about what should happen. These are things that you should understand as well.

A. Instructors have the right to expect students to arrive on time.

It is distracting and annoying to have your train of thought interrupted every time someone else enters the room. Some teachers will close and lock the door to prevent people from entering late. Others may not be quite that strict, but will appreciate a latecomer slipping in as quietly as possible.

B. Instructors have the right to expect students to behave as adults.

Students should pay attention in class, listen and take notes, not disturb the class by talking with friends, getting up, walking around, or leaving early. If you must leave early it is best to mention this to the instructor before class. If you have a disability that necessitates you moving around, let your instructor know in advance. It is perfectly acceptable for you to accommodate your needs, but this should not come as a total surprise to the instructor.

C. Instructors have the right to expect respect from students.

It should never be necessary to shout, use obscenities, or in any other way show disrespect to a teacher. If there is a severe problem that cannot be resolved with the instructor, talk to the department chairperson or the academic dean of the college.

D. Instructors have the right to be notified if students have a problem or concern about their courses.

Always use your instructor as the first resort to seek a solution for any class problem.

E. Instructors have the right to expect students to read the syllabus, to be prepared for class, and to be prepared for tests.

(Bring your own pencils, etc.)

F. Instructors have the right to expect students to seek help during posted office hours, to request make-up materials, or to check on work missed during an absence.

It is really unfair of students to expect the teacher to be a walking file cabinet, carrying all of the handouts from the last three sessions, just in case someone didn't get them or lost their copies. Many teachers have their classes scheduled back to back and in different rooms, which really makes it inconvenient to stay after class to talk to a student who missed a previous session.

G. Instructors have the right not to be expected to calculate grades in their heads or on the spot just because the student caught them in the cafeteria or parking lot.

Even if the teacher has his/her grade book at hand, don't expect to look over his/her shoulder at your grades; that's a breech of confidentiality if other students' grades are on the same page.

H. Instructors have the right to withdraw students from their class for the following reasons:

1. lack of attendance
2. plagiarism
3. lack of satisfactory progress
4. misconduct

I. Instructors have the right of academic freedom.

As degreed professionals they are granted the right to express themselves freely (within the college's code of conduct), to conduct their classes as they see fit, to assign homework, to use outside sources of information as provided by the copyright laws, and determine their own system for grading.

■ Instructor Responsibilities

Your instructors have certain responsibilities to you as students and to the college. Because they seem somewhat self-explanatory, we will not go into great detail about each. Here is a list of several that we thought were important.

It is your instructor's responsibility:

A. To arrive and start class on time.

B. To inform the students in advance if he/she knows class will be cancelled.

C. To cover the material in the syllabus.

D. To treat students and their opinions with respect.

E. To inform students of their progress without violating confidentiality.

F. To provide a learning environment.

G. To present effective lectures that stick to the subject without rambling.

H. To be prepared and organized.

I. To be considerate of the able bodied and the disabled student, i.e., not speaking too fast or in a monotone, leaving transparencies or visual aids on the screen long enough to take notes, and willingly providing reasonable accommodations for students with disabilities.

J. To explain concepts, and to repeat or reteach if necessary.

K. To be in their office during posted office hours and to keep scheduled appointments.

L. Not to:

1. keep class beyond the end of the period

2. show partiality or favoritism

3. embarrass students

4. behave as if their class is the only class the student is taking

5. behave as if their opinion is the only opinion

Becoming a Student

By this time you may already be enrolled in your first semester of college. You may have been through the admission and registration processes. In that case you have already selected your first classes and been to the bookstore to buy your first textbooks, including this one. For those of you who may be still in high school, let's talk for a moment about the admissions process.

Orientation

Most colleges provide some type of orientation program for their new students. It may be required or it may be voluntary. Participating in whatever kind of orientation your school has is always a good idea. This is your opportunity to learn about the environment where you will be spending the next years. Every attempt will be made to inform you of the services and facilities that your college offers, but if there is some service not mentioned, ask questions. It is still your responsibility to seek out help.

Registration

The registration process varies from college to college. Most offer an open registration period that lasts until the semester begins. Some schools may even allow you to register the opening week of classes. The earlier you get your schedule set, however, the better. Once a class has the maximum number of students enrolled, it will be closed. Sections with the best times and the best teachers always fill up first. I've seen popular classes become full during the first hour of registration! So, get started as soon as possible. If you ended up with a lot of leftovers this semester, that should convince you to register early next semester.

Academic Advisors

Full-time students are usually assigned an academic advisor. Academic advisors may be full- or part-time faculty, administrators, or other staff that provide assistance with deciding on a major, selecting courses, teaching study skills, or a number of other services for students. Find out what your school's policy is regarding academic advising. Is there an Academic Advising Center? Have you been assigned to an academic advisor? Be sure to make good use of any service that is offered in this area. Find out who your advisor is and schedule an appointment. When you meet with him/her, bring along the college catalog, your placement test results, the schedule of classes for the semester, an advisor summary listing all previous courses taken at your institution, and/or transcripts from other colleges and universities. By having everything you need, you will make the best use of your time with your advisor.

Your advisor can also help you rearrange your schedule, if that becomes necessary. If you find out within the first week of classes that your work/practice schedule has changed, or that a particular course or instructor isn't what you thought and you know you'll never survive an entire semester, try to rearrange your schedule immediately. There is probably a refund period during which you can get your money back if you withdraw from a class. Make sure you follow the college's add/drop procedure for making those changes. There may be penalties for procrastination or not following the proper procedure. Failure to follow all the steps may result in your not being withdrawn during the refund period. Remember, too, that there is a final withdrawal date after which you cannot drop a class for any reason. If you don't withdraw by that date, the instructor must give you a grade for the course.

Core Curriculum

Most colleges have some kind of core curriculum. This means that all students are required to take the same group of courses. The purpose of these courses is to provide you with a well rounded education, not just to prepare you for an occupation.

Grades/Grade Point Average

Grades are used to evaluate your success in school at the end of each semester. Students who intend to transfer or graduate need to be concerned about their Grade Point Average (GPA). Your grade point average is determined by the number of credits you attempt during a term. Each grade is assigned a value and is worth a certain number of quality points. Most colleges use a 4.0 grading system, although some colleges have a 5.0 grading system.

A = 4 points	A = 5 points
B = 3 points	B = 4 points
C = 2 points	C = 3 points
D = 1 point	D = 2 points
E/F = 0 points	E = 1 point
	F = 0 points

To figure your Grade Point Average, multiply the number of quality points for the grade you received by the number of credits for the course. Total the quality points for all the courses and total the number of hours you attempted in the semester. Then divide the total quality points by the total number of attempted hours. An Incomplete grade does not receive any points until the course is finished. If a course offers a grade of Pass/Fail or Satisfactory/Unsatisfactory the credits will count for graduation, but the grade for the course does not compute into your GPA.

Tuition and Fees

You will be charged tuition for every credit hour in which you enroll. Variable course fees for such things as photocopies, computer time, and lab equipment are charged in addition to tuition. The course fee is usually listed on the schedule. The college may add other fees such as a registration or testing fee, and you will also be charged a student activity fee. This money helps pay for such things as student clubs, entertainment, special speakers, the school newspaper, literary magazine, or other publications that are distributed free to students.

Financial Aid

If you need assistance with your tuition, fees, books, and supplies, visit the Financial Aid Office on your campus to see what might be available to you. This office coordinates all sources of financial aid including scholarships, grants, loans, work-study programs, and deferred payment plans. Ask any financial aid officer for the appropriate forms for federal and state financial aid programs in order to see if you qualify.

Campus Resources

The Campus

Your college has many resources to help you with a wide variety of needs. The campus itself is a resource. The buildings and grounds are maintained so that you will have an accessible place to study and attend classes. There are parking lots for staff, students, and visitors. There may be a bus stop or stops for other forms of public transportation. Every campus will have a bookstore where you can buy your textbooks, school supplies, clothes with the college logo, greeting cards, snacks, and other items. Campus maps help newcomers find their way around. There will be a campus police or security station. There may be other conveniences such as a photocopy center or ATM machine.

Food service on campus may range from vending machines to a full service cafeteria. Depending on the campus, the cafeteria may be open for breakfast, lunch, and dinner on a daily basis. Another important resource for students is the information center which is usually centrally located to help with the following services: general information, payment for everything from tuition to traffic tickets, switchboard, and student computer stations that let you personally access your schedule, records, etc.

Academic Support Services

Learning Resource Center/Library

It always amazes me when students who have been on campus for more than a semester don't know where to find the Learning Resource Center (LRC). Even if you don't have a research paper to write, the college library offers the perfect place to study in peace and quiet. Current popular books, magazines, and newspapers are available to read for pleasure in addition to the scholarly publications needed for research. The LRC offers a variety of other services such as a place to view video tapes, use computers or word processors, duplicate materials, and may be the center for telecourses.

Academic Skills Center

The academic skills center is a good place to learn. It offers assistance with study skills, time management, and note taking. It also provides free or inexpensive tutoring services for students. The academic skills center may be the place to make up missed exams, to take placement tests, or to use when you need extended time on a test. Again you will need to check your individual college's policies regarding the skills center.

Tutoring

Tutoring services are available in many schools at no extra cost or low cost to students. Find out where tutoring is available at your school. Academic skills centers and specialized programs offer these support services. A tutor may be another student, a faculty member, or a professional staff person whose primary responsibility is assisting students with their academic work. In any event that person is skilled in his/her subject area and trained to work with small groups or with a student on an individual basis. Tutoring may be available to you as a walk-in or by appointment only.

If you have made an appointment with a tutor be sure that you keep the appointment and come prepared. Do not expect the tutor to do your work for you or to make up for missed classes. Read your textbook, work your assignments, and write down any problems or unanswered questions you might have. Bring all your work to the tutoring session. If you cannot keep your appointment be sure to call the tutoring office to cancel. There may be other students waiting to use that valuable time.

Mentors

Mentors are usually volunteers who assist students in adjusting to college. They may be faculty, staff persons, or members of the community to whom you can turn when the going gets rough. These people are dedicated individuals who give of their time freely and have made a difference in the lives of many students.

Academic Computing Labs

There are places on campus where you can use computers to do your assignments. They are usually staffed with a lab assistant to help you if you need it. Academic computing labs are not where you learn how to use a computer; that's why computer science courses are offered.

Specialized Labs

Often the college will have specialized labs for practicing what you are learning in foreign language classes. Computer assistance or audio tapes may be available to increase your vocabulary, verb conjugation, pronunciation, and conversation fluency.

There may be a writing lab for students who need to develop their writing skills. This can be an excellent way to learn as some of these labs offer extraordinary supplemental instruction. If you are taking a writing course this lab should be a must on your list of sites to visit.

A basic skills lab may offer computer-based learning to enhance your skills in all areas of reading, writing, and math. This lab is a MUST for all developmental education students. Locate and become familiar with the services of any specialized labs on your campus.

Disabled Student Services

If you have a documented physical or learning disability, you are entitled by law to **reasonable** accommodations because of your disability. Most campuses have an office that coordinates these services. They might range from enlarging reading material, providing note takers, arranging for sign language interpreters, furnishing desks in classrooms to accommodate wheelchairs and other physical disabilities, and allowing instructors the facilities to give untimed tests. They may provide equipment such as tape recorders, calculators, magnifiers, automatic page turners, computer voice synthesizers, recorded textbooks, and large print dictionaries. Professional tutors may also be available to help students with learning disabilities. Students with limited English speaking proficiency, students whose academic skill level interferes with success in their classes, and students with health concerns can be eligible to receive services as well.

Your campus may have a variety of special programs to meet the needs of specific target populations. Some may provide counseling and tutorial services beyond those regularly offered on campus. The money to pay for these programs usually comes from federal or state funds, given to the college in the form of a grant. With these extra resources grant programs can enhance your opportunities to achieve your academic goals.

■ Student Services

Counseling

Most college counseling centers are staffed by professionals who have degrees in counseling or psychology. Many are licensed by the state or by their profession to help students with academic and personal issues. If you need assistance with choosing a major, selecting courses, or just feel the need to talk to someone about where you are going and what you are doing, be sure to stop in your college's counseling center. Services are usually free. Your visits and anything you discuss with the counselor will always be kept confidential.

Career Center

The career center may or may not be part of the counseling center on your campus. This is where you can find material for career exploration. Interest inventories and other assessment instruments are usually available to students for the purpose of discovering their career options. Computerized versions of career guidance information systems may also be available in your center.

Placement Center

This office on campus helps students and alumni to get jobs in their career field. The center may bring employers on campus for job fairs or recruiting purposes. Some publish a job bulletin that lists full- and part-time employment opportunities. Often this office handles student worker applications, provides resume writing workshops, helps you to acquire interviewing skills, and assists you in your job search.

Intercultural/Minority Affairs

Intercultural and minority affairs generally supports the recruitment, retention, and graduation of students from groups that are not well represented on college campuses. They may provide services to any protected class such as women, African Americans, Native Americans, Latinos/Latinas, etc.

Health and Wellness

Many people today are concerned with health and well being. The college is a great place to learn better, healthier habits for eating, exercising, and prevention of diseases. Check out the workshops and seminars offered through the health services department or program. If you have a problem with smoking, drug and/or alcohol abuse there are support services available to help you.

Graduation/Records Office

The records office (sometimes called the registrar's office) is where you will find all your student records. Your instructors will be sending your grades to the registrar and it will be this office from which you will receive your report card. If there is any doubt in your mind about the final grade you receive for a class, contact your instructor or the registrar. When transferring to another school or finding employment you will be asked for a transcript of your records.

Student Activities

Athletics and clubs on campus offer students many extracurricular activities. Find one that suits your major, interests, or hobbies.

Student Organizations

You might investigate a number of groups on campus for the sole purpose of extracurricular activities, personal development, making new friends, or just having fun. The athletic department, the health and wellness center, service clubs, awareness groups, religious organizations, music and theater groups, diversity clubs, and honor societies can all add a little spice to your life.

If you are interested in politics, student government may be the avenue for you. It is an excellent training ground for teamwork and leadership and will look terrific on any resume. If your major is media or communications, you may be interested in the student bulletins, newspaper, yearbook, photography/video clubs, or campus radio and TV stations. A number of honor societies invite students with high GPAs and/or specific majors to become members.

Campus Facilities

The college campus has a wealth of facilities that are open to students and residents of the campus. The health and fitness center, gym, swimming pool, athletic fields, tennis courts, and/or bowling alleys on many campuses contribute to the physical well being of the community. The performing arts center, art gallery, planetarium, greenhouse, and/ or arcades provide additional recreational opportunities. For many adult students who are parents of young children, the child care center or preschool on campus makes it possible to attend classes and activities with peace of mind. They don't have to worry about finding a reliable babysitter, it is convenient, and they are close at hand should an emergency arise.

Community Outreach Programs

Colleges seek to serve the people living in their community. They offer general interest courses to develop a hobby, to learn a new skill for fun, or for social interaction. These are non-credit classes provided at a reasonable fee as a service to the public. Continuing education courses let people in various professions upgrade their skills, keep current with new trends, and qualify for recertification.

For those who need help with basic reading, writing, and math skills, the college is the place to go. Adult education departments usually offer courses at no cost to the students, and often even provide the textbooks. Volunteer literacy tutors give one-on-one instruction to adults who wish to learn to read (or to read better). Some colleges have programs that give books to needy families to encourage children and their parents to read. English as a Second Language (ESL) classes help beginners and advanced speakers master the English language. GED test preparation, though, is probably the most popular feature of adult education. Special graduation ceremonies are often held to honor those who have attained their high school equivalency diploma.

Most colleges reach out to business and industry. They provide assessment and training for employees, help with small business development, and may have special programs for dislocated workers (people out of work because of lay offs, plant closings, or downsizing).

Music, art, and theater events are open to the public and provide cultural opportunities for the community. Youth college offers children a chance to be involved with fun and educational classes at their own level, while elder college encourages senior citizens to stay active. Other community outreach programs might include support groups, athletic events, family activities, job fairs, college fairs, and providing facilities for meetings, festivals, or research.

Community Services Available

The community, in turn, provides the college with many services to benefit students. Bus transportation is often available to most campus centers and satellites. Local newspapers, radio and TV stations inform the public of current events on the campus, and the college has an outlet for advertising their activities to the community. Health care services, counseling, community hot lines, programs such as the Private Industry Council, Displaced Homemakers, and Public Aid supplemental projects assist students.

■ Summary

We have explored your expectations for college. We also discussed in detail the rights and responsibilities of you, the student, and the rights and responsibilities of your instructors. The remainder of the chapter acquaints you with the resources on campus and in the community, all of which will enable you to become good college students.

In addition, one of the best campus resources is your faculty. They want you to succeed and get a good education so that you will have a strong foundation for life. That is the reason that they are in the classroom. If you are successful, they are successful. The faculty on your campus, however, expect that you will take responsibility for your education. Make the best use you can of all your campus resources and services. They are there to help you.

CHAPTER 3
Learning with Style

This chapter deals with learning styles and how the styles affect your learning. As you read through and do the exercises, keep in mind that there are no right or wrong answers. The goal is to help you find your learning style and use it to your advantage. In the process you will also find out more about your weaknesses. The more you know about yourself and the way you learn, the more effectively you can put that information to use in your college courses. Getting the most information from instructors and textbooks is important to your success. Discovering your learning style can help you be a better, more successful student (if you use the information).

From *Practical Approaches for Building Study Skills and Vocabulary,* Second Edition by Funk et al. © 1996 by Kendall/Hunt Publishing Company.

■ What Is a Learning Style?

Before continuing, it is necessary to make clear just what is meant by learning style. Scholars have different opinions regarding what should or shouldn't be included in the definition. For our purposes, learning style is the characteristic and preferred way one takes in and interacts with information, and the way one responds to the learning environment. Think of your particular learning style as the way you prefer to learn new or difficult information, and the way you find it easiest and most comfortable to learn.

To illustrate, suppose that you are given a learning task. What is the first thing you would prefer to do to get the new information—read about it in a book; listen to someone talk about it; or do something with the information to prove that you know it? None of the ways is the right or best way, they are simply examples of different ways to learn. You may prefer one, or a combination of those listed. There is no best way to learn, just different ways. The goal for you is to find your preferred learning style.

Depending on which expert you ask, there are many different ways to consider learning styles and many ways to analyze them. This chapter will only touch on a few. If you feel that you would benefit from a more extensive diagnosis, you should get in touch with your campus counseling or testing center.

Your learning style may be more difficult to determine now than it would have been in elementary school. The reason is that as you get older and become a more mature learner, your learning style becomes more integrated. You have probably learned that you have to use many different ways to get information depending on the learning situation. When you answer the questions on the various learning style inventories given later in this chapter, keep in mind that you want to answer them thinking about your preferences. Answer them based on what you are most comfortable doing, and what's easiest for you. The more accurate the picture of your learning style, the more you can use it to help you.

■ Why Should You Know about Your Learning Style?

One of the goals of a college education is to make you an independent learner (also, a goal of study skills). There will be many things you will have to learn after you complete your degree, and helping you learn HOW to learn is an important aspect of your education. Knowing how you learn will help you begin to monitor your learning. The more aware you are of the way you learn, the better you can be at determining where you need help and where you don't.

As you study information by reading a textbook for example, if you are not understanding what you are reading, you need to make adjustments in the method you are using. You may try one of several options—reading the material aloud, silently reading it over again, asking someone from your class to explain it, or whatever might work. If you know what your learning style is, you will have a better idea about the one or two strategies more likely to work for you. This makes you more efficient (you don't have to try everything to find a strategy that works) and it makes you more effective because you can change strategies and understand the difficult material more clearly.

Some research indicates that grades are better, and the learner is more motivated when taught using the preferred learning style. The research also indicates a tendency in learners to retain the information better. Although you can't usually make choices about how your instructors will present information to you, you can choose how you will study on your own. This independent studying is the way you will be getting more of your information in college.

Strengths and Weaknesses

Knowing your learning style can also help you understand why certain types of information are easier or more difficult for you to learn. Being aware of weaknesses can help you be prepared for them. For example, if you know that you have trouble with numbers, then you know that your math class (necessary for meeting general education requirements) is going to be difficult for you. You can be better prepared by scheduling the class at a time when you are most alert, finding a tutor early on in the class, or scheduling it during a semester when you can devote the necessary time and effort to it. Your awareness of weak areas will help you be prepared for problems and prevent some, instead of being caught by surprise.

By knowing your strengths, you can overcome the problems and weaknesses. If you know the ways you are most comfortable learning, you can use those to help you learn difficult material. If you know, for example, that you need to read information to really understand it, then you know that you have to read the text chapter before you go to the lecture class. Hearing about something is not your preferred way to get information. You have to prepare yourself to be a better listener by reading first (using a strength).

As indicated earlier, as you mature, your learning style becomes more integrated. This does not mean that you don't have preferences. It only means that you have learned how to get information and use your weaker areas better. You will not always get information in your preferred style, so you must learn to use those styles which are less comfortable for you. Some students learn this easier and more quickly than others. By helping you see your style, you can also find the areas which need attention. The ultimate goal for a student is to use any learning style comfortably depending what's best for the situation. That may not be practical, but you need to be fairly competent getting and using information in several ways. This will help you with instructors who use only one method of getting information across, and will give you more options when faced with difficult material to learn. Most of us learn better when we use more than one modality to get it.

■ What Is Your Learning Style?

Modality Strength

The first survey is an informal look at whether you prefer the auditory, visual, or kinesthetic modes. Auditory learners like to learn by listening. Visual learners prefer reading or watching, and kinesthetic learners learn by doing (touching or manipulating) or using their hands in some way.

Answer the survey by checking those statements which are MOST like you, or are like you most of the time.

Brain Dominance

The next inventory will help you determine your brain dominance. The results of this inventory and what brain dominance means will be discussed later in the chapter. Answer the questions using the answer sheet given.

Information Style

The final inventory will help you determine your preferences for taking in information and the way you work with that information. Answer the questions according to the instructions given.

Results

Now that you have these results, you can begin to see the way you prefer to learn. The results of the surveys are informal, and if you think you could benefit from a more in-depth diagnosis, you should contact your campus counseling or testing center. They will have other tests which will give you more information.

■ How Can You Use Your Learning Style?

Going back to the checklist for your modality strengths, look at your preferences regarding auditory, visual, and kinesthetic. If you have a strong preference for one over the others, you probably have some idea that you learn better if you receive information in a particular way. You would prefer to work with or react to information in that same mode.

If you don't find that you have a strong preference for one learning style over the others, you may have found that you prefer to receive information one way, but you would rather react to it or work with it in another way. Or you may have found that you are well integrated in these areas, and show no strong preferences in receiving or reacting to information.

The following suggestions will be categorized according to the modality area. It's a good idea to read over all of the suggestions, keeping in mind your strengths and weaknesses. The type of material you are responsible for getting in different classes should also be considered when choosing a strategy to use. Generally, the more senses you can use, the better you learn and remember the information. Sometimes it will be helpful to concentrate on your strong areas especially with difficult material.

Suggestions for Auditory Strengths

General Hints

You will benefit from hearing information—audio tapes, your own voice, or lectures.
You may want to make tapes of reading assignments or class notes.
Pretend that you are teaching someone else the information and explain it out loud.
Reading aloud notes or text material will help you.

Lecture Hints

Use a cassette tape player for pre-testing by asking yourself questions, leaving a 2–3 second blank space, and then giving the answer.
Use a cassette player to record difficult material from your notes and then listen to the information as needed.
Orally test yourself by asking questions from your notes.
Read aloud any difficult material in your notes.
If you can't read aloud, try vocalizing the words quietly.

Textbook Hints

Read aloud summary statements, headings, and subheadings before you begin reading a chapter.

Restate key ideas to yourself as you read material. Keep a "conversation" going with your text as you read (agree or disagree with the author, or question key ideas).

For difficult material, restate in your own words what you have just read.

Read aloud, vocalize, or whisper passages that are difficult.

Read vocabulary words and their definitions before you begin reading.

After reading, quiz yourself (aloud) over the vocabulary.

Orally quiz yourself over selected main ideas.

Tape yourself reading difficult text sections, and then go back and listen to them.

Suggestions for Visual Strengths

General Hints

You will benefit from seeing information—either in print or from videos, charts, or overheads.

It will be easier for you to remember what you read than what you hear.

When given information orally, you should write it down or take some notes.

Lecture Hints

Read the text before attending lectures.

Take notes over lecture material.

For difficult or confusing material, use a mapping technique along with notes (mapping is drawing a diagram of the material read, using only the main ideas, then showing the relationship among the ideas with lines connecting them).

Use white space on your page as a guide when taking notes (skip lines between main ideas).

To learn material, stare off into space and remember what the written information looked like on your page.

Textbook Hints

Preview chapters by reading the headings, subheadings, and outlines before reading the chapter.

Watch for topic sentences. Reread them to help you stay with the material being read. Underline topic sentences.

Draw a diagram, jot down a list, use mapping, or make a chart to help you retain difficult material.

Underline key words and concepts as you read. Marking your text will be very helpful.

Suggestions for Kinesthetic Strengths

General Hints

You learn best by doing. The more involved you are with material, the easier it is for you to learn.

You should try to find practical applications for information. When you can, do projects and experiments using what you learn.

Write information down.

Moving your fingers along the lines as you read may help.

Lecture Hints

Take notes and go back over them, making special marks for important material or material you need to go over more.

For difficult or confusing material, answer practice questions in writing.

Write difficult information in the air with your finger.

Use your hand as a marker as you go through your notes.

Textbook Hints

Use your hand or finger as a guide as you read.

For difficult material, draw a chart or diagram to help you understand what you read.

Underline important words and concepts as you study.

Making and using study cards will help you learn difficult material.

Use 3 x 5 cards with a question on one side and the answer on the other. You can also put charts, lists, and diagrams on small cards to use for studying.

Use your finger to point out summary information, main points, and headings and subheadings as you read.

■ Brain Dominance

Research on the two brain hemispheres began in the 1950s with Dr. Roger Sperry. Dr. Sperry found that the two hemispheres (or halves) of the brain processed information differently, and both were equally important to the whole person. The functions of the hemispheres had previously been found to be different—with speech being a left brain function and spatial (visual) capability being in the right. It was not known until Dr. Sperry's research that the processing of information was different for each of the halves. The left brain is linear and processes in a sequential manner, while the right brain uses a global process.

It seems that schools and their curriculums favor the left hemisphere. In other words, we are given a major dose of left brain learning in school, and the right brain is neglected. Most of us probably learned that success in school depended to a great degree on choosing the proper hemisphere to process information. We didn't consciously make this choice, but we could figure out what would be required of us, and we would do that to be successful. This may have caused many students problems if they were unable to use the left brain easily, or if they couldn't determine what to do to be successful.

Research findings indicate that the learning of most information is better when both the right and left hemispheres are used. If your results from the inventory indicate that you do not have a dominance in the right or the left hemisphere, and that you are integrated, you are achieving the best for learning. You can use both sides of your brain equally well. You can choose one over the other when the situation calls for it.

If you have a strong tendency or preference for either the right or the left hemisphere, you may find yourself having trouble in various learning situations. As with your modalities, integration is the key to becoming a better learner. Use the list of characteristics on the following page to find areas where you can develop or polish your weak areas. Also, use them to help you with difficult material—use your strong areas to compensate for your weak areas. The more integrated you become, the more you are free to choose different ways to process information, depending on what's best for a given situation.

The box on brain dominance characteristics lists some of the characteristics of left brain dominant and right brain dominant people. You will find characteristics in both lists that describe you, but you should find more in the list that corresponds to your results on the survey. If you are an integrated person, you should find that the two lists have about an equal number of characteristics which fit you.

■ Information Style

In the final learning style inventory, you indicated your preferences for perceiving and processing information. Look at the descriptions on the following page. This will give you a clearer picture of your preferences.

These categories came about as the result of research done by Dr. David Kolb in the early 1970s. The survey that you took is the result of Bernice McCarthy's research of the 1970s. Many other researchers have come up with similar findings over the years. The researchers have been experts in the fields of psychology, education, and business. Their findings are amazingly close when defining characteristics of people in the four areas (although their names for the different styles are different).

Most of us can perceive information either abstractly or concretely and then process it actively or reflectively, but we are more comfortable perceiving and processing in a certain way.

Whether we perceive or process information one way or another is probably the result of heredity, past experiences, and the demands of the present environment on us. We would be better learners if we used each information style equally well, based on what the situation required. When you read over the descriptions of the information styles, think about ways you can build on your strengths and develop your weak areas.

The way you perceive and process information influences the career choices you make, the way you get along with others, the way you solve problems, and the types of subjects you prefer, to mention only a few. You will probably be more comfortable if you follow your natural inclinations. The problem may be that you have had to use one information style so much up to this point, that you have stifled your more natural choice. Again, integration is the key, and the more you can refine your skills in all areas, the better off you will be. You may make some discoveries about your true preferences along the way!

Now that you have some idea of your learning style, you may begin to see how difficult it is to separate the areas. You may have found that you had trouble with some of the questions because you could think of instances when all of the answers fit with your preferences. That's good, because it shows that you can use more than one learning style when faced with a situation calling for one over another.

Refining your skills in weak areas is important to help you become more integrated. The more integrated you are, the more flexible you can be in learning situations. You can use any number of skills and strategies which will help you. Knowing your strengths helps you when you are faced with a difficult learning task because you can use the strategies best suited for your learning style.

Brain Dominance Characteristics

Left Hemisphere	Right Hemisphere
Objective	Use visualization
Rational	Intuitive
Sequential and systematic	Rely on images for thinking and remembering
Like right and wrong answers	Risk-takers
Structured	Need neat environment
Questioning	Long-term memory good
Need constant reinforcement	Short-term memory bad
Contract-liking people	Prefer subjective tests
Organized	Random learning and thinking
List makers	Short attention spans
Time conscious	Respond to demonstrated instructions
Follow directions closely	Need touching
Rely on language in thinking and remembering	Don't read directions
Good planners	Don't pay attention
Accomplish things quickly	Pilers
See cause and effect	More flexible
Prone to stress-related ills	More fun loving
Perfectionists	Accident prone
Control feelings	Need to have goals set for them
Do one task at a time	Multi-tasks needed
Need gentle risking situations	Creative
Analytic	Visual learners
Solve problems by looking at the parts	Solve problems by looking at the whole picture
Verbal	Like humor
Recognize names	Recognize faces
More serious	Like improvising
Dislike improvising	Think geometrically
Abstract thinkers	Dreamers
Focus on reality	Assuming
Work on improving the known	Like fantasy
Like non-fiction	Inventors
Learn for personal achievement	Intrinsically motivated
Extrinsically motivated	Learn for personal awareness
Prefer objective tests	Free with feelings

■ What Other Factors Influence Learning?

In addition to your preferred learning styles, there are other factors which affect your learning. There are factors which affect your ability to study effectively and efficiently. Some of these will affect you more than others. Some may not be an issue for you at all, but you will find some you should consider when planning where, when, how and what to study.

Consider the answers to these questions regarding your preferences. Are writing assignments easier for you than oral ones? Would you rather write a paper or give a talk on a subject? (Tough choice!) Do you feel that you do a better job when you write or when you speak on a subject? Is it easier to get your thoughts down on paper or to talk about them? The answers to those questions will help you determine your preference for oral or written expressiveness. You will have to do some of both, but you can make course choices based on this knowledge.

Another option you may have in some of your classes is whether to participate in study groups. If you are the type of person who is comfortable in a group, then they will help you. Others, who learn better alone, may find a study group a liability. There are times when working with a group can help you understand material because the group can exchange ideas. Material may become clearer as you discuss it among the group members. Know your preferences and study accordingly.

Motivation plays a role in your learning. Are you learning for the pleasure of learning—to become more aware of the world around you, and to broaden your knowledge? Or are you learning with that one goal in mind—a degree? If the achievement of that goal is the only reason you are learning, you are approaching your education differently than the person who is learning to increase knowledge.

Being aware of your locus of control can help you understand your motivation. Locus of control is your perception of what accounts for the successes or failures in your life. It can be either external or internal. If external, then you attribute success or failure to outside forces (family, peers, fate, enemies). If internal, you attribute success or failure to the consequences of your own actions. You probably have a tendency toward one or the other, but do not see everything one way or the other. If this is a problem for you, you may need to work on changing your outlook.

Other factors which may influence your ability to learn or study are given in the following list.

   Noise level—from complete quiet to lots of noise
   Light—from low to bright
   Temperature—from warm to cool
   Time—early morning to late evening (the time you feel most alert)
   Position—sitting to lying down

Try to choose your ideal learning environment taking these factors into consideration. Consider others that impact you. Complete the sentences in the Environmental Factors Worksheet with your preferences for YOUR ideal study environment. Answer with the first thing you think of, and don't spend too much time thinking about them.

Analyze what you have just written. You may want to go back and revise, but you should not change answers unless the new one is definitely a stronger preference. Use the information to set up your study environment. Think about what you can change, and how you can adapt to those you cannot change.

■ What Are Teaching Styles?

Faculty members are learners from way back (and should still be learning). They also have learning style preferences. Those preferences had something to do with the choosing of their academic fields. The instructors also have teaching styles as a result of personality traits, learning preferences, goals, motivation for teaching, job satisfaction, and other factors.

Information Style Descriptions*

CONCRETE EXPERIENCE: A high score in this area indicates a receptive, experience-based approach to learning where feeling-based judgments are most important. These individuals tend to be people oriented. Theoretical approaches don't hold much weight with them. They prefer to treat each situation as a unique case, and this is a problem with a theory. They learn best from specific examples and being involved. Individuals who emphasize concrete experience tend to be oriented more toward their peers and less toward authority figures in their approach to learning. They benefit most from feedback and discussion with fellow "concrete experience" learners.

ABSTRACT CONCEPTUALIZATION: A high score in this area indicates an analytical, conceptual approach to learning where logical thinking and rational evaluation are most important. These individuals tend to be oriented toward things and symbols and less toward other people. They prefer to learn in authority-directed, impersonal learning situations. They learn best when theory and systematic analysis are emphasized. They benefit little from unstructured learning approaches where discovery is important. They find these situations frustrating.

ACTIVE EXPERIMENTATION: A high score in this area indicates an active "doing" orientation to learning and processing information. These individuals learn best when they can engage in such things as projects, experiments, and homework. They will prefer small group discussions over passive learning situations such as lectures. They tend to be extroverted.

REFLECTIVE OBSERVATION: A high score in this area indicates a tentative, impartial, reflective approach to learning and processing information. These individuals make judgments based on careful observation. They prefer learning situations such as lectures where they are allowed to be impartial, objective observers in a learning situation. They tend to be introverted.

You can also analyze your "Information Style" one step further by looking at the specific ways that you prefer to perceive or take in information and then the way that you prefer to process or do something with that information. Do this by determining which of the following is your strength: CE or AC _____ and RO or AE _____. This gives you a clearer picture of your preferences, and descriptions follow. You will want to look over each definition, but the one which describes your two strengths as suggested above will be most likely to best describe you.

ABSTRACTLY PERCEIVE (AC) & REFLECTIVELY PROCESS (RO): Look for facts; need to know what the experts think; learn by thinking through ideas; prefer to learn by watching and thinking; more interested in ideas and concepts than people; like to collect data and critique information; thorough and industrious; will re-examine facts in perplexing situations; they enjoy traditional classrooms—schools are designed for them; function by adapting to the experts. Possible careers: basic sciences, math, research, planning.

ABSTRACTLY PERCEIVE (AC) & ACTIVELY PROCESS (AE): Need to know how things work; prefer to learn by testing theories in ways that seem sensible to them; learn by thinking and doing; need hands-on experiences; enjoy solving problems and resent being given the answers; have a limited tolerance for fuzzy ideas; need to know how things they are asked to do will help them in "real" life. Possible careers: engineering, physical sciences, nursing, technical areas.

CONCRETELY PERCEIVE (CE) & ACTIVELY PROCESS (AE): Need to know what can be done with things; prefer to learn by doing, sensing, and feeling; adaptable to change, and love it; love variety and situations calling for flexibility; tend to take risks; at ease with people, but sometimes seen as pushy; often reach accurate conclusions in the absence of logical reasoning. Possible careers: sales, marketing, action-oriented jobs, teaching.

CONCRETELY PERCEIVE (CE) & REFLECTIVELY PROCESS (RO): Look for personal meaning; need to be involved personally; learn by listening and sharing ideas; prefer to learn by sensing, feeling, watching; interested in people and culture; divergent thinkers who believe in their own experience; excel in viewing concrete situations from many perspectives; model themselves on those they respect; function through social interaction. Possible careers: counseling, personnel, humanities, organizational development.

*Source: Concept & Ideas created by Bernice McCarthy and David Kolb.

When you are in a classroom setting where you feel comfortable and everything feels right, you are probably with a teacher whose learning style matches yours. When you are uncomfortable and feel out of place, the teacher may be someone whose learning style is different from yours. Since it isn't always possible to be matched up with a teacher who learns as you do, you must learn to adapt to the teaching style being used by each instructor. The more you can learn to use different styles, the more readily you can identify and adapt to teaching styles.

Many instructors have a tendency to teach the way they learn. You can make some guesses about their preferred learning styles by analyzing the predominant way material is presented and the atmosphere of the classroom. Material can be presented visually—videos, demonstrations, or diagrams on the board or overhead. It can be primarily an auditory presentation with lecture or audio tapes. Hands-on activities and experiments would be kinesthetic. You will find a combination in most classrooms, but look at the predominant one, or the one your instructor seems most comfortable using.

When you are in a classroom that is unlike your preferred style, you will have to work harder at concentrating and understanding. You may have to find extra materials to help you understand. It's imperative that you adapt to be successful.

A number of factors are used to describe teaching styles, and there are different ways of looking at and determining what constitutes a certain style. One area that will be important to you is the way an instructor communicates and interacts with students. At one extreme, there is the instructor who is formal and authoritative, and at the other extreme, the instructor who is very informal and casual. Most teachers fit in somewhere between the two extremes. If you find yourself not getting along with an instructor, think about this aspect and what you are most comfortable with, and you may have a clearer picture of the problem.

Again, you can't always be matched up with someone just like you, but you can ask around about specific teachers' styles. If you prefer a lecture setting, where students work independently and are expected to assume responsibility for learning, then find an instructor who is like that (especially for difficult classes).

However, if you are more comfortable in an informal setting where the instructor uses small and large group discussions and acts as a guide through the learning process, you will want to look for this kind of instructor for the more difficult classes.

You should be aware of teaching styles. You may find it helpful to analyze your teachers a little at the beginning of a class. You will then know whether you are going to feel comfortable in the class or need to adapt somewhat. The earlier you know this, the better your chances for success in the class.

■ Summary

Learning style has been defined as the way you perceive or take in information, the way you process that information, and the way you react to the learning environment. You were given inventories to determine your modality strengths, brain dominance, and information style. Knowing about your learning style is important to you because it can make you aware of your strengths and weaknesses. You can use this information to be a better learner by using your strengths to help you with difficult material. Your weak areas are where you need to develop or improve your skills to become more integrated. Being more integrated means being able to adapt to the best learning strategy for the learning situation.

Many factors influence your ability to learn and study. The more awareness you have of these and your preferences, the better you can set up your learning environment to be the most efficient and effective for you.

Teaching styles of instructors also influence your classroom experience. Being aware of the different teaching styles you may encounter will help you be prepared to adapt when necessary.

Complete the following with what you have found in this chapter.

MODALITY STRENGTH: Auditory   _____

                     Visual   _____

                     Kinesthetic   _____

BRAIN DOMINANCE: Left   _____

                     Right   _____

                     Integrated   _____

INFORMATION STYLE: Concrete Experience   _____

                     Abstract Conceptualization   _____

                     Active Experimentation   _____

                     Reflective Observation   _____

                     (CE or AC) + (AE or RO)

                     _____   _____

LEARNING STYLE REFLECTIONS:

_____

_____

_____

_____

_____

Name: _Bibi Begum_ Date: _09/23/08_

■ Modality Checklist

Check the statements below which are most like you, or like you most of the time.

1. ☐ My emotions can often be interpreted by my general body tone.
2. ☑ My emotions can often be interpreted by my facial expressions.
3. ☑ My emotions can often be interpreted by my voice (quality, volume, tone).
4. ☑ When I'm angry, I usually clench my fists, grasp something tightly, or storm off.
5. ☐ When I'm angry, I usually "blow-up" verbally and let others know I'm angry.
6. ☐ When I'm angry, I usually clam up and give others the silent treatment.
7. ☐ The things I remember best are the things I do.
8. ☐ The things I remember best are the things I hear.
9. ☑ The things I remember best are the things I read.
10. ☐ I remember what was done best, not names or faces.
11. ☑ If I have to learn something new, I like to learn about it by reading books and periodicals or seeing a video.
12. ☐ I like to learn through real experience.
13. ☑ I enjoy learning by listening to others.
14. ☐ I am easily distracted by sounds.
15. ☐ I am easily distracted. I have a short attention span.
16. ☐ I am easily distracted by visual stimuli.
17. ☐ I understand spoken directions better than written ones.
18. ☐ I remember what I have read better than what I have heard.
19. ☐ I like to learn most by building or making things.
20. ☐ I remember names, but forget faces.
21. ☑ I remember faces and forget names.
22. ☑ I tend to be quiet around others, and may become impatient when listening.
23. ☐ If I have to learn something new, I like to learn about it by having it told to me (lectures, speeches, tapes).
24. ☐ I enjoy learning by reading assignments and class notes.
25. ☐ To remember things, I need to write or copy them.
26. ☐ I generally gesture when speaking, and am not a great listener.
27. ☐ I really enjoy talking and listening with people.
28. ☐ When solving problems, I prefer to attack them physically, and often act impulsively.
29. ☐ When solving problems, I prefer to organize my thoughts by writing them down.
30. ☑ When solving problems, I like to talk the problem out and try solutions verbally.

Score by marking the numbers below that you checked. Add up the total number of statements checked in each category. You will find that one area probably had more statements checked than the others. This would be your modality strength. If you do not find one clear strength, you probably are well-integrated in these areas, and can use the modality which best fits the learning situation.

AUDITORY:	3	5	8	13	14	17	20	23	27	30	Total _____
VISUAL:	2	6	9	11	16	18	21	22	24	29	Total _____
KINESTHETIC:	1	4	7	10	12	15	19	25	26	28	Total _____

■ Brain Dominance

Check the statements below which are most like you, or are like you most of the time.

1. ☐ I prefer to have things explained to me.
2. ☐ I prefer that someone shows me things.
3. ☐ I don't have a preference for verbal instructions or demonstrations.
4. ☐ I prefer classes where things are planned so I know exactly what to do.
5. ☐ I prefer classes which are open with opportunities for change as I go along.
6. ☐ I prefer both classes where things are planned and open to changes.
7. ☐ I prefer classes where I listen to "experts."
8. ☐ I prefer classes where I try things.
9. ☐ I prefer classes where I listen and also try things.
10. ☐ I prefer to take multiple choice tests.
11. ☐ I prefer essay tests.
12. ☐ I don't have a preference for essay tests or multiple choice tests.
13. ☐ I don't like to play hunches or guess.
14. ☐ I like to play hunches or guess.
15. ☐ I sometimes make guesses and play hunches.
16. ☐ I decide what I think by looking at the facts.
17. ☐ I decide what I think based on my experiences.
18. ☐ I decide what I think based on facts and my experiences.
19. ☐ I respond better to people when they appeal to my logical, intellectual side.
20. ☐ I respond better to people when they appeal to my emotional, feeling side.
21. ☐ I respond equally well to people when they appeal to my intellectual side or emotional side.
22. ☐ I prefer to solve problems by reading and listening to the experts.
23. ☐ I prefer to solve problems by imagining and seeing things.
24. ☐ I prefer to solve problems by listening to experts and imagining things.
25. ☐ I am primarily intellectual.
26. ☐ I am primarily intuitive.
27. ☐ I am equally intellectual and intuitive.
28. ☐ When I remember or think about things, I prefer to think in words.
29. ☐ When I remember or think about things, I prefer to think in pictures and images.
30. ☐ When I remember or think about things, I sometimes prefer words and sometimes prefer pictures.

31. ☐ I am very good at explaining things in words.

32. ☐ I am very good at explaining things with my hand movements and actions.

33. ☐ I am very good at explaining with words and hand movements.

34. ☐ I am almost never absentminded.

35. ☐ I am frequently absentminded.

36. ☐ I am occasionally absentminded.

37. ☐ I am very good at recalling verbal materials (names, dates).

38. ☐ I am very good at recalling visual material.

39. ☐ I am equally good at recalling verbal and visual material.

40. ☐ It is more exciting to improve something.

41. ☐ It is more exciting to invent something.

42. ☐ It is equally exciting to improve something or invent something.

43. ☐ I would rather read realistic stories.

44. ☐ I would rather read fantasy stories.

45. ☐ I don't have a preference for reading realistic or fantasy stories.

Score by marking the numbers below that you checked. Add up the total number of statements in each category. You will probably find that one area had more checks than the others. If so, you have a tendency for that area (left, right, or integrated) to be your stronger learning preference. If you are more integrated than left or right dominant, then you can use either side of your brain. A more detailed description of brain dominance is given later in the chapter.

LEFT BRAIN: 1   4   7   10   13   16   19   22   25   28   31   34   37   40   43   Total _____

RIGHT BRAIN: 2   5   8   11   14   17   20   23   26   29   32   35   38   41   44   Total _____

INTEGRATED: 3   6   9   12   15   18   21   24   27   30   33   36   39   42   45   Total _____

Concepts & Ideas created by David Kolb, Paul Torrance, and Bernice McCarthy.

■ Information Style

This survey is to determine the way you deal with information best. There are no right or wrong answers—just your preferences. Mark the statements which best describe your preferences. Mark the ones most like you, or like you most of the time.

1. ☐ I am energetic and enthusiastic.
2. ☐ I am quiet and reserved.
3. ☐ I tend to reason things out.
4. ☐ I am responsible about things.
5. ☐ I prefer learning to be "here and now."
6. ☐ I like to consider things and reflect about them.
7. ☐ I tend to think about the future.
8. ☐ I like to see results from my work.
9. ☐ I prefer to learn by feeling.
10. ☐ I prefer to learn by watching.
11. ☐ I prefer to learn by thinking.
12. ☐ I prefer to learn by doing.
13. ☐ When learning, I trust my hunches and feelings.
14. ☐ When learning, I listen and watch carefully.
15. ☐ When learning, I rely on logical thinking.
16. ☐ When learning, I work hard to get things done.
17. ☐ I like concrete things that I can see and touch.
18. ☐ I like to observe.
19. ☐ I like ideas and theories.
20. ☐ I like to be active.
21. ☐ I accept people and situations as they are.
22. ☐ I am aware of what is going on around me.
23. ☐ I evaluate things before acting.
24. ☐ I enjoy taking risks.
25. ☐ When I learn I am open to new experiences.
26. ☐ When I learn I like to try things out.
27. ☐ When I learn I like to analyze and break things down into their parts.
28. ☐ When I learn I like to look at all sides of the issue.
29. ☐ I am an accepting person.
30. ☐ I am a reserved person.

31. ☐ I am a rational person.

32. ☐ I am a responsible person.

33. ☐ I am an active person.

34. ☐ I am an observing person.

35. ☐ I am a logical person.

36. ☐ I am an intuitive person.

Score by marking the numbers below that you checked. Add up the total number of statements in each category. You will probably find that one area had more checks than the others. A detailed description of what these areas mean is given later in this chapter.

CONCRETE EXPERIENCE: 1   5   9   13   17   21   25   29   33   Total_____

REFLECTIVE OBSERVATION: 2   6   10   14   18   22   26   30   34   Total_____

ABSTRACT CONCEPTUALIZATION: 3   7   11   15   19   23   27   31   35   Total_____

ACTIVE EXPERIMENTATION: 4   8   12   16   20   24   28   32   36   Total_____

■ Environmental Factors Worksheet

1. The best time for me to study is _____

   _____

2. The best place for me to study is _____

   _____

3. My favorite study position is _____

   _____

4. My preference for noise when studying is _____

   _____

5. My favorite temperature when studying is _____

   _____

6. My favorite light when studying is _____

   _____

7. My preferred class to study first is _____

   _____

8. I can study best when _____

   _____

9. I can't study when _____

   _____

10. List anything else that you know about your preferences for studying. _____

    _____

    _____

    _____

    _____

CHAPTER 4
Study Skills

"**H**ow do I develop good study skills?" you might wonder. The first step is to manage your time effectively. You're out of high school now and on your own in college. You have to treat college like a nine-to-five job. Managing your time efficiently will help you both to study and to avoid wasting precious time. Prioritizing your goals and treating your study time like scheduled appointments will help build discipline. Use any tool, such as a daytime planner, that will help with time management and to maximize your time to study hard and to play hard. Many students who have charted what they actually do in a day realize how much time they spend doing nothing! This time doing nothing can be managed for you to be doing something productive.

From *The Essential Handbook for Academic Success*, by The California University Regents. © 1998 by Kendall/ Hunt Publishing Company.

In this chapter, we will present to you "ideal" study skills to maximize your results for the time and work you put into studying. Of course there is no "ideal" in real life. Because we learn differently, study skills that work for one person may not for others. A visual learner may need to draw pictures and study graphs. A verbal learner may prefer to discuss with and listen to others for an exchange of concepts. Our goal is to suggest study skills. You can decide and choose which study skills seem ideally suited for you.

First, you must consider which type of learner you are and which study skills would be most beneficial to you. Included in this chapter is a "learning strengths inventory" that can help you understand that realizing your strengths is the first step to utilizing them effectively. Capitalizing on what you do well already will help you to develop the best study skills for you and can ultimately lead you to academic and career success. There is no doubt that studying is hard, and there is no need to make it any harder by focusing on your weaknesses. Zero in on your strengths. This makes studying easier and more manageable.

■ Identifying Your Strengths

Follow the directions on the first page of the inventory, and select the two words in each group which best describe yourself. You must be honest. It may be possible that all or none of the words really describe you, but choose the ones that come closest. For the purposes of this inventory, the subjective descriptions are valuable in evaluating your learning strengths. On the following page, circle your answers from the previous page with each corresponding number and add the total number of circles for each column (#1–4). Continue on to the next page titled the "Learning Styles Inventory Data Sheet" and fill in the totals you got from columns #1–4. After multiplying these totals by four, this will give your total for each of the four learning styles: Concrete Sequential (CS), Abstract Random (AR), Abstract Sequential (AS), and Concrete Random (CR). The next page is a "Mind Style Graph" that you can fill in to visualize what type of learner you are. Finally, the last page of the inventory has a brief description and suggestions for each of the four learning styles.

This inventory can give you a basic idea of what your strengths are and suggest specific learning styles to foster them. If your results are lopsided in one category, then this can be interpreted as being your strongest learning style. Use the suggestions for this specific learning style to capitalize on your strengths. Perhaps your results were evenly distributed between two, three, or even all four styles. This means that you may be a bit of every style or a combination of some. In this situation, take advantage of all the suggestions that apply to your multitude of styles. Whatever your results may be, try using all the applicable suggestions to personalize your own learning style.

■ Learning Strengths Inventory

DIRECTIONS:
- ■ Read each group of four words and select the two words which best describe yourself.
- ■ You must be honest.
- ■ Think how others might describe you.
- ■ Circle the letter of your choices.

1. A Imaginative
   B Investigative
   C Realistic
   D Analytical

2. A Organized
   B Adaptive
   C Critical
   D Inquisitive

3. A Debating
   B Getting to the Point
   C Creating
   D Relating

4. A Personal
   B Practical
   C Academic
   D Adventurous

5. A Precise
   B Flexible
   C Systematic
   D Inventive

6. **A Sharing**
   B Orderly
   C Sensible
   D Independent

7. A Competitive
   B Perfectionist
   C Cooperative
   D Logical

8. A Intellectual
   B Sensitive
   C Hardworking
   D Risktaking

9. **A Reader**
   B People-Person
   C Problem-Solver
   D Planner

10. **A Memorize**
    B Associate
    C Think-Through
    D Originate

11. A Changer
    B Judger
    C Spontaneous
    D Wants Direction

12. A Communicating
    B Discovering
    C Cautious
    D Reasoning

13. A Challenging
    B Practicing
    C Caring
    D Examining

14. A Completing Work
    B Seeing Possibilities
    C Gaining Ideas
    D Interpreting

15. A Doing
    B Feeling
    C Thinking
    D Experimenting

Name: _____Bibi Begum_____ Date: ___9.25.08___

■ Learning Styles Indicator Data Sheet

1.	(C)	D	A	(B)
2.	A	C	B	(D)
3.	(B)	A	D	C
4.	(B)	C	A	D
5.	(A)	C	(B)	D
6.	B	C	(A)	D
7.	B	D	(C)	A
8.	C	A	(B)	D
9.	D	(A)	B	C
10.	(A)	C	B	D
11.	(D)	B	C	A
12.	(C)	D	A	B
13.	B	D	(C)	A
14.	A	C	D	(B)
15.	A	(C)	B	D

———	———	———	———
Total	Total	Total	Total
#1	#2	#3	#4

Continue on to next page . . .

Learning Styles Inventory Data Sheet

_____6_____ x 4 = ___24___   CS   Concrete Sequential
Total
#1

_____2_____ x 4 = ___8___   AS   Abstract Sequential
Total
#2

_____5_____ x 4 = ___20___   AR   Abstract Random
Total
#3

_____2_____ x 4 = ___8___   CR   Concrete Random
Total
#4

◼ Mind Style Graph

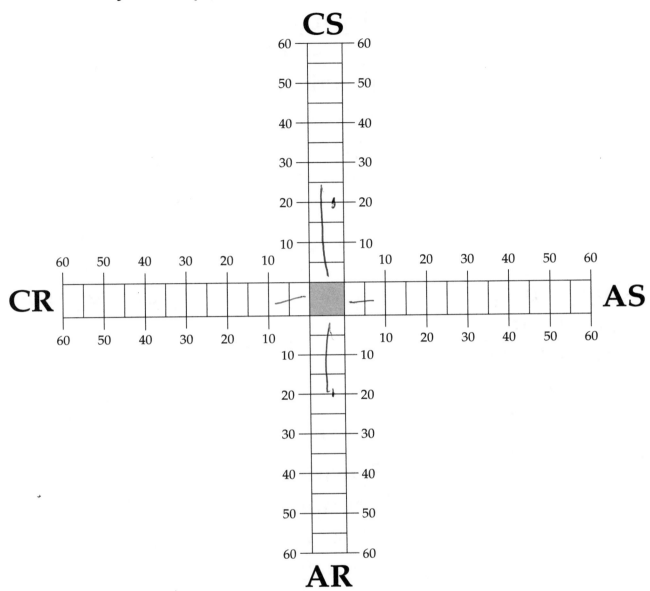

Factual
Consistent
Practical
Efficient
Organized
Structured

Creative
Experimental
Questioning
Risk Taking
Independent
Original
Intuitive

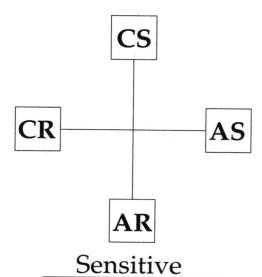

CS

CR

AS

AR

Intellectual
Logical
Conceptual
Rational
Studious
Academic
Competitive

Sensitive
Emotional
Social
Imaginative
Flexible
Understanding
Expressive

■ Identifying What Has Worked in the Past

Next, it is important to do some investigating about yourself to find out what works best for you. Thinking about what has worked in the past allows you to maximize and improve your study skills for the future. Ask yourself the following questions:

- ■ Where do I study?
  Realizing where you study is important to determine which study atmosphere is best for you. Some people like to study in quiet libraries, whereas others may study better in a coffee shop or at home. Whatever location works for you, make sure you try to utilize this facility as much as possible to do most of your studying.

- ■ When do I study?
  Think about when you study most effectively. If you are not a morning person, then be realistic and don't schedule time to study early in the morning. Studying can be hard, and there is no need to make it any harder by studying at a time when you know you will be tired or unable to concentrate. Try to schedule your specific study time each day during times you will be most effective.

- ■ With whom do I study?
  Some people study better by themselves and others study better in groups. It also depends on what you're studying. If you're studying for an essay exam, it might be better to study in a group where you can exchange different ideas and points of view. On the other hand, if you are studying for a physics or math exam, it might be better to do practice problems on your own. Another point to consider when you're studying in a group is your study partners' level of knowledge. If the rest of the group is at a higher or lower level than you are, it may be better to study on your own or try to join another group closer to your level. This will allow you to understand the concepts being shared and get more out of the session. Finally, if the group consists of your friends, it is important to make sure that the study session remains focused on work and doesn't turn into a social outing.

- ■ What do I study?
  Different classes have different material to study and therefore different study skills. For example, a psychology or biology exam may require that you know many vocabulary words. A chemistry exam may require many formulas. Flashcards would be an effective method to help memorize these terms. On the other hand, a social science or a humanities essay exam may require you to validate arguments on a number of topics. Creating an outline from the reading material and lectures is an effective way of organizing what you need to know.
  Figuring out what you need to study may require you to visit your professor. Go to office hours—get clues about what types of questions may be on the exam (i.e., multiple choice, short answers, essay) or what specific information is most important. Look at your syllabus to determine where the readings and lectures overlap—this extra emphasis is a good clue that the professor finds this information important. Realizing what you need to know will determine how you will go about studying and which specific study skills to use.

■ Specific Study Skills and Strategies

Now that you have an idea of what type of learner you are, what you're learning strengths include, and what has worked for you in the past, a list of specific study skills and strategies is presented to you. As you read the following list, keep in mind what your learning style is and what your strengths are to choose and use the skills and strategies that are best for you.

Learning Styles Suggestions

Concrete Sequential

Organize your quarter by planning out when you will begin working on certain projects and exams. Organize your week by setting aside specific times you will study. Take courses which you enjoy, and which will utilize your strengths, such as being practical, efficient, and organized. Study with and surround yourself with people who are more abstract random. They will add some creativity and flexibility to your academic experience.

Abstract Sequential

Continue to question and to debate ideas with yourself and others. Form study groups with people you feel confident sharing with. Read assigned books and find other sources of information to complement them, such as magazines, news shows, documentaries, and novels. Organize your study and work sessions so that you allow yourself enough time to complete them. Have expectations for yourself, but be sure to be flexible enough that you do not get too stressed. Know when to rest. AS people tend to get caught up in a task by being too focused on the ends. Enjoy the process. Challenge yourself and those around you, including teachers.

Abstract Random

For study groups! Get a group of people with a variety of learning styles together to discuss course material. Find specific times in your schedule that you can devote to studying. Take courses which will allow you to be interpretive, like social sciences and humanities. When you have a project for a class, try to make it a group project so you can share ideas; cooperation beats competition. Find subjects and courses which get you excited. The more emotional you are about a piece of material the more motivated you will be to learn and study.

Concrete Random

Find classes and experiences in which you can work independently. Also, get involved in situations in which you will have projects to complete, with a goal that you can work towards. Take risks, enroll in challenging courses and classes that you have no experience with. Allow yourself to be curious, your desire to understand how something works, or why something acts as it does, is a strong motivation to learn. Be creative, don't just answer a question when you have a paper due, create something special, be imaginative and original. Experiment with new ideas, concepts, and discoveries.

For Everyone

Challenge yourself to be more than you are and more than you think you can be. If you are very abstract sequential, then see how you can strengthen your concrete random traits (don't think about it AS people, do it!) Utilize your strengths and build up other areas.

In Addition

A. **Set priorities**—Ask yourself, "What do I really have to do to be successful in this class?" It is important to balance your schedule between your work, academic, and personal commitments. A quarter is only ten short weeks—you probably have realized that in order to accomplish everything you could possibly want to do, you probably need thirty-hour days! Knowing where your priorities are will help you to manage your schedule.

B. **Visit professors and T.A.s in office hours**—Professors hold weekly office hours which are a wonderful resource to use. If you give them enough time, many would be willing to read an outline or rough draft of a paper. If not, and you still want to go talk to them about something else, then consider bringing a prepared question just to get the conversation going. In large classes, visiting office hours can be a wonderful way of getting to know the professor on a more personal level. In some courses, office hours before exams may be crowded; you may learn a lot of what instructors are looking for by watching and listening to the professor talk to other students. If you live in a residence hall, talk to your Resident Assistant or Program Assistant about the specific programs that encourage faculty-student interaction.

C. **Set realistic goals**—Break down large and overwhelming tasks into smaller portions. Most likely, you would not be able to finish a twenty-page research paper in one night. If you break it down into smaller tasks throughout the quarter, it will help in avoiding procrastination and you will not have to cram at the last minute.

D. **Scheduling**—Schedule in specific study time in your day and treat studying just like any other appointment or activity that you would not miss. If you are having trouble with scheduling and pressures of last minute cramming, try giving yourself a time cushion by attempting to finish a project several days before it is due.

E. **Overestimate time on tasks**—Give yourself more time than you think that you'll need.

F. **Review material (readings) before going to lecture**—While it would be especially beneficial to complete the readings before attending lecture, time constraints often prevent this. However, by skimming through the reading before attending class, it will allow you to understand difficult concepts during the lecture. Often, professors will lecture about information which may strongly overlap the required readings; if you have completed your reading the lectures will be easier to understand, and you can focus more on listening to the professor's important points rather than furiously taking notes.

G. **Review notes after lecture**—If you don't have time after every lecture, look over your notes at the end of each week. This will help increase your retention and when it comes time to study for exams, you will have already reviewed all of your notes. You might try highlighting them.

H. **Do two hours of studying for every hour of lecture**—This is just an estimate—it entirely depends on the class, and also on how you best study. Although it can be time-consuming, some people find that retyping notes in their own words can be very beneficial. This allows you to process your notes which you are more apt to understand when you need to study.

I. **Alternate subjects when studying**—Don't study more than two hours for one subject. This technique will help you to increase your retention of the material you did study.

J. **Take study breaks**—For every hour of study, you should take a ten-minute break. This will help increase your retention and reduce burn-out.

K. Take notes while reading—Although this may take more time than simply high-lighting, it will focus your reading towards the important information. It will also improve your ability to study for exams since you will not have to go through the entire book to study—you can just review your notes.

L. Try to make connections between the material—Often, professors will have themes which connect various lectures. If you can't determine them, talk to your professor or look at the syllabus for lecture topics. Pay particular attention to material which is covered in several ways (i.e., lecture, readings, section).

M. Use past exams on file—These are wonderful study tools for exams. Although the exams won't exactly be the same, many professors keep the same general format over the years. If there are none available, get together with some friends, have each person make their own practice exam; then switch exams and take the practice test. Not only will this give you an opportunity to take a practice exam, but by making your own test, it may give you a better idea of what material is most important to focus on.

N. Utilize study groups—Use groups either before the exams as a last minute review of information or as a motivator before you begin to study to determine what you already know and what material you need to pay particular attention to. One of the best ways to determine if you understand the material is if you can explain it to someone else. If you know the information well enough to explain it to someone else, then you are probably very well prepared.

O. Tutoring—It is important to realize that if you are having trouble, it is okay to get help.

You may be feeling overwhelmed now that you're taking a full load of classes, possibly holding down a job, and attempting to have "a life" as well. But you made it this far, so you do have some knowledge about what good study skills are. The key is to find out what will work best for you, and to do it. These study skills are not meant to be "the secret formula for straight As." Try some of them out, see if they work, and then make a commitment to use them. The habitual use of many of these skills will ultimately improve your academic success.

Now that you've heard our suggestions for study techniques and what learning styles you possess, you are ready to set a plan of action. Look back at the suggestions for your learning style and at the list of general study strategies. Think about what has worked for you in the past and several ways that you can incorporate these new strategies into your study techniques. Use the information in the learning styles inventory to maximize your greatest strengths. In the following space, write down six new strategies that you think may be successful for you AND that you will make a commitment to try.

1. _____

2. _____

3. _____

4. _____

5. _____

6. _____

Now go back to each strategy, and set a specific plan of action for when you will achieve that goal. For example, "I will visit my professor's office hours by Friday of next week."

Good luck! And remember, commitment is the key—only you can improve your study skills.

CHAPTER 5
Becoming a Better Note Taker

Introduction

Perhaps you have not been concerned about your note taking skills in the past. You may have managed to get by without even taking notes. However, now that you are in college, your instructors will hold you responsible for knowing the course content and the concepts presented in class. Your tests may cover several chapters at a time. In some courses, the only tests are a midterm and a comprehensive final exam that includes material from the entire semester. It is difficult to remember everything that is said in class. That is why you need to have good notes.

Academically successful college students are not necessarily the most intelligent students in the class, but are students who use good study skills. Many students who made good grades without too much effort in high school don't do as well in college. Becoming a better notetaker is a big step toward increasing your success in the classroom. Developing good note taking skills requires *being prepared for class, actively listening* to the lecture material, *selecting a note taking style*, and learning to *use your notes* as a part of your total study system.

This chapter will help you check your note taking strengths and weaknesses and will introduce several note taking systems for you to try. You'll also learn how to identify your instructor's lecture style and to develop the note taking style that works best for you.

Pretest: Assessing Your Note Taking Skills

Check Yes or No for each item to describe your note taking habits	Yes	No
1. I check my course syllabus before each class to make sure I'm ready for each assignment.		
2. I read the text chapter(s) before class to make sure the lecture material will be familiar.		
3. I use a three-ring binder and loose-leaf paper for note taking.		
4. I review and edit my notes on a daily basis.		
5. I understand my notes when I look them over several days or weeks later.		
6. I take notes in my own words rather than trying to write down everything the instructor says.		
7. I use abbreviations and symbols so that I can note all of the important information.		
8. I make sure to include examples and all key information the instructor puts on the board.		
9. I leave enough space to fill in or add to my notes later.		
10. I pay attention in class even if the instructor wanders from the point or makes remarks with which I don't agree.		
11. I use my notes to think of possible test questions.		
12. I ask questions if I don't understand the material presented in class.		
13. I identify introductory and concluding statements and recognize transition words and phrases when the instructor is lecturing.		

Look over your responses to the pre-test. Can you honestly say that you practice most of these note taking habits? If not, use the information provided in this chapter to better your skills.

Classroom Note Taking

Preparation for note taking starts before you actually begin the class. When you purchase supplies at the beginning of the semester, don't buy a spiral notebook! Why not? Spiral notebooks are limiting; they don't offer the flexibility for using your notes in study sessions that a three-ring binder and loose-leaf paper will provide. In addition, write on only one side of the paper. Our sample notes provided later in this chapter will show you how to use your loose-leaf notes for test review.

Once you get to class and the lecture starts, you have to decide quickly what information needs to be recorded. In addition to having read the material ahead of time, you need to be able to follow the instructor's lecture. S/he will use *verbal and nonverbal* signals or clues to help you pick out the information you should record.

Non-Verbal Signals include:

- *Visually Presented Information:* If the instructor puts information on the board, uses an overhead projector, or distributes handouts, s/he is giving you a signal that the information presented is important. Remember that some instructors just jot down key words or phrases. Be sure to get down enough information to prompt your memory later.
- *Instructor Mannerisms:* Frequently when instructors are about to introduce a new topic, they will pause for a minute or glance down at their notes to gather their thoughts. This is a clear signal that you should space down and get ready for a new topic.

Verbal signals include the following:

- *Definitions:* Terms or definitions frequently show up as test questions, whether in multiple choice, matching, or true-false formats.
- *Repetitions:* You can usually assume information is important if it's repeated. Make a notation in the margin, like a circled R, to show that the information was repeated.
- *Examples:* Examples help you to understand the material when you review it later.
- *Enumerations:* Your instructor may use signals like "Five characteristics of . . .," or "The three steps in the process are . . .". Make sure you clearly identify the topic and get down each item listed.
- *Transitional Words:* Be alert for words like "consequently," "furthermore," or for phrases like "another reason for . . .". These words and phrases are clear signals to record the information provided.
- *Direct Announcement:* Some instructors may simply tell you up front that something is important, with a lead-in like "Pay attention to . . .," "This is important," or literally, "note this in your book, or put it in your notes."

Some instructors are not great lecturers and tend to stray from the point, but paying attention to the clues they provide can help you to record the information you need.

In addition to using a loose-leaf binder and learning to "read" your instructor's signals, advance preparation includes developing some personalized note taking short cuts. Most instructors speak at a rate of about 125–150 words per minute when giving a typical lecture. You can't possibly record every word, but you do want to write down as much information as possible. Using a system of abbreviations and symbols will help you to increase your note taking speed. Some common abbreviations and symbols are listed in the following chart.

Word or Term	Abbreviation or Symbol	Word or Term	Abbreviation or Symbol
About	~	Introduction	Intro.
Amount	Amt.	Months	Mo(s).
And	&	Number or Pound	#
Chapter	ch.	Organization	Org.
Company	Co.	Page(s)	Pg., p., pp.
Continued	Cont'd.	Psychology	Psyc.
Decrease	Decr.	Principal	Princ.
Definition	Def.	Significant	Sig.
Economic	Econ.	Social or sociology	Soc.
Example	Ex. or X or e.g.	Summary/summarize	Sum.
General	Gen.	Versus	Vs.
Government	Gov.	Volume	Vol.
Hour/hourly	Hr./hrly.	Year	Yr.
Illustrate	Illus. or e.g.	Equal/Not Equal	= and =/=
Important	Imp.	Less than/more than	< and >
Increase	Inc.	Positive/negative	+ and −
Information	Info.	With/without	w/ and w/o

Other personalized short cuts include using a ? in any place where you think you missed something important, using a B to indicate work from the board, and an X for examples. Using abbreviations can become especially important in later semesters when you develop a specialized terminology for your major

■ Active Listening

How do we listen actively? What does this term mean? For now, we'll use the term to mean paying attention to what the speaker *means* as well as to what s/he *says*.

In the classroom, you are given directions and assignments, and you listen to presentations and lectures. How well you understand the material will help determine the grade you will receive in the class. When working, you listen to instructions that will help you do your job. In your personal life, you listen to the concerns and problems of your friends and family members. Listening, therefore, is an essential life skill, and developing that skill can make you a better student.

We can improve our listening skills for classroom use by practicing the following strategies:

■ *Read the Text:* Make sure you know the topic for upcoming lectures and that you've completed the reading assignment. Your instructor gives you a course syllabus for just this reason! Being familiar with the topic can help you follow the instructor's lecture.

■ *Concentrate:* We all know it's easy to "drift off," so you need to concentrate on paying attention. Many instructors test primarily from lecture notes rather than from the book, so you need to keep focused. Make sure you record all main points and supporting ideas. You need to be actively involved in listening to the lecture, and writing will help you to keep your concentration.

■ *Respond to the Message, not the Messenger:* Don't let your instructor's appearance, mannerisms, or lecture style detract you from your task—writing down the relevant information.

■ *Be Accepting of Different Ideas and Viewpoints:* Many college classes will introduce you to new ideas or to value systems that differ from yours. While questions are always appropriate, the classroom is not intended for personal arguments. Don't be defensive or aggressive in class if the instructor is presenting material that differs from your beliefs. You're responsible for learning the information presented in class—not for arguing with the instructor or monopolizing class time. If you have an honest difference of opinion on an issue, make an appointment to discuss it with your instructor during his/her office hours.

■ *Pay Attention to Instructional Clues:* As discussed earlier, your instructor will use "signals" or clues to guide you through the lecture. Keeping up with these transitions will help you to write down the important facts.

■ Note Taking Styles

You've spent a number of years taking classroom notes already and may have a format or style that really works for you. Many students use a formal numbered outline format, grouping main ideas or topics, secondary topics, and supporting details. This is one of the oldest notetaking systems in use, and it can be very effective if the instructor is well organized and presents the information in an easy-to-follow, step-by-step manner.

Our sample notes will present information regarding the stages of memory in two variations of the formal outline system. We'll also take this same information and present it in a visual format that may work very well in certain classes or for certain topics in a given class. Remember that you don't need to use exactly the same note taking style for every class or even all the time in the same class.

Informal Outline

The informal outline (also known as the indented topic system) shows major topics and lists secondary points and supporting details by indenting them under the major topics, without using a numbering system. This format leaves a $2^1/_2$ inch margin on the *right* side of the paper. After class, you can jot down key words or terms in this space for use as memory prompts when you review your notes. The following notes are written in the *informal outline* style.

3/14/2001
Psyc. 101

Stages of Memory

A.   Sensory Memory

- First point of information intake—sight, sound, touch
- Lasts for a few seconds as exact copy

Digit-span exp.
Chuncking—grouping
bits together

B.   Short-Term Memory

- Temp. storage of small amts. of info.—5–7 "bit" avg.
- "Chunking" helps us to remember more—e.g. S.S. #'s are 3 bits, 2 bits, and 4 bits
- Provides a "working" memory—e.g.—Looking up phone #'s
- Sensitive to interruption—phone # lost if someone interrupts us before we dial
- After 18 secs the info. is lost w/o coding or rehearsal—e.g. Meaningless syllables experiment (in text).

Sensitive to
interruption

Info. lost after 18
secs.

C.   Long-Term Memory

- Permanent storage
- Rehearsal process (repetition, etc.) required
- Limitless storage capacity
- Info. stored on basis of meaning & imp.

Permanent
Requires rehearsal
Limitless

Informal Outline System

Cornell System

Developed by Dr. Walter Pauk of Cornell University, the Cornell System is a widely used note taking system. The example below shows a blank notebook page divided into the three sections of the Cornell system, and the next page shows our stages of memory notes recorded using this system. As the sectioned paper shows, this format leaves a blank column on the *left* side of the page. This space is used to develop questions about the material presented for later review. The horizontal column across the bottom of the page is used to jot down a quick summary of key points.

Cornell Page Set-Up	
2¹/₂" for questions	**Notes**
Summary	

03/14/01
Psyc. 101

	Stages of Memory
	Sensory Memory
	1. First point of information intake—sight, sound, touch
	2. Lasts for a few seconds only as exact copy
	Short-Term Memory
How does the process of chunking help us to remember?	1. Temp. storage of small amts. of info.—5-7 bit avg.—digit span experiment
	2. "Chunking" like bits of info. together makes it easier to remember—e.g. S.S. # has 3/2/4 bits grouped
	3. Info. from sensory memory is selected for attention—phone # you've looked up, etc.
	4. Serves as working memory
What happens to info. entering STM?	5. Sensitive to interruption—someone interrupts before you make the phone call, and the # is gone
	6. After 18 secs. w/o rehearsal, info. is lost and doesn't get to LTM.
	7. Coded, rehearsed info. goes into LTM
	Long-Term Memory
	1. Permanent storage
	2. Limitless storage capacity
How does info. get moved from STM to LTM?	3. Rehearsal process (repetition, etc.) required
	4. Info. stored on basis of meaning & imp.

Info. must go through 3 stages—sensory, S/T, and L/T. Rehearsal process required for retention. Info. stored on basis of meaning & imp.

Notes Using Cornell Note Taking System

Charting, Mind Mapping, and Clustering

These note taking systems allow you to "picture" the information visually. Mind mapping and clustering usually begin with the main topic circled in the middle of the page, with arrows or smaller circles radiating out from the middle to show supporting topics or details. Charting is a more linear format, using horizontal or vertical arrows or lines to show a sequence of events. The figure below shows our memory notes in a horizontal chart, with the process moving from left to right and top to bottom across the page.

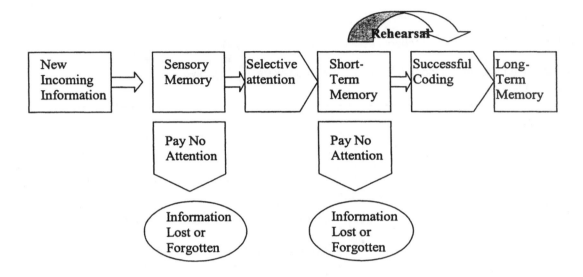

Choosing a Note Taking Style

We've looked at three different styles of taking notes. How do you know which method will work the best for you? Look over some of your previous notes. How are they arranged? Do they seem to match one of the styles we've discussed, or do you have an original style? Have your notes provided you with the information you needed? Are you comfortable with the system you've been using? If so, you don't need to change.

As you reviewed the descriptions of these three note taking systems, you probably thought one of them seemed easier to use than the others. Many psychologists and neurologists think that we are primarily either linear or holistic thinkers. Let's look at these two preferences in greater detail. See which one sounds most like you. By understanding how we tend to organize and process information, we can learn to develop a note taking style and study system with which we feel comfortable.

Linear thinkers like things to be logical and use rational, step-by-step problem-solving techniques. Holistic thinkers, on the other hand, like to see the whole picture and respond strongly to visual stimuli. Look over the characteristics identified with primarily linear or holistic thinkers and see if one pattern seems to describe the way you work.

Linear Thinkers	Holistic Thinkers
■ Make lists ■ Keep track of time ■ Prefer to work alone ■ Like a neat, orderly desk ■ Plan and organize work & study schedules ■ Usually take linear, outline format notes ■ Notes clearly identify main ideas and supporting details ■ Complete one task or assignment before beginning another ■ Are comfortable with deadlines and work according to a schedule ■ Use facts and reasoning to come up with answers and solutions	■ Use visuals and colors when getting down ideas ■ Not worried about time—concentrate on the present ■ May have a messy desk or work area but feel comfortable with the mess ■ Like to study or review with others ■ Study whenever time allows; sometimes have energy bursts and work non-stop ■ May use arrows or lines in their notes to show connections and relationships ■ Sometimes work on several projects at once ■ Use intuitive feelings and "hunches" to problem solve

If you feel comfortable with the style described in the linear column, you'll probably feel comfortable with either the indented outline format or the Cornell method of note taking. If the holistic style seems to describe you better, you might want to try one of the more visual note taking methods. With these systems, you can easily add symbols and diagrams and can color code information to show relationships between ideas.

You may feel comfortable with several items from either side of the chart. If you seem to have a balance between both styles, you have strengths in both areas and can use those strengths to your advantage. For example, you may usually plan your work and follow an organized schedule like a linear thinker. However, you may occasionally get a burst of energy and work non-stop until you finish a job like a holistic thinker. Remember, too, that you may need to change your note taking style depending upon the demands of a particular class, so be adaptable. It's also a good idea to find a study partner of the opposite thinking style so that you can each add creative input to a study session.

■ Using Your Notes

Developing a good note taking system doesn't help you do well in your classes if you don't learn to use your notes as a part of your total study system. Follow the steps below to maximize the usefulness of your class notes.

■ *Editing:* Your first review of your notes should take place as soon as possible after class. Use this time to rewrite illegible words, finish incomplete thoughts or ideas, clarify any abbreviations you used that you may not remember, and fill in any information you might have missed getting down. This first review is a repetition step that serves as a rehearsal, and it will help you move the information into long-term memory.

■ *Weekly Review:* At the end of each week, you should complete a second review of your notes. Concentrate on relationships, time sequences, and organizational patterns at this point. Think about how your notes and your text material overlap. This second review is critical to processing the information for long-term memory storage.

■ *Test Preparation:* If your instructor has notified you of the test format, try to predict both objective and essay type questions. For math class, try straight calculating as well as word problems. Remember to look over your notes for information that was put on the board or that the instructor announced was important.

It is at this point that the questions developed from the Cornell note taking system can be especially useful if you've followed our advice to use loose-leaf paper for your note taking. Remove your one-sided notes from your binder and overlap them so you can only see the question or key word column as shown in the example that follows.

Use a blank sheet of paper to cover your notes from the top sheet. Quiz yourself by answering the questions listed. If you're not sure, you can quickly flip the page to find the correct answer. Once you're sure you know the material, put those notes back in your binder. Continue working on the material you still haven't mastered.

Pg. 1	Pg. 2	Pg. 3
Which memory stage holds information for only a few seconds? Describe the effect of interruptions on short-term memory. How does the digit-span test affect memory?	Why can you remember your social security number when shorter strings or numbers or information may be forgotten? What process is necessary to transfer information from S/T to L/T memory?	What did the meaningless syllable experiment prove? How is information in LTM stored?

Test Review with Cornell Note-taking System

■ *After the test:* Your final review should come after your test has been returned. Were you prepared? Were your notes adequate? If not, what kind of information was missing from your notes? What percentage of test questions seemed to come from lectures? What percentage came from the text? Think about what you need to do to improve your test scores next time.

■ Summary

This chapter stressed that taking good notes requires being prepared for class, actively listening to the lecture, selecting a note taking style, and using your notes as a part of your total study system. You learned to key in to the verbal and nonverbal signals your instructors use to guide you through the lecture, and you were encouraged to use abbreviations, symbols, and other shortcuts to help you record as much information as possible.

Remember that your notes are only as good as the information you record and the way in which you use them. Students who test well have usually practiced the editing and review techniques covered in this chapter.

■ Journal Assignment

Write a one-page, typed essay in which you describe how you actually take notes in class and how you use your notes. Identify three or more specific changes you can make in your note taking. These changes can be from any part of the note taking process: advance preparation, active listening, note taking style, or use of notes as part of a total study system.

If you receive notes from a note taker or use a tape recorder instead of taking notes in class, identify which style of note taking you prefer. List three or more reasons why you prefer this style in relation to your study habits, your learning style, and the type of course for which the notes are being taken. Describe your own advance preparation for class, what you do in class to ensure that you are getting all of the correct information, and how you use and adapt the notes to help you study more effectively.

Name: _____Bibi Begum_____ Date: ___9/25/08___

■ Homework Activity, Part 1

Checking Out Your Instructor's Lecture Style

DIRECTIONS: Use the statements below to evaluate the lecture style used by one of your instructors for this semester.

Course Name _____Osl_____

	Yes	No
1. My instructor begins each class with a quick review of the last session.	✓	
2. My instructor is well organized and clearly introduces each new topic.	✓	
3. My instructor lectures at a comfortable pace; s/he doesn't speak too slowly or too fast.	✓	
4. My instructor speaks clearly and at a voice level I can understand.	✓	
5. My instructor is focused and doesn't wander off the topic.	✓	
6. My instructor includes illustrations and examples that help me to understand the material s/he is presenting.	✓	
7. My instructor uses a vocabulary (words) that I can understand and defines new terms when needed.	✓	
8. My instructor is open to questions and encourages classroom discussion.	✓	
9. My instructor frequently provides visual input by his/her use of the board, an overhead projector, or handouts.	✓	
10. My instructor uses the last few minutes of the period to summarize main ideas and/or to clarify new assignments.		

How do your instructors measure up? If your responses cluster on the "No" side, the note taking strategies presented in this chapter are especially important. They should help you to make the most of your classroom time.

■ Homework Activity, Part 2

DIRECTIONS: Complete *one* of the assignments listed below:

1. Photocopy at least two pages of notes you've taken in another class. Using the editing technique described in this chapter, rewrite any illegible or incomplete words or phrases, fill in any gaps, and clarify any abbreviations used. **Do this with a different colored pen so your editing changes stand out.**

2. Photocopy at least two pages of notes you've taken in another class. Use the margin of the paper to develop questions from the main ideas and topics presented in class. Develop *at least five study questions,* concentrating on "How" and "Why" questions. Write your questions in a different color so they are obvious.

Special Instructions—

Please do not submit your original notes from another class unless you have another copy to use for study.

You may use notes taken by a notetaker to complete this assignment as long as the editing changes or study questions are your own. The purpose of this assignment is for you to demonstrate that you can apply and use the note taking techniques described in this chapter.

How and why questions

History notes

1. How were the hebrews captured?

2. why did they not revolt?

3. How were they captivated for so long?

4. why was the zhou Dynasty so Powerful?

4. How was Confusious able to be so influental

CHAPTER 6
Taking Tests
Making the Grade

It has been estimated that in your college career you will spend from 25–40 percent of your time preparing for or taking tests! Evidently, this is a crucial skill to master if you want to succeed in college! It is very probable that no one has tried to teach you how to master this test taking skill, yet your grade point average is affected more by this ability than by any other single thing! Every student has felt at one time or another the butterflies, nausea, or extreme terror caused by the mention of the word "test." No one likes to think that their life could possibly be changed by their performance on a mental examination, but that is often the feeling that we give ourselves (or is given to us by our professors). Maybe it is time to put some thought into the basic strategies that could make test taking less traumatic.

There are just two basic problems caused by the necessity of tests—test anxiety and test smartness. Test anxiety is probably familiar to all students. It's that fear of failure, the

From *Practical Approaches for Building Study Skills and Vocabulary,* Second Edition by Funk et al. © 1996 by Kendall/Hunt Publishing Company.

fear of going blank, or the fear of feeling out of control, and it can have a negative effect on test scores. You actually may have learned the material, but forget it due to test anxiety. Test smartness is just as much of a problem, but few students may realize it. The "A" is on the paper due to good test-taking skills, but the knowledge is quickly forgotten or never applied. Since most students could fall easily into one of these two problem areas, we may need to rethink our view of test-taking.

■ What Could Take the Trauma out of Test Taking?

In the first place, we expect too much out of our memories! Due to the myth that cramming is effective, too many students believe that the best way to study for a test is to cram all the information possible into your mind the night before the test. That way all the information will be fresh! In no other area of life would we expect so much out of our abilities. Would you ever consider that you were physically fit for life because you had worked out at the gym last night? Or would you ever take a bath and feel that you had completed that task and would never have to do it again? Of course, these examples are obvious, but until we get in our minds the idea that information must be reviewed consistently to be remembered, test scores will consistently point out that we have not quite mastered the material. Many students make the mistake of trying to "view" the material the night before rather than "review." Information is retained by systematic, spaced overlearning. There is no other effective means. Cramming MAY give you a passing grade, but it will not show much practical benefit as far as retaining the material—and isn't that why you are in college?

■ Okay, What Are the Rules for True Test Preparation?

Three basic rules—plus omitting the word cramming from your vocabulary—will make a great difference in your view of test-taking preparation (and the possible trauma it creates).

Rule 1: Start studying for each test the first day of class. Do not feel that you do not need to study biology today since you just had a test last Thursday. The way you study the material being learned this week will determine your test grade just as much as the way you study the night before the test.

Rule 2: Don't get behind on assignments! Finish each day's work on that day, if at all possible. Stay caught up on reading assignments and text-note taking, revising lecture notes, and extra assignments. Don't procrastinate or your grade will reflect it.

Rule 3: Incorporate the use of all three types of review—daily, weekly, and test taking. EACH DAY spend a few minutes revising your lecture notes from that day and reviewing them. Read your text assignment, take notes, and review them. Do this for each class taken on that day. Sometime during the week, you need to go back and review all the PAST lecture and text notes from the current semester. Don't wait until test-time! Now is the time to start preparing. Think of what a difference you will feel if you have already reviewed each set of notes four or five times BEFORE you start to study for the test! Two or three nights before the actual test you can do an IN-DEPTH REVIEW of all the material, but it won't be cramming filled with panic and pressure. You will have built a solid foundation on which to study for the test.

■ What's the Difference between Recall and Recognition?

Along with these three test taking preparation rules, you must also be aware of one more way that we need to change our view of test taking. For many students, to study for a test means to be able to RECOGNIZE the material when it is presented on the test. That's why multiple choice test items seem to be easiest for most of us—we can recognize what we have studied. But if the test is a short answer, fill-in-the blank, or essay test, our memories may fail us. There's nothing to recognize! We have not studied to the point of RE-CALL, and we cannot pull up the information from our memories. We stopped short of effective learning because we stopped reviewing when we felt we could recognize the material. To realize the difference between recall and recognition is the major step towards "de-traumatizing" test taking. You must learn the material to the point that you do not need clues to aid your memory, and studying with the use of *questions* and *recitation* is the way to conquer this crucial difference. Effective students do not just read over their notes—they make questions over the main ideas, cover up the material, and recite the questions and answers aloud. Extra work? Yes. Does it make a difference? You won't believe the difference!

■ What Are the Different Types of Tests?

There are really just three types of tests—objective, subjective, and a combination of the two.

a. Objective tests include multiple choice, true-false, and matching items. These questions have only one right answer because the grader is looking for a specific letter or word. These items are all recognition items, because the choices are spelled out for you. You may choose true or false, or you may choose from a list of two or more possible answers.

b. Subjective tests are also called essay tests. The question will call for a very broad answer, and the correct answer depends on the "subject" who is grading it. What one grader might call an acceptable and complete answer could be viewed as incomplete, or even completely wrong, to another grader.

c. A combination of subjective and objective characteristics could involve sentence completion items (or fill-in-the-blank, as they are commonly called) or short answer items. These are more of a combination of objective and subjective traits because, even though one basic idea is being asked for, more than one specific word or concept could be the correct answer. Therefore, a little bit of subjectivity is being used.

■ What Are the Advantages of Each Type?

Objective tests are probably used more often than subjective tests for several reasons. An instructor can test over a lot of material in a very short amount of time with this approach. They are easy and fast to grade, and a student worker could help the instructor in the grading if time is a priority. Many instructors like to use these tests because they are less subjective and involve less decision-making when grading. No matter who grades the test, or when it is graded, the credit will be the same. So it may appear that this type of testing is a little more fair to all. But, as we all know, objective items can be worded in such a way that they may not appear "fair." Even so, ease in grading and equality in fairness are two definite advantages of objective tests. Also, since the student is not required to write long answers on objective tests, many instructors feel that these tests do not let a student's writing ability interfere with the test score. Poor writing ability does not hurt the grade; neither can a good writer cover up for lack of knowledge with outstanding writing ability. So in several ways the objective test may appear more fair.

On the other hand, subjective tests really do what a test is supposed to do—show what you really know. When you have to write out detailed answers on a topic, it quickly becomes obvious if you really LEARNED the material! Subjective tests force recall learning, and that's the best kind! Subjective tests are also much easier and faster for the professor to compose than objective tests.

■ What Are the Disadvantages?

Even though there are advantages to either of these two major types of tests, there are also disadvantages that make the choice hard for instructors to make. Objective tests may end up only testing "test-awareness," or the ability to play the game of test taking. Many students become good guessers, and they are able to recognize enough and bluff enough to make the grade. But the test has not accomplished its purpose—that of trying to show true knowledge learned. As mentioned previously, good objective items are fairly difficult and time consuming to write. Questions may end up being tricky or testing for details only.

Perhaps the main disadvantage of subjective tests is that they are very difficult to grade. This difficulty involves two aspects—time and fairness. It does take an enormous amount of time to grade essay tests. So if an instructor has several sections of one class, time factors make these tests a real trial to grade. This time and pressure factor may influence how fairly each test is graded. It may be all too true that one essay test could receive many different scores, based on the person who grades the test, the time of day it was graded, and even the order in which it was graded. Fatigue plays a role in fairness, time limits add to the problem, and personality factors of the grader complicate the matter. A student's writing ability may also influence the grader. Neat handwriting, correct spelling and grammar, a "way with words," and overall neatness of the paper may sway the judgment of the grader. Unfortunately, the opposite kind of paper may do the same thing—only in the opposite direction!

■ What Are the Causes of Poor Test Performance?

Even though the most obvious answer as to why students might not perform well on a test would be INADEQUATE KNOWLEDGE, this is certainly not the only answer. Part of the purpose of this chapter is to help you to analyze your typical test behavior and sort out the hindrances to your success. It is true that many students do not perform well on a test simply due to the fact that they did not study enough—or in the proper way. It is vital that you understand that it is not how MANY hours you study for a test that makes the difference. It is the QUALITY of those hours and the way they are DISTRIBUTED that spell out your success rate. Weekly reviews based on questions and recited answers over thorough lecture and text notes are the secrets to mastery. Intense cramming sessions the night before the test will not assure you that the information will be there when needed.

LANGUAGE-RELATED PROBLEMS can also affect your performance on tests. If you read the textbook but do not comprehend it, you will not perform to the best of your ability. If you have trouble understanding the test items, or knowing specifically what the question is asking for, your answer cannot be top-notch. Therefore, reading problems do influence many students' test grades.

Also, many students simply do not know how to take a test. Even though they may have taken hundreds in their lifetime, INEFFECTIVE EXAM-TAKING SKILLS may still be hindering their performance. Test-taking is a game one must learn to play—a skill that can be learned with practice. Certain rules must be learned and adhered to or the results will not please you. We will cover these "rules" in the next several sections.

Finally, TEST ANXIETY can cripple your test scores. You may have studied adequately, and you may feel you really do know the information, but if you panic during the test, your memory will not cooperate. Take a minute now to TEST YOUR TESTING SKILLS. Complete the inventory that follows to see if exam anxiety is a problem for you, or if you suffer from other "testing deficiencies."

■ Test Your Testing Skills!

Answer yes or no to the following questions to check up on your ability to play the testing game.

Before a Test, I

	Yes	No

1. usually wait until a test is announced before reading text assignments or reviewing lecture notes.

2. often think of tests as trials that can't be escaped and must be endured.

3. often do not read my textbook because the instructor will cover it if it's important.

4. feel that I have a good memory, so I do not usually take notes over lectures.

5. sometimes have to memorize formulas, definitions, or rules that I simply do not understand.

6. generally have trouble deciding what I really need to study.

7. depend mainly on last-minute cramming to prepare for the test so that it will be fresh in my mind.

During a Test, I

	Yes	No

8. am sometimes unable to finish answering all the test items within the allotted time.

9. sometimes am forced to leave an item blank because I cannot decide on the correct answer.

10. often find I cannot decide what the question is really asking for in an answer.

11. frequently feel that I have not studied enough, or that I have not studied the correct information.

12. start with the first item and answer each question in its correct order, regardless of difficulty.

13. catch myself thinking about how much smarter other students are than myself.

14. worry about what will happen if I flunk the test.

15. get so nervous that I feel sick to my stomach and have trouble remembering what I studied.

16. often think, "The more I study, the less I remember!"

17. then realize I would much rather write two essays than take one test!

After a Test, I

	Yes	No
18. almost always feel that I could have done better.	_____	_____
19. often find that I have made careless mistakes or left unintentional blank answers.	_____	_____
20. find that I should have changed an answer, but I did not because I felt my first answer is usually best.	_____	_____
21. try to forget about the test as soon as possible so that I can start fresh on new material.	_____	_____
22. only look over my mistakes, because the rest of the questions were correct and therefore do not need to be analyzed.	_____	_____

SCORING: Count up your yes responses. As in the game of golf, the lower your score, the better you play the game of test-taking. If you answered yes to three or more of questions 13–18, you have some problems with test anxiety also. What's a GOOD score for this test on test-taking? If you scored higher than a 7, practicing the suggestions from this chapter could completely change the way you feel about tests!

■ How Can You Become More Test-Wise?

We have already discussed the problem of test-smartness, but the goal is to be test-wise—to know how to play the game of taking tests successfully. Three main areas of test preparation need to be considered: physical, emotional, and intellectual preparation.

Be Physically Prepared!

You need to be in top physical condition to do your very best in a test situation. We don't mean you need to be able to run a marathon, but on the other hand, don't handicap yourself by not being physically prepared. Although you would not do this purposefully, you are in effect handicapping yourself if you do not accomplish these physical tasks before a test:

a. *Attend class*—each and every one. The worst class to skip is the one before the test. Never skip class in order to study more. Important reviews may take place right before the test session, so don't miss them!

b. *Ask questions*—These questions may include the type of test (objective or subjective), length of exam, time allowed, material covered, possible points and percentage of total grade, examples of test questions, and if any aids are allowed, such as pocket dictionary, calculator, etc. These answers may influence the way that you will study.

c. *Eat properly*—Don't skip breakfast, and try to include some protein in the meal before your test. Give yourself "brain fuel!"

d. *Sleep properly*—Don't skip study time to sleep, and don't skip sleep time to study. Schedule each for its proper time. Don't plan all night studying sessions. Sleeping seems to "cement" learning, or help your memory to consolidate what you have studied. If you do not get an adequate amount of sleep, your spontaneity and originality may be hurt, and your level of anxiety may be heightened. Also, the worst time to "party hardy" is the night before the test! You need a clear head and quick thinking ability to do your best on the test, and drinking will not help you in either of those areas!

e. *Study in a simulated test-taking atmosphere*—Try to make your study sessions like the real thing! Set time limits, sit at a desk, don't allow interruptions, and don't peek! Anxiety may be increased in a testing situation simply because it is so different than what you are used to.

f. *Use a multi-sensory approach to studying*—Remember to use your eyes to see, but also your voice to recite, your ears to listen, and your hands to write the information you need to learn. The more ways you put the information in your mind, the better chance you have of it sticking!

Be Emotionally Prepared!

Now that you've mastered the physical aspects of test-preparation, consider these emotional aspects:

a. *Think positively!*—Push for success, not just to avoid failure. Too many of us think as the little boy who reluctantly told his father, *"Dad, I'm afraid I flunked that math exam."*
   "Son, that's negative thinking!" admonished his father. *"Think positive!"*
   "Then, Dad, I'm positive I flunked that test!" the son replied.

Don't dwell on the past or even what the future will bring. Think only on the OP-PORTUNITY of this one test. A test is not a trial, but a chance to show what you know, and learn what you've missed. Use it to its full advantage!

b. *Visualize a good grade*—Although this is similar to the suggestion above, it is so helpful that we want to include it separately. See an A+ paper in your mind. Tell yourself, "It will be just like me to ace this test!" Instead of putting yourself or your ability down, pump yourself up! These "coping statements" will make a big difference in your attitude and confidence!

c. *Tie main ideas in with your life*—Try to apply the big ideas of what you have studied to your own situation. The more applicable you can make the information, the more apt you are to remember and benefit from it.

d. *Avoid pre-test hall chatter*—Have you ever noticed the typical statements of students before they go in to take a test? You hear things such as, "I didn't study at all for this test! Did you?" or "I hope to goodness I don't flunk this thing!" You don't need this type of talk! Whether you have studied enough or not, don't erode what you do have!

e. *Remember that some anxiety is helpful*—Although you can suffer from too much test anxiety, a little bit of nervousness will keep you alert and on top of things. Accept this as natural and helpful!

Be Intellectually Prepared!

Intellectual preparation for testing is the ONLY area that many students feel has to be dealt with, but as we have discussed, physical and emotional preparation are essential also. However, this area of being intellectually ready for the test is obviously crucial. Consider these vital components of being intellectually prepared:

a. *Review lecture and text notes weekly*—This vital weekly review has already been emphasized, but it cannot be stressed too much. This one step will make an enormous difference in how ready you *feel* for a test—and how prepared you REALLY are! Also remember to study handouts, past assignments, previous tests, and make use of study guides if they are provided. As much as possible, try to make your study notes manageable with mnemonic systems, questions, highlighted vocabulary, etc.

b. *Always study as for essay tests*—Many students tend to worry more about essay tests than objective tests. They feel that essay tests are harder, and in some respects they are because recall is necessary—not just recognition. Therefore, you should study for ALL tests as if they were essay, whether they are or not. Think in terms of main ideas, and recite questions and answers aloud. Force learning by recall, and all tests—whether essay or objective—will be easier and more beneficial.

c. *Get old tests and talk to "old" students*—If your instructor has old tests in his or her files, ask to see them or have a copy of them. Your library may even keep a "test bank" of past tests for you to look through. Former students of your current class are excellent resources. Ask them questions about what they remember of the tests, and see if they possibly still have their old tests. Is this cheating? No! You are studying the instructor's format of testing, and you are also studying in the best possible way—with questions and answers.

d. *Anticipate test questions*—Some ways to do this have already been mentioned in the previous paragraph, but also think about some other clues for your instructor's possible test questions. Information that was written on the board is usually a good resource. The teacher may have even told you during lecture that certain information was important, or asked you to particularly note that section. You should have

Understanding Test Words

Learn the meanings of these testing words because they are usually not interchangeable! You must know what the instructor is asking you to do before you can do it!

1. *COMPARE—bring out points of similarity AND points of differences*

2. *CONTRAST—show differences when placed side by side*

3. *CRITICIZE—give YOUR judgment of; approve OR disapprove; give good and bad points*

4. *DEFINE—give the meaning of, explain the nature of*

5. *DESCRIBE—tell about, give a word picture which characterizes; do not just name or label*

6. *DIAGRAM—make a drawing, chart, or graph, and usually add labels; possibly add a brief explanation*

7. *DISCUSS—examine, analyze carefully, and give reasons pro and con; be complete and give details*

8. *ENUMERATE—give a numbered list; name over one by one*

9. *EVALUATE—cite both advantages and disadvantages; include appraisal of authorities and your own appraisal*

10. *EXPLAIN—make clear, interpret, make plain*

11. *IDENTIFY—name, label, classify, or characterize*

12. *ILLUSTRATE—make clear by stories, examples, or diagrams*

13. *INTERPRET—translate, give examples, give your judgment*

14. *JUSTIFY—prove your point, give your argument; discuss bad and good points and conclude with it good*

15. *LIST—write a numbered list*

16. *OUTLINE—give the main ideas in organized arrangement; use headings and subheadings to give a well-ordered list*

17. *PROVE—establish that something is true by citing facts or giving logical reasons*

18. *RELATE—stress associations or connections between ideas*

19. *REVIEW—analyze a subject critically*

20. *STATE—present the main points briefly*

21. *SUMMARIZE—give the main points briefly*

22. *TRACE—give a description of progress in a definite order; follow the trail of*

emphasized this in your notes in some way (such as a star, or a box). Information that is mentioned in both text and lecture would be good test questions. Don't forget vocabulary words that are often in italics or boldface print! They make excellent matching questions. Review questions at the beginning or the end of the chapter are also an easy way for your teacher to get a question. Don't omit any of these clues to help you to anticipate test questions.

e. *Understand question words*—This suggestion is especially crucial for success with essay tests. To be asked to diagram a concept is not the same as to explain it. To summarize does not mean to criticize. You cannot get full credit for an answer if you do not answer the question! Study the chart that follows to make sure you are doing what is called for!

■ What Causes Test Anxiety?

In the TEST YOUR TESTING SKILLS worksheet, you may have been able to see if test anxiety is a problem for you. Many things can cause this problem, but you can help yourself by deciding to eliminate the following characteristics if they describe you during testing.

Test anxiety may strike if you:

- focus on yourself rather than the task at hand.
- associate a test score with your self-worth.
- allow negative self images.
- compare your performance with others around you.
- continually rethink an answer.
- allow panicky self-talk.
- begin to feel out of control.

You must stay in control and take care of your job one step at a time. Recognizing what causes test anxiety is the first step toward solving the problem.

What's the Cure for Test Anxiety?

The real cure for panicking during a test is over-preparation BEFORE the test! Better planning will replace panic with confidence. Then when you get into the testing situation, do not focus on yourself OR on what others are doing. Focus only on the task in front of you. If that scares you, focus on some other object for a minute, such as your shoe! Regroup your thoughts and talk positively and confidently to yourself. Remind yourself that you are competent and in control. Then start to work on the test. Only think of that one task. Don't allow negative thoughts to enter into your thinking. Plan to arrive a little earlier on test day so you won't be rushed. Then you could do some relaxation techniques (as discussed in the chapter on stress) to help you to relax. Always start with the easier questions on the test to build your confidence, and keep encouraging yourself with positive self-talk. Perhaps the best strategy is simply to realize that test anxiety is a learned set of responses that are only detrimental to your performance and that can be changed. Focus on changing them!

■ How Can You Improve Test Scores?

There are many strategies that will help to improve your test scores—regardless of the type of test or the content. Take the WHAT'S YOUR TESTING IQ? inventory that follows to see how many strategies you already know that are essential for test-wiseness—whether you know the information needed for the test or not. Some of the questions are serious, some are trivial, and some are downright silly, but they all illustrate test-taking strategies that every college student must master. The answers will be given to you also, and we will give you suggestions for test-taking in general and for each type of test specifically. You need to practice these suggestions for EVERY test, including pop quizzes, unit tests, and comprehensive finals. Learn to play the game!

What Are Some General Test Taking Suggestions?

1. Avoid rushing. Get to the test early. Think calmly and act calmly.

2. Pick a good spot to sit and recite notes calmly. The best spot is usually your normal seat, because you will feel more comfortable there. But the best spot is also usually away from distractions and close to the front. That's why it's important to pick the right spot the FIRST day of class and stick with it. It is a good idea to study up to the last minute, as long as you can do so calmly.

3. Get rid of undue anxiety by relaxation techniques, positive self-talk, and focusing only on the task at hand.

4. Wait for oral instructions. Do NOT begin the test as soon as you receive it. After you put your name on the paper, WAIT. You may miss vital information or clues if you do not listen to instructions.

5. Jot down memory clues before you begin. If there are dates, names, or mnemonic strategies you are afraid you may forget, jot these down on the back of the test. This may relieve some stress immediately!

6. Skim the entire exam, reading directions carefully. This is a crucial step that is often overlooked. As you quickly look over the test, look for:

   a. point allotment—All questions are not created equal, and you should spend the most time on items worth the most points.

   b. type of questions—Which will take more time for you? What order would be best to answer the questions?

   c. clues—Often, test questions may have clues farther on in the test, or perhaps you may even find the answer!

   Although reading the directions is not a difficult step, it is one to which you should learn to give strong emphasis!

7. Ask specific questions if needed. Notice that you wait until the instructor has had time to explain, AND until you have had time to skim the test! Many questions can be answered by these two steps. If you still have questions, ask pointed, specific questions.

8. Do the easy ones first. This suggestion will make a big difference in your confidence level. It will also help you with the time problem, because you will make sure you complete the ones you know quickly, and you will have the rest of the time to concentrate on the harder ones.

9. Skip the harder ones, mark them so you will remember to come back to them, and return to them after you complete the easy ones and have warmed-up. A little mark beside the more difficult ones will also make sure you note these as you get your test returned after grading. Of course, you will notice it if you miss it! But if you get it correct, you may not remember the correct answer two weeks later unless you take special note of it.

10. Do all tests four times. Most of us hate the thought of doing a test once, but you need to go through four steps to do your best. First, skim the test as stated. Then do the easier ones while you mark and skip the harder ones. Return to do the harder ones, and finally, look over the entire test to check that you have answered all questions.

11. Change your answer if needed. Although this policy has been hotly debated, recent research seems to point out that when an answer is changed, more often than not it is changed from a wrong answer to a right one. But you also need to analyze your pattern. What usually happens for you? If the answer was clearly just a guess, perhaps your first guess IS your best answer. But, if after second thought you feel the need to change the answer, do so!

12. Budget your time. Do this before you start by considering the point value of the question. Also, make sure you allow enough time to complete the whole test with time to double-check.

13. Never leave blanks! A guess is better than a miss, so don't guarantee an error by leaving a blank. You may luck out. Usually a middle answer in multiple choice questions or true answers in true-false questions are more apt to be correct.

14. Write answers clearly. Do not try to fool the instructor by making your T also resemble an F in true-false items. Don't try to make the "a" also pass for a "c" in multiple-choice items. All you will probably succeed in doing is aggravating the grader who may check the item wrong with a flourish.

15. Make the test serve you after it's over. You have paid for it, so get your money's worth. Don't purposely try to put it out of your mind. Talk about strategies with other students. Look up the ones you weren't certain about. (You will remember the answer much longer than any other question if you do!) When you get the test back, check errors and also guesses that turned out to be correct. If you have marked the difficult ones, this will be easier. Analyze why you missed the question. Learn for the next test—and there's ALWAYS a next one! Make the doing of the test in itself beneficial.

Okay, now that we've gone through helpful strategies for test taking in general, let's see about your TEST TAKING IQ!

◼ What's Your Testing IQ?

Answer these questions to the best of your ability. Use every test-taking strategy that you know.

A. True-False

Answer + for each true statement and—for each false statement. Each item is worth 1 point.

1. _____ Smart students always study 2–3 hours each day for every class.

2. _____ Frequently, students leave too much studying to do until finals week.

3. _____ Some students study a lot, but no one studies as much as they should.

4. _____ The way to learn the most efficiently is not to succumb to distractions.

5. _____ Hunger leads to decreased concentration and increased apathy when studying.

6. _____ According to the textbook, most students study at a 1-1 ratio of hours studied versus hours in class.

B. Multiple Choice

Write the letter of the correct choices for each item in the blank. 4 points each.

7. _____ Test-taking can cause:
   a. hardening of the arteries.
   b. students to study harder.
   c. professors to have papers to grade.
   d. late night studying.
   e. all of the above
   f. answers b, c, & d
   g. answers b and d
   h. none of the above

8. _____ Students go to class because
   a. since it is necessary.
   b. information is being taught.
   c. it is the most fun way to spend the day.
   d. the law of xfghot recommends it.

9. _____ Which statement(s) is(are) not correct?
   a. Students often study in the library.
   b. Students do not study enough.
   c. Most students should try to study more.
   d. Professors should never give essay tests.

10. _____ Colleges often
   a. blow up.
   b. get torn down.
   c. try to educate students in the best possible manner with the least amount of expense.
   d. change their names.
   e. try to educate students in the worst possible manner with the greatest amount of expense.

11. _____ The distance from Paris to New York is approximately
    a. 3000–4000 miles.
    b. 10–20 kilometers.
    c. 9000–10,000 miles.
    d. 500–1000 miles.

12. _____ Mass hysteria can result when large numbers of people
    a. believe something that is not true.
    b. fear an invasion.
    c. share delusory perceptions.
    d. all of the above

C. Matching

Write the letter of the correct answer in the blank. 2 points each.

13. _____ preview
14. _____ test-taking
15. _____ survey
16. _____ time schedules
17. _____ quixotic

a. a writing system
b. to manipulate data
c. used for evaluation
d. getting an overview of a chapter
e. used for efficient studying
f. idealistic, but impractical
g. determines the appropriateness of using a dictionary

D. Sentence Completion

Write the missing word in the blanks. 10 points each.

18. _____ is the process for becoming a citizen.

19. The largest animal in the world is a _____ .

20. _____ _____ _____ is the collective name of Superior, Huron, Erie, Ontario, and Michigan.

21. Lions are most likely to be found in _____ .

E. Short Answer

Answer concisely but completely. 1 point each.

22. Describe the best way to make a time schedule.

_____

_____

23. Evaluate the practice of previewing in studying a chapter.

_____

_____

F. Essay Question

24. Trace the history of your immediate family. Enumerate how many people are included, list their occupations and ages, and discuss their personalities. State if you care for them or not, and make a decision as to their honesty when considered as a group.

■ Answers for "What's Your Test-Taking IQ?" Worksheet

Before you started taking the test, you should have skimmed over the entire exam to see the type of questions and to budget your time according to point value. Notice that you could have missed ALL of the True-False questions and only have done the damage of missing three Matching questions. Missing all of the Matching questions would have been the same as missing ONE Sentence Completion question. Also notice that the Short Answer questions were only worth one point. Therefore, it was not worth your time or effort to spend a lot of time on these answers. Examine the point value carefully before you take a test, and spend more time on the most points! Below are the correct answers. If there was a "clue word" in the sentence, it is given also.

A. TRUE-FALSE
    If you did not answer with a "+" or a "–", you missed all six questions. You must follow the directions to get the credit!
    1. – (always, each, every)
    2. + (Frequently)
    3. – (no one)
    4. + (not)
    5. – (Hunger)
    6. + (According to the textbook)

B. MULTIPLE CHOICE
    Notice that the directions said you might have more than one answer (the word was CHOICES).
    7. f
    8. b
    9. b, d
    10. c
    11. a (kilometers)
    12. d

C. MATCHING
    Note that the directions clued you in to the fact that you would only have one answer for each question, but it did not say that you could not use the same option more than once! If this had been a real test, you may have needed to clarify these points.
    13. d
    14. c
    15. d
    16. e
    17. f

D. SENTENCE COMPLETION
    18. Naturalization
    19. whale (a)
    20. The Great Lakes (3 blank spaces)
    21. Africa

E. SHORT ANSWER

22. Possible answer—Denote class time, work time, and other necessary time by the hour and plan the best times to study and take care of other responsibilities.

23. Possible answer—Experts say previewing is crucial to effective studying of a chapter because it increases concentration and comprehension, and I would agree.

F. ESSAY

24. (If you were REALLY bored enough to answer this monster of a question, you should have first shown some type of a chronological review of your family history. This would be followed by a numbered list of the job and age of each person in your immediate family, and a brief description of their personalities. You should have stated your feelings for each one, and finally stated an opinion as to whether your family could be considered honest or not. This question really involved seven questions—trace, enumerate, list jobs and ages, discuss, state, and decide—and would have best been answered in six or seven paragraphs with the key word repeated in the topic sentence of each.)

By the way, how many points was this awful essay question worth, or does it matter? Would it make any difference how long you spent on it if it was worth *10* points rather than *100* points? Of course it would—or should! You need to ask, if point values are not given, and then write accordingly. If the essay is worth 100 points and you don't have anything to say, you had better come up with something! If it is only worth 10 points, don't spend three pages answering the question. BUDGET TIME BY POINTS AND DIFFICULTY!

■ Can You Follow Directions?

This is a test to see how well you read and understand test directions. You should do this test as quickly as possible. First, read through the entire test. Then go back and do what the items instruct you to do.

1. Write your name in the upper right corner of this paper.
2. Circle the word name in the first sentence.
3. Draw five small squares in the lower left-hand corner of this page.
4. Put an X in each square mentioned in Number 3.
5. Put a circle around each square.
6. After the title, write "YES, YES, YES."
7. At the bottom of this page, add 1991 to 2397.
8. Stand, turn around, and whisper, "I am a leader in following directions."
9. Working from top to bottom along the left margin, count by 2s from two to 32.
10. Across the bottom of this page, list your favorite four friends.
11. Recite "The Star-Spangled Banner" to yourself and write the twelfth word in the song on this line.

   _____

12. Put a box around all of the words that start with a "b" on this page.
13. Write the name of the President of the United States in the exact middle of the right side of this page.
14. Complete step one and six, disregard everything else and stop.

Did You Follow Directions?

What is your testing IQ? Points excluding the essay question add up to 82, so let's say the essay question was worth a meager 18 points to make it a nice, even 100 points. But let's also say that you got all 18 points on that essay! What is your test score? Add up your points and judge yourself on this scale, and then read ahead to find out how you might have done better, or, more importantly, how you may do better on the next REAL test!

95–100 points	A	Hey, you've got a good handle on this test-taking game!
90–94 points	B	Not bad!
85–89 points	C	Look forward to improving!
84 points or less		Have we got some great tips for you! Read on!

■ Are There Any Specific Clues about Taking Objective Tests?

If you want to "show all you know," there are specific suggestions you should follow for each type of objective test. Remember to put into practice the general suggestions that have been given for all tests, and then study the specific suggestions that follow. Look back at your WHAT'S YOUR TESTING IQ? answers to see how these strategies work. We have included the reasons for the answers after each item.

True-False Tests

1. Watch for qualifiers. These include words that are absolutes or limiting words, and those that are tentatives.

   a. Absolute or limiting words indicate a false statement. These include: always, every, all, no, never, none, only, entirely, invariably, guaranteed, great, or much. They leave very little room for exceptions, and sentences containing these words would seldom be true.

   b. Tentative words leave room for exceptions and would tend to indicate true statements. These words include: seldom, sometimes, some, often, most, many, few, usually, generally, frequently, or ordinarily.

   This suggestion explains why question 1 is false (always, each, every), and question 2 is true (frequently).

2. Remember, if any part is false, the whole thing is FALSE! Every word must be true before you would answer the statement as true. As some great test-taker has said, "Whatever is almost true is quite false." Question 3 is false because we cannot say that NO ONE studies as much as they should.

3. Watch for negatives or negative prefixes. Words such as not, none, no, or except often confuse you as to what the question is really asking. Negative prefixes, such as il-, im-, ir-, dis-, un-, non-, or a- may do the same thing. It is suggested that you circle or underline these negatives so that you do not disregard them, as test-takers are prone to do. Question 4 would be made less confusing by omitting the word **not,** deciding the answer is false, putting the word back in, and reversing the answer to true.

4. Don't read more into the statement than is actually there. Look for qualifiers, but then read the statement as it is. In the statement, "Hunger leads to decreased concentration and increased apathy" (Question 5), the word is hunger—not extreme hunger or starvation. This kind of statement would probably be false, in most cases.

5. Guess true if you have to guess. Teachers usually dislike writing false statements for two reasons—they are afraid you will believe the false item, and good false statements are difficult to write. They either wind up being obviously false (and a little bit stupid) or being tricky because they are so near the truth. For this reason, you will usually find more true statements than false. So if you didn't know the answer to question 6, you should have guessed true.

6. If you have to guess, consider a possible pattern. Don't count on it, but consider it. True-False tests are difficult to grade because the grader can easily get confused. Therefore, some teachers incorporate a pattern. Check it out. (Notice the T-F-T-F-T-F pattern of the True-False section of the test.)

Multiple Choice Tests

1. Read the directions carefully. How many correct answers are possible? Do the directions say choose the correct answer, the correct answers, or the BEST answer? Ask for clarification if you are not sure.

2. Read the question and each option separately, making sure you consider all options. If you consider each as a true or false statement and mark it to the side accordingly, you will help yourself immensely by ruling out distractors, as in question 7. Watch for grammatical matches that might give you hints, as shown in question 8. Option **a** did not fit with the question grammatically, so this is a clue that it is not the correct choice. Usually your professor would have pointed out the mistake if it was a correct answer.

3. Don't choose unfamiliar or foolish options—as in question 7 (option a) or question 8 (option c or d). If you've never heard the word before or never heard the idea mentioned in class, chances are THAT is not the correct answer.

4. Be suspicious of negatives and absolutes. Circle or underline these to make sure you are aware of them. Question 9 could be tricky if you do not take out the negative and decide without it. Option b implies that ALL students do not study enough, and we cannot say this is true. Option d has the absolute word "never," so we can rule it out as a distractor.

5. Consider carefully similar options, opposite answers, longer answers, more general, or more inclusive options. Usually, one of these will tend to be the correct answer. Options c and e of question 10 illustrate opposites and longer answers.

6. Number answers tend to be in the middle range of options. Question 11 shows that you could rule out the second option because it is the only one that is in kilometers. Why would the right answer be so obviously different? You then have a range of 500 to 10,000 miles. Consider only the options that are in the middle range, and you have narrowed your odds considerably!

7. Try to answer before you look at the options to lessen your confusion. The distractors will be more obvious if you have already formulated an approximate answer.

8. Consider "all of the above" carefully, especially if it is not used very often. All you have to do is find two answers that are correct. As question 12 demonstrates, even if you do not know about the third option, it must be true IF you can only choose one answer and IF there are no options like "answers a and b."

Matching Questions

1. As always, read the directions carefully, and ask questions if necessary. Since our test said to write the correct *answer*, we assume only one will be possible. But we would need to ask if options could be used more than once to know what to do with questions 13 and 15. If we can use an option twice, option d could be the answer to both. If we can't, option b **or** c might answer number 15.

2. Get an overview of number comparisons before you start.

   a. If you have equal numbers of questions and options, it will be easier to eliminate distractors, so be sure and do so systematically.

   b. If the numbers are not equal, start with the *longer* column and look down the shorter column for matches, even if it is the option side. It is important to consider each option each time.

3. Always answer the easier ones first to better your odds!

4. Consider grammatical clues. Are you trying to match up nouns, adjectives, events, dates, etc.? Question 17 is an adjective, so look for an option that describes an adjective, not one that describes a noun.

5. Guess if necessary, but only as a last resort! Work mainly with eliminating distractors.

Sentence Completion or Fill-in-the-Blank

1. Reword the question so the blank is at the end, if possible. Use all the words in the question as your best clues. (See question 18.)

2. Watch carefully for grammatical clues. Question 19 gives you a clue that the blank must start with a consonant due to the word "a," so you have a good guess that the animal must be a whale instead of an elephant. Check to make sure that there will be subject/verb agreement with your answer. Is the blank calling for a name, date, event, noun, verb, adjective, or what?

3. Check to see if length or number of lines indicates a clue, as in question 20.

4. Ask very specific questions if needed. If you tell your instructor that you are not sure what should go in question 21, you will probably hear, "I'm sorry, but I cannot help you." But if you ask for clarification on whether the question is asking for a country or a continent, you will probably get an answer, and a very good clue at the same time. If you are completely off track, you will also probably get a clue about that too!

5. Never leave blanks! Consider every possible clue and then guess, and you might be amazed at the partial credit you may receive!

Short Answer Questions

1. Think before you write, and then start off by restating the key words of the question in your answer.

2. Watch for the key question words (describe, evaluate) to make sure you do what it says.

3. Give direct, concise answers.

■ How about Suggestions for Subjective Tests?

Many students may give an unconscious shudder at the sound of the words "essay test." Why do we fear them so much? Maybe because we feel in these tests we really have to KNOW what we're being tested over! The word recall is the key word again. But another major problem with subjective tests is that HOW you answer is almost as important—if not more so—than WHAT you answer. Organization, relevancy, writing ability, and even neatness all enter in as a vital part of your grade. Students typically do two things wrong with essays: they write everything they can think of about the topic (whether it is relevant or not!), or they write only their feelings to fill up space, rather than the facts that were asked for in the question.

> ### Critical Thinking
>
> *It may be an error in judgment to assume that most students do not score their best on tests because they do not know the material. Look back at one of your past tests and analyze your errors. Were they due to lack of knowledge, or was it possibly lack of reading skills, lack of exam skills, or exam anxiety? Before you can correct your test-taking errors, you have to know what is causing them. Then you can decide what steps to take to correct them.*

The Lab Bowl System

L—ook over the entire exam before you begin. Read the directions carefully, and underline the testing words (verbs) that are crucial to your answer. As you answer, it is a good idea to come back and check off each verb to make sure you have done what the question asked.

A—sk for point allotment if it is not given. Don't assume all of the questions have equal value, and don't spend the same amount of time on each question.

B—udget your time based on the point allotment. Make a tentative time schedule before you begin to make sure you allow enough time to finish the test, and to make sure you spend the most time on the questions that are worth the most points. (But you know the most information about the question that's only worth three points? That's the way it usually goes, but you had better come up with more information for that 30-pointer!)

B—egin with the easiest question. This is an important practice in all testing, but especially when you have to write essays! This will increase your confidence, get you warmed-up, and get a large portion of the test done quickly. If you start each answer on a separate page, the order that you answer will not matter. You can then put the answers in the correct order before you turn in the test. You also have a way to add more information to a question later in the test if you allow this space.

O—utline each question before you begin on a pre-essay page. This page will be a thinking page to help you get started. Your time schedule could be figured out here, along with the order that you will answer the questions. You might want to copy the testing words here to make sure you answer in the correct way. Make an outline of each answer before you start to write, and the writing will be much easier and faster. Label this page Pre-essay Page and you will really impress your professor! As you try to outline question 4, you may remember something else you needed to add to question 2, and you can jot that down on this thinking page. Don't spend TOO much time here. You still have to write, so include this thinking time in your time schedule.

W—atch those key testing words! As mentioned before, to diagram does not mean the same as to discuss. Be very aware that you do what you are supposed to do!

L—ook over the exam again before you turn it in to correct errors or omissions. Teachers sometimes seem to make snap judgments on your grade based on the way your paper looks, so make it look good!

■ How Can I Raise My B's to A's?

Because HOW you answer is just as crucial as WHAT you say in an essay, there are a few impressive things that you can do to make your test give a good impression, and hopefully add points to your score. Your instructor may not consciously give you more points, but there **is** a natural tendency! So consider these steps to add the "icing to the cake":

1. Write in essay form. This means use paragraphs, topic sentences, transition words between paragraphs, complete sentences, etc. Also, repeat part of the question (usually the testing word) in the first sentence of each portion of the essay.

2. Be accurate grammatically and with spelling. You may want to bring a pocket dictionary with you to the test. It will pay off!

3. Start each answer on a new page and number the answers correctly.

4. Neatness is vital! So:
   a. Write in pen.
   b. Write on one side of the paper only.
   c. Remember to leave margins—side, top, and bottom.
   d. Use unlined paper with a line guide underneath if you really want to impress!
   e. Put your name on each page and staple all pages together.

5. If you run out of time because you did not budget correctly, outline your answer. You may get partial credit.

■ Two Final Considerations!

What If You Have to Cram?

Even though we feel that it is vital to distribute your studying throughout the weeks, you may find yourself in a bind occasionally. It may be the day before the test and you have not started your preparation. Should you cram? Definitely! If you haven't been reviewing, your memory level is somewhere between 2–20 percent—a definite F percentage! You are starting from scratch the night before the test. So there are two words that you must abide by: SELECTIVITY and RECITATION. If you try to study it all lightly, you will probably forget it all. Pick the main ideas and recite them until they are solidly in your mind. You will do a better job on the test knowing the main points well rather than trying to remember the details fuzzily!

Can You Guess Successfully on a Test?

Although some students seem to be better at this "skill" than others, we do not suggest you count on guessing. However, as we have stated before, never leave blanks! Check and double-check to make sure you have an answer for each question. There is no reason to throw a point away! Take a minute to fill in the blanks of our multiple choice test with random "guesses" to see if it **might** pay to guess.

■ Objective Exam Analysis Worksheet (Example)

Student ___ Nicole ___ Course: ___ Health ___ Exam: ___ #2 ___

Grade: ___ 69% ___ Date: ___ 2/10 ___

ANALYSIS RESULTS — COMMENTS AND OTHER INFORMATION

A. 61% missed due to exam skills

B. 39% missed due to poor retention/lack of knowledge

	Lack of Knowledge					English Skills				Exam Panic				Exam Skills					Other				Comments
Test Item Missed	Reading/Textbook	Inadequate Notes	Application of Knowledge	Poor Retention	Other	Reading Comprehension	Reading Speed	Vocabulary	Other	Decreased Concentration	Mental Block	Forgot to Use Exam Techniques	Other	Did Not Focus on What Question Asked	Failed to Consider Options Carefully (True, False, ?, etc.)	Poor Use of Time	Changed Answer	Other	Math	Carelessness/Clerical Error	Other	Other	
A 1				X																			Info on Diet
2				X																			Info on Medication
4															X								Need to T.F. each option
6																	X						Need to ask for clarification
12																	X						Did not read carefully
13				X																			Info on Diet
14														X									Did not note key word
16														X									Need to formulate own answer 1st
19															X								Need to T.F. each option
24														X									Failed to note key word
28															X								Need to T.F. each option
30															X								Need to T.F. each option
31				X																			Info on Diet
33				½											½								Needed to T.F. each option
B 4				X																			Info on Disease
6															X								Needed to T.F. each option
16																	X						Practice "except" questions
20				X																			Info on Medication
22				X																			Info on Medication
Items				7½										3	5½		3						
%				39										16	29		16						
% Totals			39%													61%							

Objective Exam Analysis Worksheet

Student _____   Course _____   Exam _____

Grade _____   Date _____

Test Item Missed	Lack of Knowledge					English Skills				Exam Panic				Exam Skills						Other		ANALYSIS RESULTS
	Reading/Textbook	Inadequate Notes	Application of Knowledge	Poor Retention	Other	Reading Comprehension	Reading Speed	Vocabulary	Other	Decreased Concentration	Mental Block	Forgot to Use Exam Techniques	Other	Did Not Focus on What Question Asked	Failed to Consider Options Carefully (True, False, ?, etc.)	Poor Use of Time	Changed Answer	Carelessness/Clerical Error	Other	Math	Other	
																						Comments:
Items																						
%																						
% Totals																						

■ Summary

We have explored the idea that most students have an incorrect view of test taking. Taking a test may be traumatic because we view it as a trial instead of a challenge for which to prepare and "show all we know." We have discussed objective and subjective tests, and a combination of the two. The advantages and disadvantages of each have been pointed out, along with possible causes why students might not perform well on tests. Many suggestions have been given to help the student become more "test-wise" in general test-taking situations and for each of the specific types of objective tests. Test anxiety has been analyzed along with the best possible cure—over-preparation. Finally, the dreaded essay tests have been discussed along with a systematic way to tackle taking them. Several worksheets have been given to help you analyze your testing behavior and your testing skills. Now it is up to you, the student, to put these discussions and suggestions into practice. If you want to show all you know, learn how to de-traumatize test taking, and master the evaluation process. Prove to yourself that you are the master of the test-taking game and that you can "make the grade!"

■ Does It Pay to Guess?

Finish taking this multiple choice test by filling in the blanks with random a, b, c, or d answers. Then grade your "test."

Multiple Guess Test!

1. _b_	11. _a_	21. ____	31. _c_	41. ____
2. _d_	12. _d_	22. _d_	32. _a_	42. _b_
3. ____	13. ____	23. _a_	33. _a_	43. _b_
4. _d_	14. _a_	24. ____	34. ____	44. ____
5. _c_	15. ____	25. ____	35. _b_	45. ____
6. ____	16. _b_	26. _a_	36. _b_	46. _d_
7. _a_	17. _d_	27. _b_	37. _c_	47. _b_
8. _a_	18. ____	28. ____	38. _c_	48. _c_
9. ____	19. _b_	29. ____	39. _d_	49. _b_
10. _c_	20. _c_	30. _a_	40. ____	50. _c_

If you had turned in the test with the blanks, your score would be no higher than 68 percent—usually a D. Now "grade" your test and see how guessing may have helped.

3. c	15. b	25. a	40. d
6. d	18. c	28. d	41. a
9. b	21. c	29. d	44. a
13. a	24. b	34. b	45. c

To compute your score, take the amount you "missed" times 2 and subtract that number from 100. What is your new percentage? How does that compare with 68 percent? Would it have been to your advantage to guess? For most students, guessing pays off, and it is certainly better than a guaranteed miss!

CHAPTER 7
Managing the Stress of Life as a College Student

Introduction

You probably didn't expect college to be easy, but many students are unprepared for how stressful going to college can be. As a community college student, you are likely to have more roles than the average person. Most students work at least part time, but many are full time employees. If you live at home, you may have additional responsibilities. If you are married and/or a parent, you know the time and energy involved in building strong relationships and running a household. If you're just starting to live on your own, you have the pressure of paying bills, grocery shopping, etc.—things that your parents used to do for you. Many of you are also involved in extra activities either on campus or in the community. Now you've added the hours of homework and studying it takes to maintain good grades. In addition, if you were not

From *The Community College: A New Beginning* Third Edition by Linda S. Aguilar, Sandra J. Hopper, and Therese M. Kuzlik. Copyright © 2001 by Kendall/Hunt Publishing Company. Used with permission.

a strong student in high school, or if it has been a few years since you were in school, you might be feeling anxious about taking tests, math classes, or writing papers. The pace of college courses goes at least twice as fast as regular high school courses. It can become overwhelming by midterm as you start thinking about all you have to do before the end of the semester.

This chapter is going to look at stress objectively so you can identify the things in your life that cause you stress. Then, several ideas for reducing stress will be presented along with a description of a few relaxation techniques. Finally, some specific student stressors such as math and test anxiety will be discussed. So, if you're feeling a little stressed-out these days, read on; this chapter is for you.

Pretest

Identify the major changes that are happening in your life right now. Check as many as apply to you *within this past year*.

Family changes:
- Death of spouse, parent, sibling
- Death of grandparent or other close relative
- Divorce or marital separation (you or your parents)
- Marriage
- Pregnancy
- Gaining a new family member/s (birth, adoption, stepfamily, elder moving in, etc.)
- Major changes in health or behavior of a close family member

Health changes:
- Serious personal injury or illness
- Major change in sleeping habits
- Major change in eating habits
- Quitting, starting, or major increase in smoking, drinking, or other drug use
- Major change in amount of exercise or activities

Financial changes:
- Sudden loss of income
- Major change in financial status (a lot better or a lot worse off than usual)
- Taking on a mortgage
- Foreclosure on a mortgage or loan
- Taking on a loan

Employment changes:
- Being fired from work
- Retirement from work
- Major change in responsibilities at work (promotion, demotion, transfer)
- Changing careers
- Major change in working hours or conditions
- Major conflict with your boss/supervisor, or co-workers

Personal changes:
- Detention in jail or other institution
- Death of a close friend
- "Breaking-up" with girlfriend/boyfriend
- Conflict with spouse, in-laws, parents, or a close friend
- Beginning or ceasing formal schooling
- Moving to different residence / Major change in living conditions
- Outstanding personal achievement
- Revision of personal habits (dress, manners, associations, etc.)

Social changes:
- Changing to a new school
- Major change in usual type or amount of recreation
- Major change in church and/or social activities
- Vacation
- Major changes in holiday celebrations, and/or number of family get-togethers

What does it mean? Change causes stress. The more check marks, or the more changes you have going on in your life, the higher your risk for a stress related illness. If you have major changes taking place in all the areas of your life (check marks in each category), that can also signal the potential for trouble.

What Is Stress?

Stress is the body's reaction to an occurrence or an event. You're driving to class and suddenly notice the flashing lights and siren of a police car behind you. Your body instinctively reacts. You look down at your speedometer. It shows 10 miles over the speed limit. Tension mounts. You prepare for what may follow. You don't really have time to stop and certainly can't afford a ticket. Your heart starts beating faster, and your mind is racing as you try to think of what to say. Even if the police car continues down the road, you may still feel a little shaken. Your adrenaline is high; you're stressed. A police car driving with its lights and siren turned on is not in itself a stressful event. If you were stopped at a red light on a side street or driving in the opposite direction, you would have a much different reaction to that event. The event is neutral, but your reactions can be positive or negative.

Our reactions come from a variety of sources. Some of them are the importance we place on the event, the expectation of certain consequences or results, our previous experiences, and our ability to handle a variety of situations. Our perceptions, beliefs, habits, level of self-confidence, and physical, mental, and emotional health also influence our reactions. No two people will react exactly alike. What may be a challenge for one person may be distressful for another.

We usually think of stress as always being from negative or bad events, but it can come from happy occasions as well. Starting college, planning a wedding, the birth of a child, celebrating the holidays with family, getting a new job, moving to a new house, or remodeling your current one are usually considered positive events. Yet, all of these can produce stress. Change of any kind may produce stress. That's why the pretest asked you to identify how many major changes are going on in your life right now. A little tension may be just what you need to motivate you. However, if you get too much in too short a time period, it can cause your body to become overloaded. When that happens, your body's natural immune system may be unable to defend itself against all of the germs, bacteria, and viruses that surround us. Your resistance is lowered, and you succumb to whatever illness is "going around." Being overloaded for a long period of time can be very damaging to your health. That's why it is important for you to use common sense and practice good health habits as your first line of defense.

Stress is unavoidable and affects everyone. We all have events in our lives that cause us to react positively or negatively. Some of the common ones are the conditions and circumstances that surround our families, friends, money, health, work, school, and relationships with others. In addition to major life changes, stress can be the result of improper reactions to every-day irritations, conflicts, frustrations, and over-extension of ourselves. Stress is often self-imposed. Sometimes we set unrealistic goals for ourselves or set our standards too high. When we expect too much of ourselves by overrating our abilities, we may fail to make satisfactory progress toward (or achieve) our goals. Failure can produce a state of depression that prevents us from functioning effectively. The opposite is also true. We may set our standards too low or not try to achieve. Then, we're stressed by the consequences of our laziness and irresponsibility.

Another cause of stress is a conflict in our values. When we are in situations where we act contrary to our core beliefs and values, we feel the pressure of being phony. Time constraints or the feeling of always being overloaded is yet another huge stressor. When we lack the proper support and/or resources, or feel that school or job demands interfere with our personal activities, we may exhaust our abilities to reduce or resist stress.

■ How to Reduce Stress

We cannot control all of life's stressors, but we can control how we react to them, and we can control the degree of anxiety they place on our lives. Learn how to reduce stress by identifying what is causing it and then implement your own personal stress-reduction program. If you alter your beliefs and your way of thinking, you can reduce anxiety levels. You can also condition your body to resist any ill effects that remain. Stress is manageable, providing it does not approach a life-threatening level.

Step One—Look for Stress Symptoms—Be aware of the symptoms of stress. Awareness always precedes action. Recognize the symptoms, and don't deny that you have them. Then you can start to solve the problem.

Step Two—Identify Stressful Times, Situations, and People—Identify the times and places when you feel stressed out. Did you relate to any of the typical sources of stress listed in the previous section? Think of the current causes of anxiety in your life right now. If it helps, keep a diary to pinpoint the sources of your stress. Record what happened and your reaction. Think of other possible ways you could have reacted. List the kinds of things that were helpful in relieving your anxieties.

Step Three—Eliminate Unnecessary Stress—Whenever possible, eliminate the causes of unnecessary stress. From your diary you might have noticed a pattern of things or people that always bother you. When you come to that situation/person again, think ahead. Try to anticipate what will happen. Then, avoid those stressful situations. "That's easier said than done," you say. Yes, some events and conflicts with people in our lives are unavoidable. In those cases you may have to develop a tolerance for what you cannot resolve. You cannot change someone else, but you can change yourself and your attitudes. Don't let conflict with the significant people in your life become a way of life. It's too exhausting and frustrating. Learn new skills such as assertive communication to improve and soften all your relationships.

Step Four—Reduce the Effects of Unavoidable Stress—For the stress in your life that you can't eliminate, try to control and reduce its effects. Remember to keep your perspective. Think about how important this event really is. Will you even remember it next week? Next month? If not, why get upset about it? Keep your stress at a minimum and don't over-react. People have successfully dealt with the stress in their lives by using some of the following techniques.

Common Stress Reducers

1. *Establish Support Systems*—Maintain the positive, supportive relationships you already have and build new ones. Feeling isolated increases stress, so join clubs or organizations with others who have similar interests or needs. Spend quality time with family and friends. Everyone needs nurturing and satisfying relationships. Ask for help when you really need it. It's OK to acknowledge that you can't do

everything on your own. Having someone who you trust and with whom you can share your troubles makes them more tolerable. In addition, don't overlook the resources available through the helping professionals on campus and in the community. The college, area hospitals, social service agencies, civic groups, and churches often have support groups or classes to meet a variety of needs.

2. *Maintain a Healthy Lifestyle*—Take care of yourself. Good nutrition and diet are always important in managing stress, anxiety, and tension. Eat balanced meals each day (as opposed to a day full of junk food or waiting until late at night to pig out). Get plenty of sleep. Research studies and surveys on college campuses reveal that most students do not get enough sleep. People who are under a great deal of stress need more, not less, sleep, just as they do when they have a physical illness. Don't neglect exercise. When you're busy, it's easy to put off things like extra sleep and exercise because you don't have time for them. That's a big mistake. Regular exercise of 20–30 minutes at least three times per week will help you work off your tension, reduce your anxiety, and improve your overall health.

   Remember, too, that drugs, including alcohol and tobacco, do not remove the stressful conditions of life. Most drugs are habit-forming and expensive, and that creates additional stress. Alcohol and nicotine are depressants that decrease your energy and make you feel down. They may mask the symptoms for a while, but they really make the problem worse. In short, the healthier you are, the better you are able to cope with everything.

3. *Practice Emotional Control*—This one should probably be at the top of the list. Emotional stress is so commonplace. We live in an angry, violent society these days. Consider the shootings at schools, in the streets, and at workplaces. Road rage is epidemic. There are a lot of people who do not have control over their emotions and have no way to deal with their problems without exploding. Many people live with a great deal of unresolved anger and resentment.

   Freedom comes from letting go and forgiving. Live at peace with yourself and others. Choose emotional health for yourself even if others in your life don't make that choice. Another emotion to keep under control is self-pity. Get rid of self-defeating, negative thoughts. They will only add to your stress. Put your problems in perspective and be grateful for the things you do have.

4. *Use Humor*—Lighten your emotional load. A good sense of humor and laughter always puts things into a positive perspective. You know the old saying, "laughter is the best medicine." Norman Cousins actually proved that to be true. In his book, *Internal Jogging*, Cousins describes the healthful benefits of laughter. It exercises the lungs, relaxes the diaphragm, increases the oxygen level in the blood, burns calories, and tones the entire cardiovascular system. The relaxation response after a good laugh can last as long as 45 minutes. Smile more, too. It brings out the best in other people.

5. *Learn to Communicate Effectively*—Being able to express yourself is such an important concept, we're going to devote an entire chapter to it. Pent-up feelings can eat away at you and increase your stress. You need to be able to let others know how you feel. It's so frustrating to be misunderstood. If that happens on a daily basis, it's probably a source of constant irritation. Try to improve the situation by becoming more assertive. Respect yourself and others. Be honest about your feelings. Be aware of your body language and the indirect ways you communicate, too. You might be saying one thing with your mouth and the opposite with the rest of your body. In addition, learn to actively listen to others. Never assume you know what the other person is thinking or what s/he will say. You may reach the wrong conclusion and create a misunderstanding.

6. *Manage Your Time*—In the age of e-mail, cell phones, fax machines, high-speed transportation, fast food, automated express lanes, and instant everything, it is easy to feel like the world is spinning out of control. You can reduce stress when you simplify your life and modify your routines. Maintaining balance and moderation are the keys to good stress management. Don't push beyond your limits. Learn to say no to things that are not high priorities. Cut back where you can. If you are really stressed at this stage in your life, you might be better off with less to do. Consider what you can live without. Remember that the more things you accumulate, the more time you will need to take care of them.

Manage your schedule. We often advise our students to concentrate on getting good grades in a few classes rather than poor grades in a lot of classes. It will take you longer to graduate if you take fewer classes each semester, however, it will be a lot less stressful, less expensive, and take less time than repeating courses that you failed or dropped because you were trying to do too much at once.

7. *Understand Yourself*—Examine your value system. Earlier I mentioned that value conflicts cause stress. If you are not sure of your values, you won't be able to act consistently. Spend some time thinking through what you really believe and why you believe it. Often college is the first time people are really challenged about their beliefs and values. The diversity in the student body and faculty may bring in new or different perspectives you have not considered before. In addition, college is supposed to teach you to think critically. Students who don't know what they believe are often easily swayed by someone else's opinion. They swing back and forth depending on who they're with at the time. When it comes time to make an important decision, they don't know what to do or whom to believe.

8. *Try Changing Your Behaviors*—Sometimes we get stuck in a rut of dysfunctional, stressful behavior. We do things the same way, and we get the same unpleasant results. Seek alternative solutions to your problems. Decide what outcome you want and think of ways to get there. Don't be intimidated by big problems. A situation may seem overwhelming and unmanageable in its entirety, but taking the first step toward resolution isn't so bad. Another stress reducer is to use cooperation instead of confrontation. Learn how to compromise and work out conflict rather than avoid it. If you have stressful habits you need to break, seek the help of a counselor and try some behavior modification techniques.

9. *Enjoy Leisure Activities*—Reward yourself for your accomplishments. Give yourself a break and combat built-up tension. A few quiet minutes can provide a change of pace from daily routines that produce anxiety. Soft, gentle music can soothe tension. The sound of waves lapping the shoreline, listening to birds chirping in the sunlight, or watching a crackling fire in the fireplace can help you relax. It is difficult for your body to be uptight and fearful when your mind and heart are singing. Take time out for yourself to play, have fun, and re-charge. Make time for hobbies, sports, interests, and activities you love. Read a novel, go to the movies, take a bubble bath, walk in the woods, or do something new. Start small, vary your activities, and be flexible. It is not always possible to stick to a regular schedule. Remember to enjoy some free time alone. You're worth it.

10. *Cry/Scream/Vent*—Crying is a healthy way to relieve anxiety. It could prevent a headache or other more serious symptom of stress. Socially, it may be embarrassing, but psychologically, it is a proper response to overwhelming stress. It is cleansing, healing, and effective. When screaming or venting, be sure you do it when you're by yourself—*not in public and not at another person.*

11. *Learn New Skills*—Look toward a bright future. Develop a happier, more motivated self. One of the most effective ways to combat depression is to learn something new. It energizes and revitalizes your spirits. Improved skills that increase productivity will help you accomplish more in the same amount of time and with the same effort. Learning how to cope with a crisis makes you feel more competent and in control. If you see the problem that used to cause anxiety as an opportunity for growth, you can change that deficit into an asset. Become a lifelong, perpetual learner.

12. *Try Massage Therapy*—No longer a luxury reserved for the rich and famous, massages are now affordable and as convenient as a local hair or tanning salon. Devices designed to massage your neck, feet, or back are available in most retail stores. Many community colleges and park districts offer classes in massage techniques. Check the personal interest/non-credit/continuing education section of the schedule.

    If massages are too much trouble, try aromatherapy. A variety of products such as candles, body lotion, or bath gel can cater to your individual needs and tastes. The point is, do something that soothes and relaxes you.

13. *Don't Forget Your Faith*—Perhaps more than any other intervention, a strong faith can pull you through the toughest times. Whatever your beliefs, prayer and meditation can take you beyond your personal troubles and help you focus on the important things in life. Many people find that starting and/or ending their day with prayer, scripture reading, and/or time for quiet reflection significantly helps keep them balanced and peaceful.

14. *Learn to Accept Change*—Accept change with a positive attitude. Change is an inevitable part of life and not always a negative experience. Allow yourself time to adjust. Fighting change causes additional stress. Now that we're in the 21st century, we are faced with many challenges as a result of increasing technology and fewer support systems.

Relaxation Techniques

It is difficult to eliminate all the stress in your life, but you can learn to cope by practicing relaxation exercises. Some are more involved, but some are simple enough to do anywhere—even at the college. If you are one of those people who blank out during a test and then remember all of the right answers after you walk out of the room, it could be that you are overly stressed about the test. Once your tension has been released, your mind and memory work just fine. If you could release that tension right before, or even during the exam, you might be able to remember the answers when you need them. Try one or more of the following exercises whenever you feel yourself becoming anxious.

1. *Deep Breathing*—Shallow, rapid breathing occurs when one is stressed. Deep, slow breathing can reduce stress and help you relax. Oxygen is the body's natural stress reducer. By increasing your intake of oxygen, you relieve tension. Begin by closing your eyes. Exhale slowly and clear the air from your lungs. Then inhale deeply through your nose and hold your breath for a count of five. When taking a deep breath, your stomach/diaphragm should be expanded. Slowly exhale, using your lips to control the rate of air that you move out of your lungs. Begin the cycle again. Repeat several times until you feel calmer. You can do this anywhere and any time you feel stressed, even while you are taking an exam.

2. *Deep Muscle Relaxation*—One of the most common reactions to stress is muscle tension. Deep and progressive muscle relaxation will help you to relax your entire body from head to toe by first tensing and then relaxing the various muscle groups. The whole process can take anywhere from one to twenty minutes. Find a comfortable

position either sitting or lying down. If you have privacy, you may want to loosen any tight clothing. Close your eyes. Begin with your head and facial muscles—scalp, brow, eyes, lips, jaw, etc. Tighten your muscles and hold tense for ten seconds, then relax. Continue contracting and relaxing your muscles by moving through your neck, shoulder, back, and chest areas. Keep doing this through every major muscle group. Concentrate on taking slow, deep breaths while you work your way down to your hips, legs, and feet.

When you have completed all the muscle groups, you will feel refreshed and relaxed. This type of relaxation may also help you sleep better. You can do a shortened version of this exercise in class or almost anywhere. Close your eyes; tense up all of your muscles for a couple seconds; then release them slowly, one body part at a time.

3. *Meditation*—Is one of the oldest techniques that can help you clear stressful thoughts from your mind, but it may take time to learn how to do it effectively. Find a location where you are comfortable and won't be disturbed. Close your eyes and focus on a peaceful word or image. Your goal is to find a quiet, peaceful state of mind. Concentrate on something calming, and do not let any other thoughts enter your mind. Learning to abandon all thoughts is the hard part. Return to the one image or word you have selected, clearing your mind of any stress and worry. Breathe deeply. At the end of your meditation session, you will feel calm and relaxed.

4. *Imagery*—Is another other type of mental exercise. It is like taking a mini, mental vacation, or daydreaming with a purpose. You can achieve the same feeling of tranquility that you do with meditation, but the technique is different. Rather than concentrating on a single thought, you create an entirely relaxing, though imaginary, place of your own to which you can escape. Once again, close your eyes and visualize the perfect place to relax. It might be in the woods by a brook, on a warm, sandy beach, in the mountains, floating on a cloud, wherever seems right to you. See yourself there, calm and satisfied with life. You can go to this special place in your mind whenever you need a few seconds of escape time. You can also use this technique to build confidence. While in your perfect place, visualize yourself accomplishing one of your goals.

5. *Autogenic Exercises*—Another way to control your stress is to use conscious thoughts to influence the way your body functions. With intense concentration, you focus on any part of yourself that you feel is tense in order to develop a more relaxed and tranquil frame of mind and body. This technique requires total concentration, so start by lying down alone in a darkened room. Begin with deep breathing; then slow your breathing to its most relaxing pace. Focus your thoughts on the part of your body that you wish to relax. Repeat each statement several times. Examples: "My head is heavy, my mind is calm." "My body is heavy and relaxed." "My breathing is calm and regular." "My body is warm and comfortable." You can keep your focus on one part of your body or you can move through all of your muscle groups individually as you did in the deep muscle relaxation exercise.

■ Student Stressors

Adjusting to new and unfamiliar situations is a cause of stress for most people, and students are no exception. A new school, new course, or new instructor can cause some students a great deal of anxiety. How much depends on their personality and past experiences. For some students, quizzes, tests, and final examinations can induce stress. A more extreme form is called test anxiety. Another high stessor for students is their fear of math. Both of these kinds of anxiety could be caused by a history of not doing well in school or on tests, having poor study skills, fear of failure, and outside pressures.

Test Anxiety

It is not abnormal to be anxious about a test. Almost everyone, even good students, feel some apprehension, fear, uneasiness, or worry about taking a test. A little pressure can be beneficial if it is moderate and controlled. For example, some students view an exam as an opportunity to show what they can do. Their attitude is similar to that of an athlete who enjoys competition because it promotes a higher level of performance. If moderate anxiety keeps you alert and on your toes or provides you with a burst of energy, it can help you rise to meet the challenge before you.

Test anxiety, though, is usually the result of pressure to maintain good grades. Grades are important to students for many reasons: to qualify for scholarships or financial assistance, to be accepted into a specific university or program, to meet with parental approval or please a significant other, to remain in good academic standing, to make the Dean's list, to maintain athletic eligibility, and to create or maintain a good self image. However, grades are still not the whole picture. Many colleges consider other factors *in addition to grades* when making decisions regarding admission. If you suffer from anxiety because you think you have to be perfect, you need to let go of some of your unrealistic expectations.

Concern arises when stress and anxiety are extreme, acute, disabling, and so intense that they affect your performance or become detrimental and threatening to your well-being. At that point, you may need the help of a professional to get your anxiety under control. If your anxiety is less extreme, you may be able to use the following strategies to handle it yourself.

Test Anxiety Reduction

- **Attitude Adjustment**—Be realistic about the importance of any single test or exam. What is the worst that could happen? You could get a lower grade than you wished, you could be embarrassed about your performance, you could fail the test, or a poor test grade could cause you to fail a course in which you are struggling. You might even lose an opportunity for a scholarship or have to pay back some of your financial aid. Yes; these are all terrible consequences, but none of them will determine the outcome of the rest of your life. A test is just a test—usually part of your total grade for one course in any one semester. Recognize that your value as a person is not dependent on what you do on any one test or course.
- **Effective Study Techniques**—Previous chapters have introduced you to strategies and techniques designed to increase your ability to perform successfully in the classroom. Faithfully practicing the note taking, time management, and test-taking strategies outlined in this book will give you the confidence you need to go into the test with a winning attitude. Be sure to use tutoring and other academic support services as needed.
- **Positive Self-Talk**—Negative thinking increases your anxiety levels. Recognize any self-defeating thoughts you might have and replace them with positive thoughts designed to increase your confidence levels. Believe that you have the ability to control what happens and visualize yourself doing your absolute best. Practice using positive statements to boost your confidence and self-esteem. In your mind, tell yourself, "I am well prepared; I am confident; I will do my best."

Math Anxiety

The physical and psychological reaction to math that affects performance in class and keeps you from remembering what you learned when taking a math test is termed math anxiety. It is usually the result of negative past experiences. Most students with math anxiety can trace its roots to a teacher or school experience that humiliated them. Students who were punished or ridiculed for not grasping math concepts as readily as their peers developed a fear or hatred of the subject. Sometimes the pressure to do well, or conversely, the excuse to do poorly came from parents or other family members.

If you suffer from math anxiety, think about your first negative experience with math. Was it failing to learn the multiplication tables right away? Was it being made to stand at the board in front of the class until you could work out a difficult problem? Was it the result of someone telling you, "You'll never be good in math?" To combat the causes of math anxiety you need to recognize their sources, reject the untrue things you've been programmed to believe, and adopt a new approach—a willingness to go at it with a fresh start. If math anxiety can be learned (and it is), then it can be unlearned.

Math Anxiety Reduction

Effectively reducing math anxiety requires most students to combat negative self-images about their ability to be successful in math by taking positive steps to change their attitude. First, they must develop and practice strong math study skills. Each small success in math performance will build confidence levels.

How can you change a negative attitude about math? Start by examining the following math myths, and become aware that these common assumptions are, indeed, myths.

False assumptions about math:

- Math is linear and logical; therefore, creative people cannot be good in math.
- There is only one right way to solve a math problem.
- Women are not good in math. It's genetic. Variation: No one in my family is good in math, therefore, I can't/won't be good in math.
- Math has no value in the real world.
- I haven't been good at math in the past, and it's too late for me to learn math now.
- Math is hard and boring.
- It doesn't help to ask questions because I won't understand the explanation anyway.
- I've always been good in English, so I can't expect to be good in math.
- Math isn't logical.

Now that you've recognized these math myths, take a look at the following **math facts**:

- Math is sequential, building upon itself, so it is important to study every day. Studying once a week will not produce the same results as keeping up daily, especially if you have a class that meets three or more times per week.
- The key to solving math problems is practice. Keep up with your homework and work the problems whether or not the instructor collects or grades homework.
- It is just as important to understand the concepts, principles, and relationships as it is to memorize the formulas and work the problems.
- You are better off taking a five-hour math class that meets every day for one hour than you are taking the same course that meets once a week. Fewer, concentrated sessions tend to produce stress, especially for students who do not excel at math. If you don't understand the material, you may have to wait a whole week to ask your questions. In a five-day per week course, fewer concepts can be presented per day, which gives you time to practice before moving to the next topic.

The same logic applies to a 3 credit hour math course. Students who have difficulties in math will have less pressure if math is taken three days a week rather than only once or twice a week. Also, it is not advisable for such students to take math during accelerated summer sessions because these sessions are more intense than the traditional fall/spring semesters.

- Missing a math class can cause a real gap in your knowledge and understanding. Remember, math is sequential. Missing any material can cause confusion and lack of understanding.
- Math anxiety is learned, and it can be unlearned.

We've reviewed some common myths and some truths about math. If you have difficulties with math and/or math anxiety, how can you counteract any negative attitudes you may have developed? First, you need to examine your past math experiences. Can you remember the first time you felt unhappy with your math performance? If you can uncover the source of your negative attitude, you can work on changing it to a positive one. If your problems with math stem from knowledge gaps or not understanding some fundamental concepts, then you can correct that by working in a computerized learning center or taking a basic math course to learn what you don't know.

Take a look at your current attitude. Do you truly believe that you will never be successful at math, or are you willing to change your attitude? The following tips for improving math performance will help you build a stronger, more positive attitude.

- Confront any math myths you've held in the past and recognize that they are myths.
- Use the relaxation techniques and positive self-talk approaches discussed earlier in the chapter to help you develop a positive attitude about your math ability.
- Before registering for your next math class, talk to other students and try to identify instructors who are receptive to questions, use cooperative learning techniques, review material prior to tests, and teach in a style that matches your learning style.
- Review as soon as possible after class.
- Attend every math class, take good notes, and record all steps in the examples covered in class so you will remember them later.
- Ask questions in class and seek tutorial assistance as soon as you do not understand any material. *Don't get behind!* Remember that sequential process.

Do all of your assignments and the sample problems provided. Practice makes perfect.

Practice the following steps to help you solve math problems:

- Make sure you understand basic definitions, symbols, and other math terminology.
- Make sure you understand the formula being used.
- Read the problem aloud.
- Draw a picture to help you see relationships within the problem.
- Set up the problem.
- Estimate the end result.
- Ask yourself if your answer makes common sense.
- Check your answer.
- Practice until you understand how to do that kind of problem perfectly and completely.

■ Summary

We all live complicated lives and are faced with stress on a daily basis. Moderate amounts of stress are normal and can motivate us to do our best. Too much stress, however, can cause serious physical, emotional, and behavioral problems.

Math and test anxieties are common problems experienced by many students. Both are learned responses that can be unlearned. Practicing good study habits, having a realistic attitude about the importance of tests in our lives, practicing positive self-talk, using relaxation techniques, and dispelling any math myths we may hold will help us create successful experiences.

We need to acquire the skills necessary to control or eliminate excessive stress in our lives. A number of strategies to help you develop your own stress management program were covered in this chapter. Maintaining a healthy lifestyle, using support systems, and practicing relaxation techniques are especially effective. If you have very high stress levels that have lasted for long periods of time, seek professional help. Remember that you can reduce many of your life stressors by identifying the people and events that cause you stress. Change the things in your life over which you have control, and release the rest. Don't worry; be happy!

■ Journal Assignment

Choose one of the following topics and write a one page, typed journal entry about it.

1. Do you have test or math anxiety (or both)? To what do you attribute your fear of taking tests and/or your problems with math? What do you need to do to overcome these fears? List several strategies you will use.

2. Do you have symptoms of stress? Identify the major causes of stress in your life. Describe how you can eliminate some of them and what strategies you will use to reduce the effects of stress that can't be eliminated.

Name: _____ Date: _____

Homework Activity

Physical Symptoms

How many of these symptoms have you experienced in the last 6 months. Are you at risk? Rate yourself using a scale of 0 to 4, with 0 being "not a problem" and 4 being "I experience this all the time."

_____ 1. Tension or migraine headaches

_____ 2. Back, shoulder, neck, or joint pain

_____ 3. Excessive tiredness and chronic fatigue

_____ 4. White knuckles or cold, clammy hands

_____ 5. Grinding teeth, jaw ache, or pain

_____ 6. Rapid or irregular heartbeat, tightness of chest, or chest pain

_____ 7. Shallow breathing, shortness of breath, hyperventilation, or asthma attacks

_____ 8. Excessive perspiration or changes in body temperature

_____ 9. Digestive disturbances such as abdominal pain, nausea, upset stomach, diarrhea, frequent urination, or constipation

_____ 10. Trembling, nervous tics, shaking hands, or voice tremor

_____ 11. Increased blood pressure or increased adrenaline flow

_____ 12. Acne, psoriasis, dermatitis, hives, rashes, allergies, and other skin problems

_____ 13. Frequent colds, cough, or flu

_____ 14. Weakness, dizziness, or blurry vision

_____ 15. Excessive thirst

_____ 16. Choking sensations

_____ 17. Change in appetite or unintentional weight gains or losses

_____ 18. Impotence, decreased sex drive, or infertility

_____ 19. Menstrual problems

_____ 20. Loss of consciousness

_____ **Total score for Physical Symptoms**

■ Emotional or Psychological Symptoms

How many times in the last six months have you had these feelings? Review this list and rate yourself on a 0 to 4 scale with 0 being "I never feel this way" and 4 being "I feel this way all the time."

_____ 1. Depression

_____ 2. Hopelessness

_____ 3. Mood swings

_____ 4. Loss of interest

_____ 5. Dissatisfaction

_____ 6. Feelings of guilt

_____ 7. Preoccupation

_____ 8. Mental distraction

_____ 9. Boredom

_____ 10. Sadness

_____ 11. Loneliness

_____ 12. Fear

_____ 13. Worry

_____ 14. Feeling overwhelmed

_____ 15. Frustration

_____ 16. Confusion

_____ 17. Forgetfulness

_____ 18. Burnout

_____ 19. Panic

_____ 20. Suicidal feelings

_____ **Total score for Emotional or Psychological Symptoms**

■ Behavioral Changes

Have you noticed any of these kinds of changes in your behavior in the last six months? What about in the last semester? Review this list and rate yourself on a 0 to 4 scale with 0 being "This has not changed" and 4 being "Major change."

_____ 1. Over-eating or under-eating

_____ 2. Increased use of alcohol or tobacco

_____ 3. Sleeping too much or insomnia

_____ 4. Nightmares

_____ 5. Overspending

_____ 6. Increased reliance on prescription or non-prescription drugs

_____ 7. Impulsive behavior

_____ 8. Inability to concentrate or poor memory

_____ 9. Accident proneness

_____ 10. Compulsive or repetitive behavior

_____ 11. Excessive anger or aggressive behavior

_____ 12. Increase in risk-taking behaviors e.g. Speeding, recklessness

_____ 13. Difficulty in making decisions or poor judgment

_____ 14. Stuttering or other speech difficulties

_____ 15. Loss of productivity

_____ 16. Mood swings or irritability

_____ 17. Nervous laughter

_____ 18. Restlessness

_____ 19. Apathy, loss of interest or withdrawal

_____ 20. Self-mutilation

_____ **Total score for Behavioral Symptoms**

Finish all three parts. Total your points for each list. Write your scores for each scale on the lines below and add them together for a total score.

Physical Symptoms _____

Emotional/Psychological Symptoms _____

Behavioral Symptoms _____

TOTAL SCORE _____

- ■ If your total score is below 80, you are probably able to manage the stressors in your life.
- ■ If your total score is 80–160, you should try to reduce your stress as quickly as possible.
- ■ If your score is over 160, get help now; you are at risk for a stress-related illness.

CHAPTER 8
Maintaining a Healthy Lifestyle

Healthy Lifestyles through Wellness

How are you? You probably answered "fine" without really thinking. But, how do you **really** feel . . . about yourself, your life, your lifestyle, your health? Chances are that you may not have considered all of the many facets that constitute your true well-being. Do you eat well? Do you exercise regularly? Do you smoke or drink? Do you have close friends with whom you can share your experiences, both good and traumatic? Are you under extreme stress to get good grades, perform well on the job, or be a good parent? Do you get regular medical checkups and do you practice self-care? Are you aware of safety and environmental factors that contribute to your health? This

From *The Freshman Year: Making the Most of College* by Glenda A. Belote and Larry W. Lunsford. © 1998 by Kendall/Hunt Publishing Company.

chapter will help you develop important strategies that will enable you to live life to the fullest, both physically and emotionally.

Traditionally, health was simply defined as the absence of disease or symptoms. This concept has gradually evolved over the past fifty years so that health is now defined by the World Health Organization as a continuous and harmonious balance of physical, mental, spiritual, intellectual, and social well-being. This continuum of a "balanced," healthy lifestyle has been defined as **wellness.** True wellness involves contracting with yourself to engage in healthy behaviors and attitudes that enhance the quality of your life and personal performance.

To achieve this state of wellness, you must maintain a balance of six continually changing dimensions that affect your overall health. These components of wellness are:

Physical

Physical wellness is the ability to maintain positive lifestyle habits to enable you to perform your daily tasks. Such components of the physical dimension of wellness entail eating healthy foods, maintaining appropriate weight and body fat, performing regular exercise to maintain cardiovascular fitness, and avoiding the abuse of tobacco, alcohol, and other drugs.

Emotional

Emotional wellness is the ability to manage stress and express your emotions appropriately by recognizing and accepting your feelings about the events in your life. Stress is part of everyone's life, but your ability to properly manage life's stressful events can greatly influence your overall health potential.

Spiritual

The belief in an abstract strength that unites all of your internal energies. This strength can include religion and/or nature, but also includes your values, ethics, and morals. Your personal sense of spirituality provides meaning and direction to your life, enabling you to learn, develop, and meet new challenges successfully.

Social

The skill to interact successfully with other people at work, school, and the community. This dimension of wellness encompasses your ability to handle relationships, both intimate and casual.

Intellectual

The ability to learn and use your knowledge effectively to enhance your overall health. Knowledge of self-care techniques, disease risk factors, as well as your family history of disease, are all important components to achieving intellectual wellness.

Environmental

The physical and social setting that influences your lifestyle. This dimension includes your personal safety practices, such as wearing seat belts, to your efforts to help promote a clean environment.

These six dimensions of wellness overlap, and components of one often can directly or indirectly affect factors in another. Some health parameters are under your direct control and some are not. For example, your lifestyle behaviors (diet, exercise, habits) constitute the greatest percentage of influences on the quality of your life.

Relationships involving family, friends, and the community are also important, as are factors pertaining to the quality of health care you receive by physicians and health care facilities. Approximately 85 percent of the factors influencing your health are within your control. The remaining 15 percent are beyond your individual control and consist of heredity predispositions. If your medical history reveals a family tendency toward a specific disease, such as heart disease or cancer, your lifestyle decisions can delay the onset, minimize the disease's effects, or possibly even prevent the disease from occurring. This is why a good knowledge of preventive medicine becomes so important.

■ Health Benefits of Wellness

You can achieve wellness through improving your knowledge about health, eliminating risk factors, practicing good self-care habits and preventive medicine, and maintaining a positive attitude. Some of the benefits of wellness include:

- a decreased risk of developing chronic diseases;
- a decreased risk of accidents;
- a decreased recovery time after injury and illness;
- an improved cardiovascular system function (heart efficiency and blood vessel diameter both increase);
- an increased muscle tone, strength, and flexibility;
- an improved physical appearance—less fat, greater muscle tone;
- an increased ability to manage stress and resist depression;
- proper nutrition for optimal growth, repair, immune function, and development;
- a higher self-esteem;
- an increased energy level, productivity, and creativity; and
- an improved awareness of your personal needs and the ways to achieve them.

■ Wellness as a Challenge

Your belief in your ability to perform healthy behaviors will influence your actual choices, your degree of effort to make the change, your persistence, and your emotional reactions to the new lifestyle. Your ability to turn your health-related goals into reality is dependent on formulating a plan of action. This lifestyle modification has several steps:

Step 1. Evaluate your personal health habits. Make a list of your behaviors that promote health and make another list of your behaviors that are harmful. Once you have compiled both of your lists, note which behaviors present the greatest threat to your overall well-being. These behaviors should be targeted for change first.

Step 2. Set realistic, specific, observable, and measurable goals. Don't expect miracles. Setting goals that are too ambitious leads to failure; the fear of failure may discourage future efforts. View lifestyle change as a lifetime change. Strive for moderation rather than striving for complete behavior reversal or abstinence. Behavior changes that are "slow-but-steady" are the ones most likely to result in permanent success.

Step 3. Formulate a strategy for success. Most people want to make positive changes, but too often find reasons why they cannot make changes. They may not have the time, are too tired, or simply feel embarrassed. What are some of your reasons? These barriers to change must be avoided if you are to achieve your healthy goals.

Step 4. Evaluate your progress. How well are you doing? The only way to consistently stick with your new healthy behavior is to receive feedback by monitoring your progress. This evaluation allows you to modify the program, enabling you to better achieve your goals. Initially, the evaluation periods should be frequent, such as daily or weekly. After periods of consistent success, the time interval between evaluation sessions could be lengthened to, perhaps, monthly.

Success does not have to be all-or-nothing. This manner of thinking can be detrimental to your overall motivation to change. When your goals are not fully realized, simply reshape your goals, set a more realistic time schedule, or formulate different intervention strategies, and **TRY AGAIN**. More importantly, answer these questions:

"What did I learn from this experience?"

"What can I do differently?"

Based on your answers, make a revised contract and begin immediately. Remember that lifestyle change is never easy but its rewards will last a lifetime. The exercise on the next page will assist you in planning for a healthier lifestyle.

■ You Are What You Eat

Dietary habits play a key role in both how long we live and how well we feel. A healthy diet is one that features a proper variety and balance of foods to supply our body with nutrients, essential dietary factors required for growth, energy, and repair. There are six nutrients: proteins, carbohydrates, fats, vitamins, minerals, and water.

Protein is necessary for growth and repair, forming the basic building blocks of muscles, bones, hair, and blood. Meat, poultry, fish, eggs, milk, cheese, dry beans, and nuts are excellent dietary sources of protein.

Carbohydrates provide the body with glucose, its basic fuel. There are two types of carbohydrates: simple and complex. Simple carbohydrates are sugars, which are responsible for providing short bursts of energy. Examples of dietary sugars include glucose, sucrose (table sugar), fructose (the sugar found in fruits), honey, and syrup. Complex carbohydrates consist of starches and fiber, important ingredients of cereals, breads, rice, pasta, fruits, and vegetables. Soluble fiber, found in oats, beans, apples, and citrus fruit, has been shown to lower blood cholesterol levels and decrease the risk of heart disease.

Fats are high calorie nutrients that come in two primary types: saturated and unsaturated. Saturated fats, found in animal products such red meat, egg yolk, and butter, have been shown to increase the blood cholesterol levels and increase the risk of heart disease. In contrast, monounsaturated and polyunsaturated fats are found primarily in foods of plant origin and have been shown to lower blood cholesterol levels. Polyunsaturated fats are found in safflower and corn oils, whereas canola and olive oil are monounsaturated fats. In contrast to protein and carbohydrates, which contain four calories per gram, fat contributes nine calories per gram when metabolized in the body. For this reason, a simple way to lose weight is to decrease the amount of dietary fat.

Vitamins are organic nutrients which work with the body's enzymes to enable biochemical reactions to take place. Vitamins C and E, as well as beta carotene, serve as antioxidants, substances that protect cells from dangerous free radicals produced by normal metabolic processes. Antioxidants have been shown to reduce the incidence of heart disease and certain types of cancer.

Minerals are inorganic substances found in food that are also essential for proper metabolism. Macrominerals (sodium, potassium, calcium, phosphorus, and magnesium) are required in larger amounts than are the trace minerals (iron, zinc, selenium, iodine, chromium, and fluoride). Calcium is the most abundant mineral in the body, responsible for bone integrity and prevention of osteoporosis, as well as for conduction of nerve impulses and cardiac contraction.

Exercise:

Do aerobic exercises (walking, jogging, swimming, cycling, etc.) for 30 minutes three to four times a week.

Incorporate exercise into your daily activities (e.g., take the stairs).

Always do warm-up and cool-down exercises and stretch before and after your aerobic session to improve flexibility and decrease risk of injury.

Nutrition:

Eat foods high in complex carbohydrates (breads, cereals, fruits, vegetables, pasta) to constitute 48 percent of your total daily calories.

Limit simple sugars (table sugar, soft drinks, candy); consume only with meals.

Limit saturated fat intake (animal fats, whole milk, etc.); consume more fat calories as monounsaturated (canola and olive oil) and polyunsaturated (vegetable oils) fats.

Drink at least eight glasses of water daily.

Stress management:

Improve your time management and organizational skills (set priorities, don't procrastinate, make a daily schedule with flexible time and follow it).

Practice progressive muscle relaxation, meditation, yoga, and deep-breathing exercises.

Self-care:

Don't smoke.

Only drink alcohol responsibly; (e.g. don't drink and drive, no more than two or three drinks in one sitting, etc.).

Perform breast or testicular self-exams monthly.

Have regular medical screenings and physical exams.

Know your blood pressure and cholesterol numbers.

Practice abstinence or safer sex (always use condoms).

Sleep at least seven to eight hours daily and develop a regular sleep-wake cycle.

Read about current health topics and medical discoveries; check the Internet.

Safety:

Always wear a seat belt.

Learn cardiopulmonary resuscitation (CPR).

Check smoke detectors in your home annually.

Figure 1 ■ Wellness Strategies for Top Performance: Academically and Athletically

I, _____, pledge that I will accomplish the goals listed below.

—Personal Goal: *Improve my fitness level.*

—Motivating Factors: *I want to have more energy and feel better.*

—Change(s) I Promise to Make to Reach This Goal: *Jog for 20–30 minutes at least three times a week.*

—Start Date: *January 1*

—Intervention Strategies:

1. *I will walk early in the morning before classes.*
2. *I will walk after classes on days when it is raining in the morning.*

Plan for Making This Change:

First week: walk for 10 minutes three times a week.

Weeks 2 to 4: Increase the amount of walking time by five minutes every week until I walk for 20–30 minutes each session.

Week 5: Evaluate my progress.

Weeks 5 to 9: Gradually increase my speed.

Week 10: Evaluate my progress.

After the first 10 weeks: Continue my morning jogs three times a week.

—Target Date for Reaching Goal: *March 15*

—Reward for Reaching Goal: *Buy a new, expensive pair of jogging shoes.*

—If I Need Help: *I can call my friend _____ to walk or jog with me.*

Signed: _____

Witness: _____

Date: _____

Figure 2 ■ A Sample Contract for Lifestyle Change

Approximately 60 percent of your weight consists of **water**. Water helps to digest foods, maintains proper body temperature, lubricates joints, and eliminates the body's waste products via urine. Water is necessary for survival, as we would die after only a few days without water. In contrast, we could survive for several weeks without food. You should drink at least eight glasses of water a day, not counting alcohol and drinks that contain the diuretic caffeine, such as coffee, tea, and certain soft drinks.

How Much Should I Eat?

According to the American Dietetic Association, 12 percent of your daily calories should come from protein; 58 percent from carbohydrates (of which 48 percent should be complex carbohydrates and only 10 percent simple sugars); and a total of 30 percent from fats (10 percent saturated fats, 10 percent monounsaturated fats, and 10 percent polyunsaturated fats). In contrast, the typical American diet consists of too much saturated fats and simple sugars, and lacks sufficient amounts of complex carbohydrates. To best help you determine what your daily nutrient intake is, you need to understand the food pyramid.

The Food Guide Pyramid

In 1992, the United States Department of Agriculture published the Food Guide Pyramid, a guideline to simplify the selections of foods that constitute a healthy diet. As shown in Figure 3, the Food Guide Pyramid incorporates five food groups plus fats, oils, and sugars. Foods in one category cannot replace those from another.

The foods at the base of the Food Guide Pyramid form the foundation of a healthy diet and consist of foods high in complex carbohydrates—breads, cereals, rice, and pasta. The foods at the Pyramid's base are high in fiber, iron, protein, and B vitamins, and should be consumed in the largest quantities, namely six to eleven servings daily. The second tier of the Food Guide Pyramid consists of vegetables and fruits—foods that are high in fiber, low in fat, and high in vitamins A and C. Scientific studies have revealed that vegetables and fruits may prevent cancers of the lung, colon, stomach, bladder, and breast. According to the Food Guide Pyramid, three to five servings of vegetables and two to four servings of fruits are recommended daily. Foods in the "Milk, Yogurt, and Cheese" group are high in calcium, protein, and vitamins A and B-12. Two servings per day are recommended. Foods in the "Meat, Poultry, Fish, Dry Beans, Eggs, and Nuts" group are excellent sources of protein, iron, zinc, phosphorus, and B vitamins. These foods are also high in fats and cholesterol; thus, you should choose low-fat varieties. Finally, foods at the apex of the pyramid (the smallest part of the pyramid) should be consumed in very small quantities. Fats, oils, and sweets are high in calories but supply little or no vitamins or minerals. Select foods from this category that are high in monounsaturated fats, such as canola or olive oils.

Using Your Resources

Visit the campus health center, a primary care physician, or a registered dietician to receive a personal nutrition consultation. A licensed health professional can help you lose weight or gain weight; prescribe a diet to help control blood pressure, diabetes, or high cholesterol; or provide guidance concerning dietary supplements.

Food Guide Pyramid

A Guide to Daily Food Choices

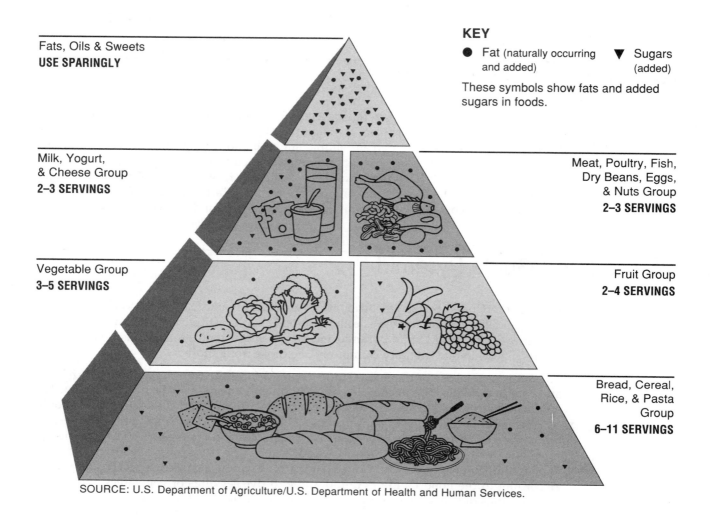

KEY

● Fat (naturally occurring and added)   ▼ Sugars (added)

These symbols show fats and added sugars in foods.

Fats, Oils & Sweets
USE SPARINGLY

Milk, Yogurt, & Cheese Group
2–3 SERVINGS

Meat, Poultry, Fish, Dry Beans, Eggs, & Nuts Group
2–3 SERVINGS

Vegetable Group
3–5 SERVINGS

Fruit Group
2–4 SERVINGS

Bread, Cereal, Rice, & Pasta Group
6–11 SERVINGS

SOURCE: U.S. Department of Agriculture/U.S. Department of Health and Human Services.

What counts as one serving?

Bread, Cereal, Rice & Pasta Group	Vegetable Group	Fruit Group	Milk, Cheese Group	Meat, Poultry, Fish Group	Fats, Oils, Sweets Group
1 slice of bread	1 cup raw leafy veg.	1 medium fruit (apple, orange, banana)	1 cup nonfat milk	3 oz cooked lean meat+	butter, margarine*
1/2 cup of rice	1/2 baked white potato	3/4 cup juice	1 cup nonfat yogurt	3 oz sliced turkey+	corn, safflower oil
1/2 cup of pasta	1/2 baked sweet potato	1/2 cup canned fruit	1.5 oz natural cheese*+	3 oz chicken breast+	olive oil
1 oz of dry cereal	1/2 cup steamed veg.	1/2 cup grapes	1.5 oz processed cheese*+	1.5 cups kidney beans	canola oil
1/2 cup oatmeal	1 cup lettuce	1/2 cup melon chunks	1/2 cup low-fat cottage cheese*+	3 eggs	palm, coconut oil*+
1/2 bagel	1/2 cup carrot sticks			6 tbsp peanut butter	cakes, pies, cookies
				1.5 cups lentils	sugared drinks

* = foods that are high in fat
+ = foods that contain saturated fat or cholesterol

Figure 3 ▪ Food Guide Pyramid

Responsible Drinking

According to a number of studies, abuse of alcohol is the number-one problem facing college students today. Although more students are choosing to abstain, approximately 85 percent of college students use alcohol. A small percentage of these students drink irresponsibly, either binge drinking (drinking five or more drinks at one sitting), drinking while under the legal drinking age, or driving under the influence of alcohol. The leading cause of death among college students is alcohol-related automobile accidents. The use and abuse of alcohol is also associated with most cases of campus violence, arrests, vandalism, rape, accidents, homicides, unwanted sex, sexually transmitted diseases and HIV/AIDS, unwanted pregnancies, poor grades, and drop-outs.

Alcohol can also impair your judgment. You may actually have sex with someone whom you would normally not even go out to lunch with! However, the consequences of your decision, such as an unintended pregnancy, a sexually transmitted disease, or an accident resulting in a lifelong disability, may last a lifetime.

By definition, any drink containing 0.5 percent or more ethyl alcohol by volume is an alcoholic beverage. However, different drinks contain different amounts of alcohol. For example, one drink is defined as any of the following:

- one 12 oz can of beer (5 percent alcohol);
- one 4 oz glass of wine (12 percent alcohol); or
- one shot (1 oz) of distilled spirits, such as whiskey, vodka, or rum (50 percent alcohol). The alcohol content is expressed as **proof**, a number that is twice the percentage of alcohol: 80-proof gin is 40 percent alcohol, etc.

To determine the amount that you can safely drink, you need to determine the blood-alcohol concentration (BAC), the percentage of alcohol in the blood. The BAC is usually measured from your breath. Most people reach a BAC of 0.05 percent after consuming one or two drinks; at this level, they do not feel intoxicated. If they continue to drink past this BAC level, they start to feel worse, with decreased reaction times, slurred speech, and loss of balance and emotional control. The legal BAC in most states is 0.08 percent. Persons driving a motor vehicle with a BAC of 0.08 percent or greater are cited for driving under the influence and are subject to severe legal penalties and fines. At a BAC of 0.2 percent, a person is likely to pass out and at a BAC of 0.3 percent, a person could lapse into a coma. Death is likely with a BAC of 0.4 percent or higher.

These factors will influence your BAC and response to alcohol:

- **How much and how quickly you drink.** If you chug drink after drink, your liver, which can only metabolize 0.5 oz of alcohol per hour, will not be able to keep up, resulting in a rapidly rising BAC.
- **The type of drink.** The stronger the drink, the faster the rise in BAC, and the consequent symptoms. If the drink contains water, juice, or milk, the rate of absorption will be decreased, slowing the rate of BAC rise. However, if you mix an alcoholic drink with carbon dioxide (e.g., champagne or a cola), the rate of alcohol absorption will increase.
- **The temperature of the alcoholic drink.** Warm drinks result in a faster rate of absorption.
- **Food.** Food slows the rate of absorption by interfering with the intestine's absorptive membrane surface. Certain high-fat foods can also prolong the time it takes for the stomach to empty its contents, resulting in delayed absorption times.

- ■ **Your size.** Large people who have excessive fat or muscle tend to have a larger water volume, which dilutes the alcohol consumed. Therefore, large people can drink more alcohol and will get drunk more slowly than small or thin people.
- ■ **Your gender.** Women tend to get drunk more quickly than men. Women possess smaller quantities of a stomach enzyme that metabolizes alcohol. The hormone estrogen also plays a role, as women are more sensitive to the effects of alcohol just prior to menstruation and when they are taking birth control pills that contain estrogen. One drink consumed by a woman will produce roughly the same physiologic consequences as two drinks consumed by a man.
- ■ **Your age.** The older you are, the higher the BAC level will be after consuming equivalent drinks.
- ■ **Your ethnicity.** Certain ethnic groups, such as Asians and Native Americans, are unable to metabolize alcohol as quickly as others including Caucasians and African Americans.
- ■ **Other drugs.** Mixing alcohol with certain common medications, such as aspirin, acetaminophen (Tylenol), and ulcer medications can cause the BAC to rise more rapidly.

Prolonged alcohol consumption can lead to physical tolerance, as your brain becomes accustomed to a certain level of alcohol. You need to consume more alcohol to achieve the desired effects. This could lead to abuse and alcoholism.

■ Alcoholism

Alcoholism is a chronic disease with genetic, physiologic, and psychosocial consequences. Like other addictions, alcoholism is characterized by the following: drinking more alcohol than intended; persistent desire but unsuccessful attempts to stop drinking; frequent withdrawal and absenteeism; decreased performance at school or work; continued drinking despite the realization that his or her drinking is causing physical, social, or psychological problems; the presence of withdrawal symptoms when not drinking; and the need for increasing amounts of alcohol to achieve intoxication.

■ Drinking Responsibly

Abuse of alcohol is no longer the cultural norm, even in many segments of the college student population. Responsible drinking is always up to you. Alcohol does not need to be present to have a good time with friends. However, if you choose to drink alcohol, it is imperative that you also eat, to slow the rate of alcohol absorption into your body. Set a limit in advance on how many drinks you are going to have, and stick to it. Always go to a party with a designated driver, a friend who, in advance, commits to not drinking. Do everything possible to prevent an intoxicated friend from driving.

Don't rely on alcohol or other drugs as a means to relax; find alternative measures such as exercise, listening to music, reading, meditation, yoga, guided imagery, biofeedback, and hobbies to help you unwind.

Finally, don't drink alcohol just because you observe others drinking or because you believe "everyone else is doing it." According to national surveys, more students **believe** that others are using alcohol (95 percent) than what is actually reported (85 percent). Students who choose not to drink excessively report "second-hand" effects of the irresponsible use of alcohol by their friends. These non-drinking students are more likely to be physically abused or assaulted by their drinking friends, or become a victim to sexual harassment or assault. Academic performance may also suffer because of time spent caring for a roommate who had too much to drink; decreased study time, lack of sleep, and poor concentration may also be "second-hand" effects when friends or roommates drink irresponsibly.

■ Using Campus Resources

The health center on most campuses sponsors student organizations which provide information and consultations concerning alcohol and drug abuse prevention. BACCHUS (Boost Alcohol Consciousness Concerning the Health of University Students) is a national student organization that provides programs on responsible alcohol use, including National Collegiate Alcohol Awareness Week and the Safe Spring Break campaign. To find out more information, contact your campus health center or counseling center. They may have physicians or mental health professionals who can assist you or refer you to a community organization for treatment.

■ HIV Infection and AIDS

We are experiencing an epidemic in the United States that is actually a worldwide pandemic. Infection with the Human Immunodeficiency Virus (HIV) has become the number-one challenging public health problem today, with far-reaching medical and psychosocial consequences. It is estimated that over 30 million people worldwide are infected with HIV, with approximately 16,000 new infections occurring daily. In the United States, it is estimated that over one million people are living with HIV infection, with about one-third having Acquired Immunodeficiency Syndrome (AIDS), the terminal phase of the continuum of HIV infection. States with the highest incidence of HIV and AIDS are California, New York, Florida, and New Jersey. The incidence of HIV infection is highest in individuals between the ages of 20 and 29 years, with the incidence of AIDS highest during the fourth decade of life (i.e., between 30 and 39 years of age). In the United States, AIDS is now the second leading cause of death among people aged 25 to 44, and in many parts of the country, AIDS is now the number-one cause of death among men in this same age range. Although the rate of infection is still highest in men, the incidence of infection is steadily rising in women. HIV infection is disproportionately higher among African Americans and Hispanics, when compared to Caucasians.

■ Epidemiology

The Human Immunodeficiency Virus is difficult to acquire. It is not spread through respiratory droplets or through casual contact, like the common cold or influenza viruses. You cannot acquire HIV by touching, simple kissing, hugging, or sitting next to someone who has the infection. HIV is not transmitted by sharing eating utensils, handshakes, using toilet seats, donating blood, or by mosquitoes.

There are only a few modes of HIV transmission. The virus is present in significant amounts only in blood, semen, vaginal secretions, and breast milk. The virus is present in very small concentrations in saliva, but there is essentially no risk of transmission via deep kissing. Transmission of HIV can occur as a result of:

- **Sexual activity.** HIV can be spread in semen and vaginal fluids during unprotected anal, vaginal, and oral sexual contact with an infected partner. Transmission is more likely to occur during anal intercourse than vaginal intercourse, and more likely to occur during vaginal intercourse than oral sex. Women are more likely to acquire HIV from an infected male partner than are men acquiring HIV infection from a female partner. The largest number of cases (55 percent) of HIV transmission involves homosexual sex, usually unprotected anal intercourse, between men; however, the incidence of heterosexual transmission has risen steadily over the past seven years, and is currently at 18 percent.
- **Injections using shared needles.** Any contaminated needle can transmit the virus, making steroid use, tattoos, and body piercing potentially risky unless sterile needles are used.
- **Perinatally.** A baby may **acquire** the virus before birth via the mother's circulation through the placenta, during the birth process via vaginal secretions, or after birth via infected breast milk. Mothers who are HIV positive have a 25 percent chance of infecting their unborn baby; this number decreases to less than 10 percent if the mother receives treatment during pregnancy.
- **Transfusions of blood, blood products, or organ transplants from HIV-infected individuals.** Since March 1985, the blood supply has been tested for the presence of HIV, significantly decreasing the incidence of HIV transmission via this means. Changes in the methods of screening blood donors have also helped with this decline. However, the risk still is present albeit very small.

Testing for HIV

The most widely used tests to determine the presence of HIV infection actually do not detect the virus itself, but measure the presence of antibodies that are formed in response to infection with HIV. The standard laboratory blood tests that are most commonly used are the Enzyme Linked Immunoassay (ELISA) and the Western Blot. The Ora-Sure is a type of ELISA test that detects the presence of HIV antibody in the mouth mucosa rather than in the blood; the accuracy of the Ora-Sure test is about the same as for the blood test.

The Western Blot is a more specific and expensive test and is therefore primarily used as a confirmatory test when the ELISA comes back as positive. The Western Blot is performed on the same blood specimen which resulted in the positive ELISA. If the ELISA is positive and the Western Blot is negative, the person does not have HIV infection. If the ELISA and the confirmatory Western Blot tests are both positive, then the person is diagnosed as having the HIV infection.

Since it takes at least two weeks to six months for the body to produce enough HIV antibodies to be measured by the tests, a negative result obtained on a test done too soon after the last risky behavior may not be accurate. It is imperative, therefore, that the ELISA be performed at least one additional time, preferably about six months later. Approximately 95 percent of people who have been infected with HIV will have positive blood tests within the first six months.

Anyone who feels they may be at risk should be tested for HIV. Early testing is important because treatments with AZT, ddI, ddC, and the powerful protease inhibitors suppress proliferation of HIV and, in most cases, lower the number of viruses in the bloodstream to undetectable levels, leading to a delay in the onset of AIDS symptoms. The use of AZT and the protease inhibitors, however, does not represent a cure. To date, there is no cure for HIV, and education remains the key ingredient in prevention.

- *Always use a latex condom rather than a natural membrane condom.*

- *Store condoms in a cool, dry place; never store them in the car or in your wallet.*

- *Do not use condoms beyond their expiration date.*

- *Only use water-based lubricants, such as K-Y Jelly; oil-based lubricants will break down the latex.*

- *Use spermicide containing nonoxynol-9, as this compound inactivates HIV.*

- *Know how to use a condom properly; practice if necessary.*

- *Do not reuse a condom.*

- *ALWAYS use one!*

Figure 4 ■ Guidelines for Condom Use

■ Limit Your Risk

NO ONE IS IMMUNE! Your risk of acquiring HIV infection is not dependent on who you are, but is dependent on your behaviors. The only absolutely safe way to protect yourself is by reducing or eliminating risky behaviors. If you do choose, for example, to have sexual intercourse, you should ALWAYS use a condom, even if you think that your partner is not infected. You can never be certain of your partner's past sexual history or drug use history, because he or she may have acquired HIV from a previous partner several years ago. Unknown to both of you, your partner may have slept with someone who slept with someone who once secretly abused injection drugs. Remember, once individuals become infected with HIV, they can remain completely asymptomatic for many years and may not even know that they have the infection! Next to abstinence, the safest way to protect yourself is to always use a latex condom with the spermicide nonoxynol-9. How confident do you feel that you will practice safer sex? Complete Exercise 2 to find out.

■ Summary

We discussed several important ways to enable you to live a balanced, healthy life. Health is something to be cherished. A healthy student is one who will excel academically, be more productive, and have time to pursue recreational pursuits and spend quality time with family and friends. A healthier student is a happier student, a happier employee, and a happier member of the community. Healthy decision making while in college will pay big dividends, with many benefits that will last far after you graduate.

■ Exercise 1. Wellness Lifestyle Assessment

DIRECTIONS: Using the following scale, answer each statement by placing the number that most closely corresponds to your lifestyle and feelings in the space preceding each statement.

KEY: 1 = "no/never" or "don't know"
2 = "rarely" or "1–6 times a year"
3 = "occasionally" or "1–4 times a month"
4 = "often, frequently" or "2–5 times a week"
5 = "yes/always" or "almost daily"

A. Physical Assessment

_____ 1. I perform aerobic exercises for twenty minutes or more per session.

_____ 2. When participating in physical activities, I include stretching and flexibility exercises.

_____ 3. My body fat composition is appropriate for my gender. (Men: 10–18 percent; Women: 16–25 percent)

_____ 4. I have appropriate medical checkups regularly and keep records of test results.

_____ 5. I practice safer sex or abstinence. I never have sex when intoxicated.

B. Nutritional Assessment

_____ 1. I eat at least 3 to 5 servings of vegetables and 2 to 4 servings of fruits daily.

_____ 2. I eat at least 6 to 11 servings daily of foods from the bread, cereal, rice, and pasta group.

_____ 3. I choose or prepare foods that tend to be lower in cholesterol and saturated fat.

_____ 4. When purchasing foods, I read the "Nutrition Facts" labels.

_____ 5. I avoid adding salt to my food.

C. Alcohol and Drugs Assessment

_____ 1. I avoid smoking and using smokeless tobacco products.

_____ 2. I avoid drinking alcohol or limit my daily alcohol intake to two drinks or less.

_____ 3. I do not drive after drinking alcohol or after taking medications that make me sleepy.

_____ 4. I follow directions when taking both prescription and over-the-counter medications.

_____ 5. I keep a record of drugs to which I am allergic in my wallet or purse.

D. Emotional Wellness Assessment

———— 1. I feel positive about myself and my life. I set realistic goals for myself.

———— 2. I can effectively cope with life's ups and downs in a healthy manner.

———— 3. I do not tend to be nervous, impatient, or under a high amount of stress.

———— 4. I can express my feelings of anger.

———— 5. When working under pressure, I stay calm and am not easily distracted.

E. Intellectual Wellness Assessment

———— 1. I seek advice when I am uncertain or uncomfortable with a recommended treatment.

———— 2. I ask about the risks, benefits, and medical necessity of all medical tests and procedures.

———— 3. I keep informed of the latest trends and information concerning health matters.

———— 4. I feel comfortable about talking to my doctor.

———— 5. I know the guidelines for practicing good preventive medicine and self-care.

F. Social and Spiritual Wellness Assessment

———— 1. I am able to develop close, intimate relationships.

———— 2. I am involved in school and/or community activities.

———— 3. I have recreational hobbies and do something fun just for myself at least once a week.

———— 4. I know what my values and beliefs are and I am tolerant of the beliefs of others.

———— 5. My life has meaning and direction. I have life goals. Personal reflection is important.

■ Analyzing Your Wellness Assessment

For each of the six wellness sections, add the total number of points that you assigned to each question. Place the totals of each section below:

TOTALS for each of the six sections:

A. Physical Assessment   _____

B. Nutritional Assessment   _____

C. Alcohol and Drugs Assessment   _____

D. Emotional Wellness Assessment   _____

E. Intellectual Wellness Assessment   _____

F. Social and Spiritual Wellness Assessment   _____

TOTAL POINTS   _____

Then, divide the Total Points by six to get the
"Average Wellness Score" =   _____

What do your results mean? The results apply to each of the six individual sections, as well as for determining your overall wellness assessment (after dividing your total score by six).

Total for each section (or Average Wellness Score)	RESULTS (for each individual section and for the overall assessment)
23–25	Excellent Your lifestyle choices and attitudes can significantly contribute to a healthy life. You are to be commended!
19–22	Good You engage in many health-promoting behaviors and attitudes. You care about your health. However, there are some areas that you could improve to provide optimal health benefits and wellness.
11–18	Average You are typical of the average American who tends to not always practice the healthiest of behaviors, despite having the knowledge which would suggest the contrary. Now is the time to consider making changes in your lifestyle to foster a healthier future.
5–10	Needs immediate improvement You are to be commended for being concerned enough about your health to take this assessment, but your behaviors and attitudes may be having a detrimental effect on your overall health. Now is the time to take action to improve your health!

■ Exercise 2. Can You Practice Safer Sex?

Most people know how HIV is transmitted and what behaviors are necessary to reduce their risk of acquiring the virus. However, some of these behaviors are not always easy to do. Your confidence in yourself to perform these protective sex behaviors is as important as simply knowing what the behaviors are. Assess your safer sex confidence level by answering these questions honestly, according to the key below:

KEY: A = I always could do this in all situations.

B = I could do this occasionally.

C = I could not do this.

_____   buy condoms at a store.

_____   discuss using a condom with a new sex partner before having sex.

_____   refuse to have sex with a person if he or she did not want to use a condom.

_____   talk to a new sex partner about his or her past sexual experiences and number of sexual partners.

_____   ask a new sex partner whether he or she has ever had sex with another person of the same sex.

_____   ask a potential sex partner about the use of intravenous drugs and sharing of needles.

_____   be able to avoid using alcohol on a date to help make a decision about sex easier.

_____   be able to clearly express what my sexual expectations and limits are before beginning any sexual activity.

_____   be able to resist an unwanted sexual advance or stop sexual activity if a condom wasn't available.

_____   be able to resist an unwanted sexual activity even when slightly intoxicated after a few drinks.

What do my results mean?

1) Multiply the number of responses you answered with "C" by 2.
2) Add to the result, the number of responses you answered with "B."
3) Responses answered with "A" do not count as points.
4) Add the answers from 1) + 2) above to get the "Confidence Score."
5) Circle your overall confidence score on the continuum below to determine your risk.

| 0 | 2 | 4 | 6 | 8 | 10 | 12 | 14 | 16 | 18 | 20 |

LOW RISK   HIGH RISK

If you scored between 10 and 20 points, you tend to doubt your ability to behave in a way that would protect you from acquiring HIV. You should evaluate your own beliefs and attitudes concerning safer sex in the four areas assessed: condom use, self-protection, sex under the influence, and sexual limits.

CHAPTER 9
Time Management

Introduction

In this chapter, we will define and discuss how cultures view time, how to set goals, how to make efficient time schedules and how to break the habit of procrastinating. The major objective in this chapter is to help you integrate your academic and non-academic life into a realistic and workable schedule so that you can achieve your goals. We will offer you many tips on how to plant your time around social/personal obligations, school, and work.

How you use your time and what motivates your use of your time are probably the most important factors which will determine if you will be successful. According to Alan Lakein,

---

From *Keys to Excellence*, Fourth Edition by Cooper et al. © 1997 by Kendall/Hunt Publishing Company.

"Time is life. It is irreversible and irreplaceable. To waste time is to waste your life, but to control time is to master your life and make the most of it."[1]

If you already know the SECRET to time management, you probably scored very well on the self-check. If you do not, you probably fell into a time management trap. In this chapter, you will learn what time management is and how time is managed efficiently. You will also learn that in order for any skill to be developed, you must practice it, thereby learning the secret.

Temporal Orientation

From the student's point of view, time is said to be a moment or a measured period when an activity/behavior occurs or is designated to occur. If you lose this period, you cannot recapture it. With all the daily pressures, it is very easy to lose track of time. Some of these pressures come about because of today's value system which presents another way of looking at time. In a multicultural society, time is usually perceived based on one's cultural heritage. A person's use of time is based on his/her value system. Its use is learned behavior. The whole issue of time is important depending on where a person works and plays and whose orientation governs the process. For example, according to Stewart, Americans are future-oriented in terms of work and action. They believe that hard work now will bring about success in the future. On the other hand, Latin Americans look to the present and the Chinese toward the past. They are very concerned about tradition and immediate conditions rather than taking steps needed for change and future progress. No matter what your temporal orientation is, you must adapt it to the society you want to work and play in, if you want to be successful. This is not an easy task since you are talking about modifying and/or changing values. Time appears to be a resource people feel they have a great deal of but often cannot control. There is, however, one good thing about time.

No matter what culture we come from or how smart or successful we are, we all have the exact same amount of time. In this way, it is an equalizer. We just have to learn to control it for ourselves. That is a part of the secret.

Everyone has the same number of minutes in an hour and the same number of hours in a day. The problem procrastinators have is that they cannot save up these hours. Yet they continue to put off and/or delay when they know they must complete a task (chore, assignment). Are you a procrastinator? Do you usually put off the task when it looks overwhelming? What should you do?

Steps to Break the Habit of Procrastinating

1. Define your goal. It will give you a sense of direction. It will help you determine what you must do.

2. Determine what your needs are.

3. Assess the task and/or situation.

4. Set up a plan of action with a specific time-frame to do a little at a time.

5. Get to work. Set your clock. TRY IT OUT.

6. Reevaluate if your plan is not effective.

---

[1]W. Herlin and C. Mayfield. *Successful Study Skills* (Dubuque: Kendall/Hunt Publishing Company) p. 9.

Goal-Setting

Manage your time. Plan your life. *In case you have not caught on yet, you are talking about managing yourself. You are talking about getting rid of habits that tend to interfere with what you need to do.* You need to set goals and priorities around your commitment to obtain a college education and a profession. Managing your time will help you successfully achieve these commitments. If you are having problems on the job, evaluate the situation, set goals and give yourself a specified period of time to complete them.

Time management calls for planning. You cannot plan without making decisions about what you want to do and where you want to go. *Effective time management requires you to be a decision-maker.* When you make the decisions about what you want and where you want to go, you have established GOALS. *Goals are important because they allow you to put your values into action. Goals are no more than your aims in life and they give you purpose and direction in which to focus your energies.*

To develop a goal is the first step in time management. *The next step is to write your goal down in explicit and concrete terms. Until it is written, it is just an idea. A goal should have the following characteristics:*

REACHABLE—Set it up in small increments so you don't bite off more than you can chew at one time. If you do, you will only become frustrated. Set only moderate goals you know you can reach.

REALISTIC—*Know your limitations and capabilities. Don't ask more of yourself than you know you are capable of doing.* Set a realistic time-frame to achieve it.

MEASURABLE—*State your goal in such a way that you as well as others will know when it has been achieved.* Be very specific and concrete about what you want to do.

For each goal, always write out a step-by-step plan as to what you are going to do to achieve it. Be concrete and specific. Each goal should always have a time-frame. Some people would put-off and put-off and never carry out the plan.

Goals are described as short-term and long-term. Long-term goals usually take a while to accomplish while short-term goals help you achieve the long-term goal. They are activities you carry out on a daily, weekly, or monthly schedule.

Now that you have your goal, you must develop a "TO-DO LIST" which may be daily, weekly, or monthly. Then PRIORITIZE. As a student, you should develop a "daily to-do list." Look at an example of how goals and priorities can be utilized.

According to the example above, the number one priority on August 31, _____ is to go to work. The second priority is to study, and the third is to practice essay writing. This is good prioritizing since this student's short-term goal is to pass English and social environment.

Long-Term Goal
I want to get my associate in arts degree in business in _____ (year).

Short-Term Goal
I want to pass English and Social Environment with a grade of "C" or above this semester.

Daily To-Do List
August 31, _____ (year).

Rank
Ordering

4 Visit with Mark and Gary
__ See "Star Trek" movie
3 Practice essay writing
__ Watch television
1 Go to work 8:00 a.m. to 12:00 noon
2 Study chapters 1 and 2 of Social Environment

Remember, you must set your goals and then begin to organize your time by using "to-do" lists which you prioritize. Most students tend to function better if they divide their goal-setting into three levels:

DAILY—WEEKLY—SEMESTER

Goal-setting should be established at the beginning of each term. This includes analysis of information on course selection, what grades you want to receive in each course, how you plan to go about it, and the evaluation of your first class sessions. Put all of this information together before setting time schedules. Remember, a goal is no good unless it is explicit and concrete. For example, to say you want to do well would be too general and vague. "I plan to make an 'A' in Psychology" is better.

Planning Your Time?

If you have not purchased your academic calendar planner for the year, you should rush right out and do it now. It should be large enough so you can write in your assignments. The ideal one would also have space for your daily "to-do" list. However, do not worry about that space since all you have to do is buy a pack of 3"x5" cards and on a nightly basis before going to bed, write out all the tasks you are planning for the next day. Don't forget to prioritize. Before writing in your planner, use these tips when planning your time.

Tip 1

Balance your time.

Balance your work, travel, sleep, domestic chores, class, study, personal, and recreational times. All work and no play truly do make Jack a dull boy. You will no doubt become frustrated if you spend too much time in some areas and your goals are not being met in other areas.

Tip 2

Plan for the semester.

Plan your school work for an entire semester based on the school's calendar. This refers to due dates for papers, hours for study time, dates for major exams, etc.

Tip 3

Set goals for each study session.

Always set a goal for each study session and be definite in your schedule about what you plan to study. Be definite about what you plan to do in each session.

Tip 4

Know how long your study session should be.

Study in short sessions. The idea is to avoid marathon sessions where you remember little of what you tried to learn. Plan to take at least a ten-minute break during every hour. During the break, try exercising or doing something else that will refresh your mind/body. This will help you maintain your concentration.

Tip 5

Study in the right place.

Select a quiet and not-too-comfortable place to study. It should allow you to concentrate on the task at hand. Make sure it has proper lighting, ventilation, and a comfortable temperature.

Tip 6

Let others in on your plans.

Let your friends and significant others know your study schedule so they will not disturb you. You are the person who must control someone else's use of your time. If you have children, plan activities for them while you study.

Tip 7

Plan to see your professor.

Make sure you understand your notes and/or assignment before trying to study. If you are not clear on what you have to study, make an appointment to visit your professor for clarification. Don't flounder. Record your appointment to see the professor if it is necessary in your appointment book.

Tip 8

Know how much time you should study for each class.

Plan two hours of study for every hour you are in class.

Tip 9

Prioritize subjects to study.

Study the subject you like least first since it will no doubt require more of your time and energy. Once you have completed this task, reward yourself by doing something you like.

Tip 10

Know when to review notes.

Review, study, and/or rewrite your lecture notes within 24 hours to help with memory and effective note taking. Forty-eight hours should be the maximum amount of time you allow to lapse before reviewing.

Tip 11

Know purpose of studying.

Study to pass tests. When reading and/or reviewing notes, always practice asking and answering questions. Study as though at the end of your study session, you will be required to pass a test.

Tip 12

Know how to begin reading text material.

Survey required chapters (material) before you begin to read.

Tip 13

Develop questions you should ask as you study.

Ask questions about what you must learn during the study period. Turn all headings into questions and then answer them.

Tip 14

Always read with a purpose.

Read the assigned chapters and/or material. Look for answers to questions posed in order to complete the assignment. Read with the purpose of finding the answers.

Tip 15

Memorize.

Go over the content which you want to remember. If necessary, orally recite and make notes to help you remember.

Tip 16

Review.

Review the material and ask questions.

Tip 17

Decide when you should study.

Determine your best time of day and schedule your study time then. In addition, a brief review before class and immediately after class is strongly suggested.

Tip 18

Use your time productively.

Don't waste time. If you are waiting, use that time for review. If you have recorded your notes and you are driving, listen to the tape. If you are riding with someone else, read your notes.

■ Taking Control of Your Time

Now that you have looked at goal-setting and establishing priorities, you are ready for the next phase in understanding how you use time-taking control. The first step is to see how you actually use your time. Once you truly know what you are doing with your time, you should plan a weekly schedule for the semester using the time management tips in this chapter. Remember there are only 168 hours in a week.

Summary

Managing time, procrastinating, and setting effective goals are major problems for students. This chapter has offered six steps to break the habit of procrastinating. The first step is to set reachable goals. All goals must be reasonable, realistic and measurable, and controllable. If you have many tasks that you must complete, then you have to make a "to do" list and then prioritize your activities. A number of tips are given to help you make the most of your time. The second step is to determine your needs. The third is to assess the task or situation. The fourth step is to set up a plan of action with a specific time frame for achieving the goal. This is the time to map out in a schedule how much time you are going to use each day and when you are going to so this task. The fifth step is to get to work and try out the plan. The final and sixth step is to reevaluate and see if the plan is working.

Journal Questions

1. What do you expect to learn from this chapter?

2. (a) In which areas do you spend too much time?

   (b) What adjustments must you make in your schedule to improve your time management?

3. Give at least two things you learned about yourself from this chapter.

4. Did this chapter give you what you expected? If not, what more do you need?

References

Ellis, David. *Becoming a Master Student*. Rapid City, South Dakota: College Survival, Inc., 1991.

Herlin, Wayne and Mayfield, Craig. *Successful Study Skills*. Dubuque, Iowa: Kendall/Hunt Publishing Co., 1981.

Merriam-Webster, *Webster's Ninth New Collegiate Dictionary*. Springfield, Massachusetts: Merriam-Webster, Inc., 1983.

Orientation and Study Skills Staff and Faculty, Miami-Dade Community College, Miami, Florida.

Siebert, Al and Walter, Tim. *Student Success: How to Succeed in College and Still Have Time for Friends*. 5th edition. New York: Holt, Rinehart and Winston, 1990.

Starke, Mary C. *Survival Skills for College*. Englewood Cliffs, New Jersey: Prentice Hall, 1990.

■ Exercise 1. Time Management Awareness Check

DIRECTIONS: Place an "X" in the appropriate box and check your responses with the answer key.

	Yes	**No**
1. Do you make a calendar and plan your coursework for the entire semester?	☐	☐
2. Do you follow a weekly time schedule?	☐	☐
3. Do you use a daily calendar or notebook to keep you aware of high priority items to do now?	☐	☐
4. When you take a course, do you know the criteria for assigning grades?	☐	☐
5. Are there times when you have difficulty starting to study?	☐	☐
6. Is it sometimes necessary for you to cram for a test?	☐	☐
7. Do you have trouble getting to class on time?	☐	☐
8. Do you have difficulty concentrating on an assignment?	☐	☐
9. Is it sometimes hard for you to finish term papers, reports, and projects on time?	☐	☐
10. Are you easily distracted when studying?	☐	☐
11. Do you become bored with the subject when studying?	☐	☐
12. Do you reward yourself when you have studied effectively?	☐	☐
13. Do you schedule large blocks of time for study?	☐	☐
14. Do you have a comfortable place where you study regularly?	☐	☐
15. Do you put off starting on a big assignment because you think it is too hard?	☐	☐
16. Do you use short periods of free time for studying effectively?	☐	☐
17. Do you plan time for rest periods when studying?	☐	☐
18. Do you plan time for recreation and relaxation?	☐	☐
19. Do you panic or become anxious in test situations?	☐	☐
20. Do you study your hardest subjects when you are more alert?	☐	☐
21. When you have a high priority assignment, do you work at smaller, routine jobs instead of the important one?	☐	☐

Model Answer Key

1. Yes	8. No	15. No
2. Yes	9. No	16. Yes
3. Yes	10. No	17. Yes
4. Yes	11. No	18. Yes
5. No	12. Yes	19. No
6. No	13. Yes	20. Yes
7. No	14. Yes	21. No

Author Unknown

Few people achieve all these ideal answers. Examine your "wrong" responses to see if you can find a better system than you have at present.

■ Exercise 2. Setting Goals

DIRECTIONS: Write out at least two of your long-term goals in the first two rows in columns A and B. At least one of them must pertain to your education or future profession. Then list at least four short-term goals under each long-term goal.

Column A	Column B
Long-Term Goal #1	Long-Term Goal #2
_____	_____
_____	_____
Short-Term Goals	Short-Term Goals
_____	_____
_____	_____
_____	_____
_____	_____

■ Exercise 3. Monitoring Your Time

1. Complete a daily log for a full week indicating how your time and energy were spent. Follow these directions:

   a. List all fixed obligations—classes, meetings, work hours, meals, travel time to and from commitments, family obligations, etc.—as you complete them.

   b. Consider and indicate time spent on class review if you prepared for class.

   c. Don't forget to indicate any time spent on health essentials such as recreation, sleep, and exercise.

   d. Be sure 24 hours per day are accounted for in your log.

   e. Use the sample time chart on the following page.

2. Summarize the time you spent each day on various activities according to the summary log sheet provided.

Sample Personal Log of Time Usage

Fill in each time block **after you have completed the activity**. Use the following categories of activities.

Class
Work
Housework
Meeting

Travel
Eating
Sleep
Recreation

Exercise
Personal (getting dressed, bathing, brushing teeth, etc.)
Other (explain)

Hours	Monday	Tuesday	Wednesday	Thursday	Friday	Saturday	Sunday
	Sample						
7:00 A.M.	breakfast	dress	breakfast	dress	breakfast	sleep	sleep
7:30	travel	breakfast	travel	breakfast	travel	dress	" "
8:00	history class	travel	history class	travel	history class	breakfast	dress
8:30	" "	study speech	" "	study speech	" "	travel	breakfast
9:00	study history	" "	study history	" "	study history	work	family
9:30	" "	speech class	" "	speech class	" "	" "	commitment
10:00	English class	" "	English class	" "	English class	" "	" "
10:30	" "	" "	" "	" "	" "	" "	travel
11:00	study English	biology class	study English	biology class	study English	" "	church
11:30	" "	" "	" "	" "	" "	" "	" "
12:00 Noon	lunch	" "	lunch	" "	lunch	lunch	travel
12:30 P.M.	" "	study biology	" "	study biology	" "	travel	recreation
1:00	travel	" "	travel	" "	travel	errands	" "
1:30	errands	lunch	errands	lunch	errands	" "	" "
2:00	work	travel	work	travel	work	study history	" "
2:30	" "	work	" "	work	" "	" "	" "
3:00	" "	" "	" "	" "	" "	study English	" "
3:30	" "	" "	" "	" "	" "	" "	travel
4:00	" "	" "	" "	" "	" "	study biology	family
4:30	" "	" "	" "	" "	" "	" "	commitment

Sample Personal Log of Time Usage "continued"

Hours	Monday	Tuesday	Wednesday	Thursday	Friday	Saturday	Sunday
Sample							
5:00 P.M.	*travel*	*work*	*travel*	*work*	*travel*	*relax*	*family*
5:30	*relax*	*travel*	*relax*	*travel*	*relax*	*" "*	*commitment*
6:00	*dinner*	*dinner*	*dinner*	*dinner*	*dinner*	*dinner*	*" "*
6:30	*" "*	*" "*	*" "*	*" "*	*" "*	*" "*	*dinner*
7:00	*study history*	*study speech*	*study history*	*study speech*	*recreation*	*recreation*	*" "*
7:30	*" "*	*" "*	*" "*	*" "*	*" "*	*" "*	*study or work*
8:00	*study English*	*study biology*	*study English*	*study biology*	*" "*	*" "*	*on special*
8:30	*" "*	*" "*	*" "*	*" "*	*" "*	*" "*	*class assign-*
9:00	*recreation*	*recreation*	*recreation*	*recreation*	*" "*	*" "*	*ments*
9:30	*" "*	*" "*	*" "*	*" "*	*" "*	*" "*	*" "*
10:00	*" "*	*" "*	*" "*	*" "*	*" "*	*" "*	*" "*
10:30							
11:00							
11:30							
12:00 MIDN.							
12:30 A.M.							
1:00							
1:30							
2:00							
2:30							
3:00							
3:30							
4:00							
4:30							
5:00							
5:30							
6:00							
6:30							

Name: _____ Date: _____

■ Exercise 3. Monitoring Your Time

Fill in each time block **after you have completed the activity**. Use the following categories of activities.

Class	Travel	Exercise
Work	Eating	Personal (getting dressed, bathing,
Housework	Sleep	brushing teeth, etc.)
Meeting	Recreation	Other (explain)

Hours	Monday	Tuesday	Wednesday	Thursday	Friday	Saturday	Sunday
7:00 A.M.							
7:30							
8:00							
8:30							
9:00							
9:30							
10:00							
10:30							
11:00							
11:30							
12:00 Noon							
12:30 P.M.							
1:00							
1:30							
2:00							
2:30							
3:00							
3:30							
4:00							
4:30							

Name: _____ Date: _____

Hours	Monday	Tuesday	Wednesday	Thursday	Friday	Saturday	Sunday
5:00 P.M.							
5:30							
6:00							
6:30							
7:00							
7:30							
8:00							
8:30							
9:00							
9:30							
10:00							
10:30							
11:00							
11:30							
12:00 MIDN.							
12:30 A.M.							
1:00							
1:30							
2:00							
2:30							
3:00							
3:30							
4:00							
4:30							
5:00							
5:30							
6:00							
6:30							

Name: ———————————————————— Date: ————————————————

■ Exercise 3. Monitor Summary

(Indicate Hours Spent in Each Area)

Activity	Monday	Tuesday	Wednesday	Thursday	Friday	Saturday	Sunday	Total
Classes								
Work								
Studying								
Travel								
Recreation								
Exercise								
Eating								
Family								
Personal								
Sleep								
Other (explain)								
	24	24	24	24	24	24	24	168

■ Exercise 4. Analyzing Your Time

According to your personal summary log, how did you spend your time?

Identify the eight areas where you spent the greatest amounts of time. Explain why.

_____

_____

_____

_____

What areas should you cut back on if you are going to accomplish your goals?

_____

_____

_____

How many hours will you reduce each one by?

_____

_____

In what areas should you increase the amount of time you spend if you are going to accomplish your goals?

_____

_____

_____

How many hours will you increase each one by?

_____

_____

Are there any other factors you should consider before actually planning and taking control of your time? If so, list them below and discuss them.

_____

_____

■ Exercise 5. Planning Your Time

This is a very important exercise because if you really follow the time management tips and are highly motivated, there is no way you can fail. The purpose of a time schedule is to give you a framework for bringing order and discipline into your life, not to make you into a robot. It will give you time to do the things you need to do. It can break the pattern of procrastinating and cut down on worrying time. **Assume that you are basically planning how the rest of your weeks will look during the semester** with the exception of a few changes for unplanned events.

1. Complete a daily log for a full week indicating how you PLAN to spend your time.

   a. List all fixed obligations—classes, work, domestic chores, travel to and from commitments, sleep, and meals—you know you must complete.

   b. Don't forget to allow time for yourself (personal time), recreation, religion, and exercise.

   c. Based on class times, indicate when you plan to study and review school work. Don't forget to consider the amount of time you need for every hour in class and when you should review for information to move from short-term to long-term memory.

   d. Go back to Exercise 4 and use the information from your analysis.

   e. Be sure to plan for 24 hours a day.

2. Now summarize the time you plan to spend each day on the various activities according to the planning summary log sheet.

■ Exercise 5. Planning Your Time

Develop a plan that will allow you to be able to do the task you know you must perform if you are to be successful. Use the following categories of activities.

Class	Travel	Exercise
Work	Eating	Personal (getting dressed, bathing,
Housework	Sleep	brushing teeth, etc.)
Meeting	Recreation	Other (explain)

Hours	Monday	Tuesday	Wednesday	Thursday	Friday	Saturday	Sunday
7:00 A.M.							
7:30							
8:00							
8:30							
9:00							
9:30							
10:00							
10:30							
11:00							
11:30							
12:00 Noon							
12:30 P.M.							
1:00							
1:30							
2:00							
2:30							
3:00							
3:30							
4:00							
4:30							

Hours	Monday	Tuesday	Wednesday	Thursday	Friday	Saturday	Sunday
5:00 P.M.							
5:30							
6:00							
6:30							
7:00							
7:30							
8:00							
8:30							
9:00							
9:30							
10:00							
10:30							
11:00							
11:30							
12:00 MIDN.							
12:30 A.M.							
1:00							
1:30							
2:00							
2:30							
3:00							
3:30							
4:00							
4:30							
5:00							
5:30							
6:00							
6:30							

Name: _____ Date: _____

Exercise 5. Planning Summary

(Indicate Hours Spent in Each Area)

Activity	Monday	Tuesday	Wednesday	Thursday	Friday	Saturday	Sunday	Total
Classes								
Work								
Studying								
Travel								
Recreation								
Exercise								
Eating								
Family								
Personal								
Sleep								
Other (explain)								
	24	24	24	24	24	24	24	168

◼ Exercise 6. Summary

1. What is the SECRET to time management?

   _____

   _____

2. Identify what you think are the three most important goals in your life and map out how you plan to go about achieving them.

   _____

   _____

   _____

3. Why is it so important to use a daily "to do" list?

   _____

   _____

4. Develop a plan of action showing how you would assist students to stop procrastinating. Be ready to share and discuss this plan with the class.

   _____

   _____

   _____

   _____

   _____

   _____

   _____

   _____

   _____

CHAPTER 10
Acquiring Financial Skills
The Buck Stops with You

Whatever name money goes by (e.g., dollar, euro, drachma, shekel, yen, ruble, baht, yuan, rupee, peso, rand), it has always served as a medium of exchange. Money was created to correct the problems imbedded in ancient barter and trading systems. Historically, a variety of materials were used as a medium of exchange. Money has taken the form of clay tablets, cowrie shells, spade-shaped bronze coins, lumps of salt, stone coins weighing up to 500 pounds, tea leaves, dried fish, and eventually metal coins. The use of metal coins for money caught on throughout the world. While this technological breakthrough eliminated many of the obvious problems associated with other early forms of money (e.g., salt-dried fish), the use of coins introduced a new set of problems. A major problem was weight, especially when a lot of money was needed for payment. Because of the weight problem with coins, paper money was invented by the Chinese centuries ago. (The Chinese experimented with other innovations. They manufactured coins in the shape of what they were intended to purchase; for example, coins shaped like human bodies were used for purchasing clothing.)

Probably since its creation, money has possessed many meanings for its users. Some civilizations produced forms of money that required a great deal of effort to manufacture. The reason for the effort was to advertise a civilization's position in the world. Of course, practical considerations also entered into the picture. For example, to prevent counterfeiting or other forms of tampering with a civilization's currency, coins were *milled*; that is, gold and silver coins were formed with ridges around the edge (which also served to deter people from scraping some of the metal off before passing the coins on to another person).

■ Money's Possible Meanings to the Individual

The Developmental Perspective

There are two things we can say about the meaning of money that apply to everyone. First, money has different meanings to people at different points along the developmental trajectory of life, because of the different tasks or expectations we face at each stage.

- Within the developmental matrix that constitutes human development, there are stages through which all people must pass to achieve effective living. Some of the stages are linked to certain age periods; others are not.
- These stages are defined by certain tasks that are representative of what needs to occur at each stage. These tasks are similar to the nuggets of gold found when panning in a mountain stream. At certain points in one's developmental journey, certain tasks shine brighter and should receive attention. Other tasks, for the time being, are returned to the "developmental stream."
- Accomplishment of a particular task is directly related to mastery of certain life-skills. Life-skills represent a sort of developmental glue that binds stage to tasks and helps to move a person on.

Money means different things at different points in our life, and the expectations concerning how we should manage money also change. Such differences often require acquiring a different set of financial skills. For example, a 16-year-old might enjoy planning how to spend an unexpected $100 from grandfather, while a parent at age 30 may worry about having enough money to provide the best for her children. Parents who spend money on themselves at the expense of their children are likely to experience some form of social censure depending on how much the children suffer as a result.

Second, money has a range of different meanings *within* each age group. Not all 18-year-olds, or 78-year-olds, view money in the same way. In any age group you can find a number of views on the meaning of money when individual members of the group are compared (either in what they say about money or what they spend money on). For example, while some 16-year-olds experience money as creating a burning sensation in their pockets, others find money to be a step to obtaining something of greater value. Years ago one of the authors knew a fellow teen who saved all the money he had earned through an assortment of part-time jobs. At 16 he had amassed a sum that enabled him to buy a small parcel of land, and he had enough money left over to finance the building of an automated carwash on the land purchased. The carwash paid for his college education. The author, on the other hand, spent all the money he earned prior to attending college and had to take out two college loans.

■ Activity

Stop and Think

1. What does money mean to you?

2. Do you think money means the same thing to your friends as it does to you? Explain.

3. Does every member of your family (e.g., brothers, sisters, parents, etc.) view money in the same way? Explain.

Money and Theories of Human Nature

Money has figured into major theories that explain human behavior. Karl Marx was a political philosopher whose theory concerning the distribution of wealth had a significant impact on political movements in the twentieth century. The psychologist B. F. Skinner, a behaviorist, proposed a psychological theory that was applied to mapping out the structure of a utopian community (Walden Two) where people received the greatest amount of external rewards (in a medium of exchange called "tokens") for doing the jobs that possessed little inherent reward. In a topsy-turvy Skinnerian world the business executive could receive a salary well below that of a garbage collector.

Theories intended to explain the role of money in our lives represent a plethora of academic perspectives. Sigmund Freud, a major thinker of the twentieth century and the founder of psychoanalysis, offered a theory of dreams that many found fascinating and strange at the same time. In his *Interpretation of Dreams*, he speculated that dreams contained personal and universal symbols. If one understood what the symbols meant, one would be able to uncover the hidden, true message of the dream. For example, Freud reviewed one client's dream that contained the theme "payment for therapy." Freud believed that this particular client was symbolically expressing a concern she harbored. According to Freud, she *unconsciously* viewed the payment as a form of avarice or greed, and essentially little more than a "filthy" exchange between two people. Freud believed his interpretation of the dream's content was valid because an adult's concern about lack of cleanliness can be traced back to childhood events. Freud wrote that unconscious concerns about filth are "often replaced in dreams by avariciousness for money" (1900/1965, p. 233). From a Freudian position it appears that money has various meanings that we are not even consciously aware of.

Even if one disagrees with Freud's interpretation of money as a symbol of repressed thoughts, it is impossible to deny that the influence of money goes well beyond issues of social status. Money has been linked to human activities such as humor (e.g., *"Money talks. It says, good-bye."*), superstitious behaviors, and common everyday expressions that have found a place in our spoken and written language. In the area of superstitious behaviors one finds many examples. Some brides place a coin in a shoe on the day of the wedding for future good fortune. New business owners display the first dollar received after opening their businesses. Visitors to Rome toss a coin into the Trevi Fountain to guarantee a return visit. Many sayings and phrases about money have invaded our language and are heard every day.

"Show me the money."

"Shop till you drop."

"It's voodoo economics."

"Share the wealth."

"Money can't buy happiness, but it helps."

"The buck stops here."

"Money makes the world go 'round."

"A penny saved is a penny earned."

"He has the Midas touch."

"You cannot be too rich or too thin."

"She is morally bankrupt."

One indication that money has a strong psychological component is the way money keeps our mind focused on a time other than the present (e.g., "What bills should I pay next month?" "Investing in ENRON for retirement was a huge mistake for my parents!" "How can I get more money next year to go to college?"). Yet while money is frequently in the forefront of our thoughts, it also passes through our hands easily and disappears sooner than we expected.

To test your awareness of the identifying features of different bills, answer these questions: Whose portrait is printed on a $10, $20, $50, and $100 bill? What scene is presented on the backside of a $10, $20, $50, and $100 bill? What is the value of the largest denomination ever printed, and whose portrait appeared on the bill? Since 1969 what is the largest bill issued? (See note below* for answers)

■ Managing Money to Achieve Academic Goals

Obviously money is important to us throughout our lives, but for the student experiencing an academic transition from high school to college there is a major change in terms of how money is used. The primary task, developmentally, is to handle your money in a way that allows you to stay in college. This investment is a good one when you consider that on the average a college graduate, over a lifetime, will increase his or her earning power by an average of approximately $1,000,000 compared to individuals who stop their educational journey with a high school diploma.

But before being able to "make the big bucks," students need to use money as a tool to stay in college and achieve their ultimate career goal. One aspect of managing money is to learn where it disappears to. The following activity will help you determine what you are spending your money on.

*Answers, in order: Portraits are Hamilton, Jackson, Grant, and Franklin. Scenes are U.S. Treasury building, White House, U.S. Capitol, and Independence Hall. Largest bill printed was $100,000 and was embellished with a portrait of W. Wilson. The largest bill printed since 1969 is $100.

■ Activity

Where Is the Money Going?

Estimate how much you spend in each of the following categories *per semester*. Then figure the percentage of the total amount that each category represents.

	$	%
Food consumed at residence	____	____
Food consumed away from residence (eating out, food from vending machines)	____	____
Nonfood groceries (e.g., cleaning supplies, laundry detergent)	____	____
Residence (dorm, apartment)	____	____
Clothing and shoes	____	____
Utilities (electric, water, gas)	____	____
Telephone (cell and residence phone)	____	____
Garbage pickup	____	____
Dry cleaning/laundromat	____	____
Transportation (e.g., car loan, auto insurance, gasoline, auto repair, parking costs, oil change and maintenance, car license tag)	____	____
Personal care (e.g., hair salons)	____	____
Health care (e.g., medicine, membership at a physical fitness center, doctor and dentist visits, glasses/contacts)	____	____
Newspapers/magazines	____	____
Club dues	____	____
Postage	____	____
Household items (e.g., furniture, cookware, repairs, decorations)	____	____
Entertainment (e.g., movies, video rentals, CDs, video games)	____	____
Loan and debt payments (other than car)	____	____
Tuition, books, etc.	____	____
Lab fees for classes	____	____
Computer equipment, software	____	____
Internet Services	____	____
Tithing/charity	____	____
Child care	____	____

Insurance (other than car) ⎯⎯⎯ ⎯⎯⎯

Taxes ⎯⎯⎯ ⎯⎯⎯

Other

⎯⎯⎯⎯⎯⎯⎯⎯⎯⎯⎯⎯⎯⎯⎯⎯⎯⎯⎯⎯⎯ ⎯⎯⎯ ⎯⎯⎯

⎯⎯⎯⎯⎯⎯⎯⎯⎯⎯⎯⎯⎯⎯⎯⎯⎯⎯⎯⎯⎯ ⎯⎯⎯ ⎯⎯⎯

⎯⎯⎯⎯⎯⎯⎯⎯⎯⎯⎯⎯⎯⎯⎯⎯⎯⎯⎯⎯⎯ ⎯⎯⎯ ⎯⎯⎯

⎯⎯⎯⎯⎯⎯⎯⎯⎯⎯⎯⎯⎯⎯⎯⎯⎯⎯⎯⎯⎯ ⎯⎯⎯ ⎯⎯⎯

⎯⎯⎯⎯⎯⎯⎯⎯⎯⎯⎯⎯⎯⎯⎯⎯⎯⎯⎯⎯⎯ ⎯⎯⎯ ⎯⎯⎯

$ %

TOTALS ⎯⎯⎯ ⎯⎯⎯

Use the space below to calculate percentages. For example, if the total was $900 and you spent $300 on rent, then the Residence category accounts for 33% of the money spent during the semester (300 ÷ 900 = .333).

The percentages below are based on figures from the U.S. Department of Labor, Bureau of Labor Statistics, Consumer Expenditure Survey. Compare your percentages to those for the age that is nearest your own. Are you satisfied with the way your money is being spent?

	Age (average income)		
	25 ($32,968)	**50** ($49,108)	**70** ($24,468)
Category			
Food at home	7.6%	6.5%	10.5%
Food away from home	5.0%	4.6%	4.4%
Shelter	7.6%	13.7%	14.9%
Utilities	5.7%	5.3%	8.3%
Clothing	5.3%	4.5%	4.8%
Transportation	15.5%	15.2%	15.3%
Health Care	3.4%	3.7%	10.7%
Personal Care	1.1%	1.0%	1.3%
Entertainment	4.6%	5.1%	4.9%
Other Spending	6.4%	8.8%	10.4%

Whether you have financial assistance (e.g., parents paying some of the bills) or not, now is the time to develop some money management skills as well as explore some avenues for bringing in additional income. Certainly one danger of being a student is acquiring too much debt. One rule of thumb to avoid acquiring too much debt is the **20% net income rule**. The rule is that you should stop and carefully consider your financial situation if your credit payments exceed 20% of your actual spending money. (If you own a condominium or house, those payments are not included in the 20% figure.) For example, using a figure of $1,000 of actual spending money (assuming none of this is going to taxes, which have already been paid), if a student is spending $350 on car payments and $100 a month on various credit card charges, he or she is spending 45% on credit payments, far exceeding the 20% rule.

■ Steps for Obtaining Financial Control

While there are many important financial goals to consider (life insurance, retirement plans, investments, and so forth), our focus will be on four aspects of money management related to students: quick money tips, budgeting, financial aid and employment, and debt stress and credit problems.

Quick Money Tips

Banks

- ■ When setting up a checking account, ask about options and determine which combination fits your lifestyle best.

Common Options
1. Overdraft privileges insure that checks written will be paid.
2. Direct deposit of income saves trips to a bank to make deposits.
3. Some banks do not pay interest if the amount in the savings goes below a certain amount.
4. Service fees can vary. Charges can run several dollars a month but by keeping a minimum amount in the checking account, you may be able to obtain free checking.

- If possible, avoid using ATMs. While the fees seem small, they add up, and you can expect the basic fees for using ATMs to rise.
- Keep receipts, even if you simply drop them into a box or some other container. ATM receipts and deposit slips provide evidence to argue your case if an error occurs (while relatively rare, banks make errors, as do other businesses). Keep in mind that there is typically a time limit set for reporting an error. Ask your bank the length of time. Generally speaking, the sooner you report an error, the better.

Credit Cards

- Credit cards are far from simple. Carefully consider the various types of charges for a credit card you are considering, and compare the credit card offers. For example, credit cards sometimes charge an "over limit" fee when you exceed your credit line. Late fees are added on when payments are past due. On many cards, even if the amount owed is very small (say, under $20), you will be required to pay a minimum finance charge, which on a small amount owed can represent a relatively large percentage. Some lenders charge an annual fee. Annual fees for regular cards can be expected to be lower than premium cards. Finally, interest rates on credit cards compared to other loans tend to be high. Find the best deal, but do not be tricked by offers of low initial rates, which are often quickly replaced by much higher rates.
- Aim to pay off credit cards by each statement. This is considered one of the best ways to use credit cards.
- Avoid paying only the minimum on a credit card. The amount owed will "never" go away, and it will generate more in terms of what is owed due to the high interest rate.
- If your balance due has grown too large, consider cutting up unnecessary credit cards. Use the simplest means to see where your cash is going—buy with cash. Making purchases with cash prevents you from spending the "imaginary money" provided by credit cards. This imaginary money materializes later in the form of debt.
- If your credit cards are stolen, contact the lender. If reported soon enough you will owe nothing; at worst, you will owe $50.

Shopping

- If impulse buying creates problems, take steps to control your urge to buy. For example, take a grocery list with you when you shop and stick to the list.
- Shop at secondhand stores. These types of stores are typically referred to as thrift stores (e.g., Goodwill, Salvation Army) or consignment stores. Both types can provide bargains.
- Avoid shopping regularly at convenience stores since their prices tend to be higher, with a few exceptions (e.g., milk may be lower, but the lower price could represent an attempt to "bait and hook" you into going in and then paying higher prices for other items).
- When shopping at supermarkets, pay attention to unit prices, which allow you to more accurately compare the cost of different products.

- Avoid buying items from end-of-the aisle displays in supermarkets. In many cases these do not offer the savings they appear to. Shoppers pause at the end of aisles, and store managers take advantage of this behavior to sell certain items.
- Try out generic brands for foods, spices, pet products, over-the-counter medicines, and so on. These store brands are frequently equal in quality but cost significantly less.
- Make salads yourself instead of buying the bagged salads that are already made (the difference can be a 50% saving).
- Eat at home instead of eating out. If you decide to eat out, seek out bargains that advertise lower prices at nonpeak times (e.g., dinner before 6:00 p.m.).

Miscellaneous Tips

- Zen Buddhists provide an excellent example of not becoming attached to worldly items. Simplify your life by reducing the number of items you buy. Review what you are paying for and ask yourself two questions.

  Do I really need or want this? For example, do you need the cell phone you are paying for? If the answer is no, get rid of the item and save money.

  Is there a less expensive (or free) way to get the item? If you really need or want an item, consider alternatives besides purchasing it. For example, join a car pool to reduce the cost of travel, bring your lunch with you rather than going out to lunch, go to the college's library to read the newspaper instead of subscribing.

- Pay bills on time to establish good credit. Sending payments in on time builds a good credit history, which means you are worth the risk of loaning money to because you pay both the money loaned to you and the corresponding interest on schedule.
- Avoid "friends" who borrow money, food, and so on without paying you back.

Budgeting

Debt is the worst poverty.

—*Thomas Fuller*

Never spend your money before you have it.

—*Thomas Jefferson*

Determine your monthly expenses. Compare the amount you are paying out to the amount of money coming in (income). In the beginning it is essential that you keep a daily record of expenses. Learn where the money is going. Once you establish the flow of cash, make suitable adjustments to gain better control if necessary. Establish a goal, or goals, and keep a budget to achieve it (e.g., "I will end each month with a few dollars, so I am not always asking my parents for help." "I will budget my money to have enough at the end of the semester to enable me to take a short three-day vacation." "I will cut back on nonessential spending to prevent that situation from occurring again—where I had to get $500 with my credit card to pay some bills.") Keep in mind the difference between money spent on wants and money spent on needs.

Use the list in the activity "Where is the Money Going" earlier in this chapter as a model to set up a budget. Include all categories listed that are appropriate, and add others that reflect your personal expenses. The greater the detail, the better you will understand where the money is going. Use this list to decide what you can cut back on, and then follow the budget you have set up. Adjust your budget after using it for a while; fine tune it to fit your financial needs and personality.

Also, if you have to buy a big-ticket item to pay for while attending college, consider ways to reduce the cost. Take the example of a car. To keep cost down, consider buying a used car. Check reliable sources of information about used cars. A *Consumer Reports* investigation found the following used cars to have better-than-average reliability: Honda Civic, Toyota Corolla, Honda Accord, Toyota Camry, Acura TL, Acura RL, Mazda MX5 Miata, Honda CRV, Toyota RAV4, Toyota Tacoma, Ford F150 2WD, and Lincoln Town Car.

When it comes to used cars, be aware that some 20% of all vehicles that are considered totaled in accidents or other mishaps are rebuilt and sold as if they are simply pre-owned vehicles (Krebs, 2002). Krebs reports that in many cases for a small fee (less than $20) the history of the vehicle you are interested in can be checked through Carfax.com or AutoCheck.com. You can also have your own mechanic check for previous damage and other problems. The cost of hiring a mechanic to check over a used car is well worth the $100 it usually costs for such a service.

Financial Aid and Student Employment

Budgeting should not simply be seen as an effort to cut back on spending. Budgeting also involves ways to increase income, looking for the amount of money available to cover certain costs. Remember the word *budget* is inseparable from the word *income*. Supplementing one's available money might take the form of seeking employment or some type of financial aid. College personnel are available who can help students find employment and learn more about various types of financial aid, scholarship applications, confusing financial terms, publications devoted to financial aid information, and steps involved in obtaining financial aid. Financial aid advisors can answer many common questions over the phone, but if you are serious about obtaining financial aid, the sooner you set up an appointment to meet face to face with a financial aid advisor, the better off you will be. There are many sources of assistance: federal and state governments, banks, the college itself, and various private donations that are intended to assist students. Several examples of ways to help fund one's education are listed below.

- *University Work Program* (student employment). In this case you earn the money needed. Jobs are usually located on the campus. Sometimes the work is even tied to a student's career interest.
- **Aid for Military Personnel.** Receipt of this form of assistance is tied directly to joining the military.
- **Grants.** This form of financial aid does not require repayment.
- **Loans.** In this case the student is expected to pay back the money borrowed. Typically, the repayment occurs after the student leaves the college, and the payment plan is based on a much lower rate of interest than is found with a regular loan from a bank.
- **Private Programs of Student Aid.** A large number of organizations or individuals provide financial aid to individual students.
- **Special Programs Providing Aid.** In this case available funding is linked to special groups of students (e.g., Donna Reed Foundation for the Performing Arts School, Women's International Bowling Congress Scholarship, Children of Deaf Adults Scholarship, Parke-Davis Epilepsy Scholarship Program, ESPN Scholastic Sports America).

The actual list of possibilities in each of these categories is long. Students interested in obtaining up-to-date information should contact their college's financial aid office. In addition, a number of publications are available to help you learn more about ways to supplement the money you currently have to pay for a college education. Some examples follow. We recommend contacting the sources listed to determine if a particular publication contains the type of information you need to achieve your financial and educational goals. Also, check with the campus financial aid office to determine if any of these publications are available for students to use.

> *Chronicle Financial Aid Guide* (order no. 502A). Source: Chronicle Guidance Publications, PO Box 1190, Moravia, NY 13118-1190 (800-622-7284)
>
> *College Money Handbook* (order no. B00514). Source: Peterson's Guides, PO Box 2123, Princeton, NY 08543-2123 (800-EDU-DATA or http://www.pertersons.com)
>
> *Earn and Learn: Your Guide In-School Educational Employment Programs* (21st ed.). Source: Octameron Associates, PO Box 2748, Alexandria, VA 22301 (703-836-5480)
>
> *Foundation Grants to Individuals* (11th ed.) (order no. GTI10). Source: Foundation Center, 79th Fifth Avenue, New York, NY 10003-3050 (800-424-9836)

Debt Stress and Credit Problems

Some students, such as, beginning students with little family income and returning adult students who have given up jobs to pursue a college degree, often find it difficult to make ends meet and might want to seek the advice of a consumer credit counselor (advisor). Usually one can find a service that is either free or only requires a small fee. Credit advising helps individuals deal with financial problems. Typically, the advisor will meet with a person (and spouse) to evaluate the financial situation and help the person develop a plan of action. The service will help the person establish a detailed budget, find the means to make payments, and even develop a plan for purchases in the future. Sometimes these services cooperate with the individual's creditors to get him or her back on a sound financial footing.

Finally, be aware of what is called **identity theft**. Identity thieves gather information about you that allows them to access your checking or savings account and to obtain credit cards and loans in your name. They acquire the needed information through a number of different avenues. They might submit a change of address form to a post office to have your mail sent to them, remove mail directly from your mailbox, or call your residence and trick you into revealing your social security number over the phone. In some cases, these thieves might have bought the needed information from unscrupulous restaurant servers who make a copy of your credit card number when you turn the card over to the server to pay a bill. Take measures to prevent the stealing of your identity (e.g., consider renting a post office box if someone in the neighborhood reports his or her identity was stolen) and to determine if identity theft has already occurred (e.g., periodically check your credit rating). Credit checks typically cost around $20. Authorities that have dealt with cases of identity theft recommend checking your credit rating once a year to uncover any problems resulting from identity theft.

■ Closing Remarks

There are many important considerations when it comes to managing money. Beyond what has been discussed in this chapter, there are other things to consider, such as savings accounts, financial plans, social security, investing, and taxes. Here we have focused on a few financial areas that have proven to be troublesome for students. We recommend that you seek additional information from an expert or one of the many published sources available to gather more information. As with the other life-skills discussed throughout this textbook, financial skills play a crucial role in our life during the college years and after graduation.

■ References

Brill, H., Brill, J. A., & Feigenbaum, C. (1999). *Investing with your values: Making money and making a difference.* Princeton, New York: Bloomberg Press.

Consumer Credit Counseling Services. (n.d.). *Client handbook.* Atlanta, GA: Author.

Editors of Rodale Press. (1994). *Cut your spending in half without settling for less: How to pay the lowest price for everything.* Emmaus, PA: Rodale Press.

Emmett, R. (2000). *The procrastinator's handbook: Mastering the art of doing it now.* New York: Walker.

Freud, S. (1965). *The interpretation of dreams* (James Strachey, Trans.). New York: Discus Books. (Original work published 1900)

Georgia Career Information System [Computer software]. (1998). Atlanta, GA: Georgia State University.

Hartman, H. (Ed.). (2001). *Time for kids almanac 2002 with information please.* New York: Family Education.

Krebs, M. (2002, April). The best used cars ever: Kick the tires and go. *Reader's Digest,* 90–95.

Morris, K. M, & Siegel, A. M. (1992). *The Wall Street Journal: Guide to understanding personal finance.* New York: Lightbulb Press.

Paris, J. L. (1997). *Money management for those who don't have any.* Eugene, OR: Harvest House.

Phillips, B. (1993). *Phillips' book of great thoughts and funny sayings.* Wheaton, IL: Tyndale House.

Pliskin, M., & Just, S. L. (1999). *The complete idiot's guide to interpreting your dreams.* New York: Macmillan.

Prather, C. L. (1964). Money. *In World Book Encyclopedia* (Vol. 13, pp. 588–599). Chicago: Field Enterprises Educational Corp.

Schemo, D. J. (2002, March 8). More graduates mired in debt, survey finds. *New York Times.* Retrieved from http://www.nytimes.com.

Shearer, L. (2002, February 23). Identity theft rising threat, expert says. *Athens Banner-Herald,* p. A10.

Temper, S. (2002). Dealing with debt dilemma. *Athens Banner-Herald,* pp. F1, F3.

U.S. Department of Labor, Bureau of Labor Statistics. (1993). *Consumer expenditure survey.* Washington, DC: Author.

■ Exercise 1. Money Management

1. Based on the material in this chapter, what area of money management do you believe you need to concentrate on the most? Explain.

2. How do you plan to work on this money management area? Be as specific as possible.

3. How does your personality affect your ability to manage money?

4. Describe how you see yourself financially in five years. What obstacles will you have to overcome to achieve your financial goals? What can you do during the next year to move closer toward these goals? How are these goals tied to your *personal values* (e.g., helping others, time, freedom, power, creativity, stability, independence, security, and so forth)?

■ Exercise 2. Investing with Personal Values

Hal Brill, Jack A. Brill, and Cliff Feigenbaum's *Investing with Your Values* provides invaluable information that allows you to select and invest money in companies that operate in ways that are consistent with your personal values. Investing in keeping with your personal values allows you to make a positive difference in the world. The Council on Economic Priorities (CEP) uses a model of evaluation (reviewed in Brill et al.'s book) to grade companies in eight values-related categories:

Environment

Community

Charitable contributions

Minority advancement

Women advancement

Work place issues

Family benefits

Public disclosure

CEP assigns points for each category listed above. After rating each category, all the points are used to calculate a grade for the company (4.0 is the highest possible grade). CEP places the top 40 companies on its honor roll. Several of these companies are listed below.

Adolph Coors Company

Avon Products, Inc.

Ben & Jerry's Homemade, Inc.

Dole Food Co.

Healthy Planet Products

Hewlett-Packard Co.

International Business Machines

Johnson & Johnson

Kellogg Co.

McGraw-Hill Co.

PepsiCo, Inc.

Polaroid Corp.

Starbucks Corp.

Sun Co.

Xerox Corp.

1. Based on what you believe is important, rank the categories used by CEP to evaluate companies.

    1) _____ (most important)

    2) _____

    3) _____

    4) _____

    5) _____

    6) _____

    7) _____

    8) _____ (least important)

2. Explain why you gave the highest and lowest rankings to the two categories you did.

■ Exercise 2. Investing with Personal Values *(Continued)*

3. Assume you have $50,000 to invest in a company for retirement. Your investment choice is either Company A or Company B.

   - ■ Company A excels in the category you assigned the highest ranking. Investing in Company A will result in $300,000 at retirement.

   - ■ Company B excels in the category you assigned the lowest ranking. Investing in Company B will result in $900,000 at retirement.

   Would you invest in Company A or Company B? Explain.

4. Would you marry a person who assigned his or her lowest rating to any of the following categories: environment, minority advancement, or women advancement? Explain.

5. Your responses to questions A–D probably tell you less about how you perceive money and more about your personal values. What did you learn about who you are by answering these questions?

CHAPTER 11
Choosing a Major

Choosing a major is a decision all college students must make. For some it can be a relatively easy decision. However, for many it is a difficult and often frustrating process. It is important to realize that having difficulty choosing a major is a very common concern for many college students. There are several factors that contribute to the indecision. First, students entering their freshman year in college do not always know what their strengths and interests encompass. Second, there are peer and parental influences. Some parents place unintentional pressure on their children by making suggestions such as "you would make a great doctor," or "you should be a lawyer." These may not be the professions which the student is interested in pursuing. Peer influences may also play a role. For example, a student may pursue a major just because many friends have decided on that major. A third factor making choosing a major difficult is if you are uncertain about your future plans; it is perhaps the most significant dilemma students

From *The Essential Handbook for Academic Success* by The California University Regents. © 1998 by Kendall/Hunt Publishing Company.

have in choosing a major. As you enter college, your future plans may change several times before graduation. Initially some students may have graduate school in mind, others may want to pursue a particular career immediately following graduation, but these plans may change several times. Despite the high frequency of indecision, students still let these future plans have a significant impact on how they determine their major. Far too often students limit their options by seeking a major that will be directly related to what they may want to do in the future. This may cause some students to choose a major that they do not have much interest in over one that they may enjoy. It is essential to understand that although choosing a major is an important decision, it will not necessarily determine the course that the rest of your life will follow.

There are several important variables to consider when choosing a major. (Only a few are mentioned here; clearly everyone has unique circumstances.) The first variable to consider is personal satisfaction and enjoyment. It is important to choose a major that is related to your particular interests or strengths because this is likely to lead to higher performance. The second variable to consider is possible future plans. Many students are not able to determine their future plans early in their college careers; as a result deciding on a major is difficult. The most challenging aspect of choosing a major is understanding that a certain major will not limit future goals or plans.

Some students wish to pursue employment immediately following college. Therefore, they seek out "practical" majors such as economics or business and accounting fields. The decision to pursue a business-related major is great for the student who may have an interest in the field; unfortunately, some will dismiss other areas of interest to pursue what they feel is practical for employment. The net result of such a decision could be an unsatisfying major and academic performance below one's potential. This scenario is far too common because many students link particular majors to particular careers. Assuming that there is a direct correlation between any particular major and a certain profession is a common misconception. Other students make the decision to proceed directly to graduate school, and some of these students also limit themselves by making a direct link between major and graduate school plans. Some graduate schools, for example, medical school, have certain prerequisites, but it is possible to fulfill the prerequisites and major in another area of interest.

An undergraduate major does not limit future plans. It is important to recognize the qualities that employers and graduate schools desire in potential candidates. Employers are looking for students that have demonstrated the ability to learn and be trained. Graduate schools are looking for academic success, diversity, and extracurricular involvement. Few employers and few graduate schools indicate a preferential major; rather, they seek potential. Potential can be determined in several ways; a particular major is not one of them. Employers and graduate schools will use a student's Grade Point Average (GPA) to assess their competence and potential. Academic success reveals the student's ability to learn or be trained. In most cases, the GPA is the first aspect which is reviewed by employers and graduate schools. If the GPA is competitive, the next step is to determine if the student is well rounded. This can be determined by looking at work experience, internships, (essential for those seeking employment) or other activities outside of academics. This demonstrates desirable qualities such as: time management, organizational skills, the ability to work with others, and initiative. These qualities are very highly regarded among employers and graduate schools alike. Finally, the next item which is evaluated is the student's major. Clearly this demonstrates that the major is not the determining factor for future plans.

The above illustrates the hierarchy starting with GPA and ending with major. Since GPA is a considerable factor for employers and graduate schools, the importance of choosing a major that one enjoys becomes even more important. If you dislike the major you have chosen, it is difficult to perform to your maximum capabilities. It is also more difficult to exert the effort required to perform well, possibly resulting in a disappointing academic record. The final outcome could be four or more years of an unenjoyable major that you thought would help with your future plans, resulting in a less than competitive academic record. An alternative outcome would be choosing a major you enjoy, resulting in a more gratifying college career with higher academic achievements which would be favorably received by employers and graduate schools. Clearly, the latter outcome is what the student should strive to achieve.

One of the first steps in choosing a major is finding one which coincides with certain interests and strengths. For example, if working with numbers and problem solving is a particular strength, a major such as math or the sciences should be explored further. Moreover, if reading and writing are preferred, majors such as English, political science, or history could be more of a match. It may help to write out some of your strengths and interests:

STRENGTHS: INTERESTS:

1. _____   1. _____

2. _____   2. _____

3. _____   3. _____

4. _____   4. _____

5. _____   5. _____

Another way to determine your strengths and interests is to take a personality mosaic, such as the one that appears on the pages following this chapter. There are several different types of personality tests, and this is only one example. It is not accurate for everyone, but it is useful to assess which majors match which type of personality. After completing the personality mosaic, it is a good idea to explore the majors that match your personality as determined by the test. The majors listed may be ones that have not yet been considered or the test may simply reinforce what you were already aware of.

The next step is to determine if any majors can be linked to these strengths and interests. One method of learning about majors at a university is to review the school catalog. Using the results from the personality mosaic, look over the majors that interest you in the catalog. Take a closer look at some of the courses offered within that major. Read the course descriptions and requirements for the major and become familiar with any possible prerequisites. Some majors are "impacted" and therefore require a certain GPA and that certain courses are passed before entering the major. Also pay particular attention to sequential courses. Some majors have sequential courses; course 1A must be completed before 1B can be attempted. Some students may prefer more flexibility in their courses. Furthermore, examine the flexibility of the major; the amount and type of courses required to complete the major. If a particular major has many course requirements, it will be difficult to take courses outside the major. All of the above steps can be labeled as preliminary research. Hopefully the aforementioned steps will assist in narrowing potential majors.

The next step is active research. After studying the catalog, a few upper and lower division courses from possible majors should be noted. One method of actively researching a major is to take a course in that major. This can accomplish two important objectives. First, it can help you to gain exposure to the types of courses in that major. Second, if applicable, you can utilize the course to fulfill General Education (G.E.) requirements. Another method of active research is utilizing one of the largest resources on a college campus, other students. More often than not students are willing to share opinions regarding certain courses and certain professors, which may be helpful in determining what aspects of a major fit with your personality. Another step is to approach the department advisors of the majors you are interested in. Advisors can provide more detailed information about the prerequisites of a major, and can also recommend a professor or a course.

After you have completed the above steps, hopefully your list of possible majors will be a reasonable one. Ideally, this step should come sometime around the end of the second year of school, particularly for those who wish to complete their undergraduate education in four years. In addition to the above steps, students should closely monitor their academic progress with a Degree Progress Report (DPR). The DPR should be obtained at least once a quarter. It explains courses and units remaining in order to graduate, as well as courses already taken and your GPA. One useful tool of the DPR is that it can be obtained with any major. If you have completed several courses in two different subjects, you may obtain a DPR for each major. If you have taken many courses in two different areas of interest, it is possible to double major or to have a minor or specialization. Students may find that they enjoy and excel in two different majors and wish to attain a degree in both. A student wishing to double major must receive approval from both major departments. For those students who wish to graduate in four years, a double major may be difficult, but can be done.

There are always students who can't avoid the "practical" major. If this is the case, an alternative is to major in a subject where the student's strengths and interests lie, and specialize or minor in what may satisfy a practical desire. For example, you may feel that you can best use your talents as an English major, but at the same time may not feel that it is "practical" enough. A specialization or minor may be a solution. You can pursue English as a major and seek out a "practical" minor such as business administration or accounting. Alternatively, if you feel this may not allow you to graduate in four years, you can take "practical" courses outside the English major. Both options will give you an opportunity to major in something you enjoy, enabling you to perform well academically, while at the same time minoring or taking other courses that will help prepare you for future plans.

In summary, there are several important things to remember:

1. It is okay to be undecided.

2. A particular major does NOT limit future plans.

3. It is important to take the time to explore different majors and narrow the choices down through informed decisions.

4. Remember to find a major that is enjoyable because the amount of interest in the subject matter will probably be reflected by the GPA.

5. Although GPA is important, it is not the only factor that employers and graduate schools consider; they prefer students who have shown initiative by working, taking relevant courses, interning, or by participating in extracurricular activities.

6. Double majoring or minoring/specializing are feasible options.

7. Consider if graduating in four years is a priority.

Choosing a major is not an easy decision, but it doesn't need to be a painful one either. Take the time to do the research and make the effort and the result will be worth it! Good luck!

■ Coming Alive from Nine to Five

Personality Mosaic

DIRECTIONS:
Circle the numbers of statements that clearly feel like something you might say or do or think—something that feels like you.

1. It's important for me to have a strong, agile body.
2. I need to understand things thoroughly.
3. Music, color, beauty of any kind can really affect my moods.
4. People enrich my life and give it meaning.
5. I have confidence in myself that I can make things happen.
6. I appreciate clear directions so I know exactly what to do.
7. I can usually carry/build/fix things myself.
8. I can get absorbed for hours in thinking something out.
9. I appreciate beautiful surroundings; color and design mean a lot to me.
10. I love company.
11. I enjoy competing.
12. I need to get my surroundings in order before I start a project.
13. I enjoy making things with my hands.
14. It's satisfying to explore new ideas.
15. I always seem to be looking for new ways to express my creativity.
16. I value being able to share personal concerns with people.
17. Being a key person in a group is very satisfying to me.
18. I take pride in being very careful about all the details of my work.
19. I don't mind getting my hands dirty.
20. I see education as a lifelong process of developing and sharpening my mind.
21. I love to dress in unusual ways, to try new colors and styles.
22. I can often sense when a person needs to talk to someone.
23. I enjoy getting people organized and on the move.
24. A good routine helps me get the job done.
25. I like to buy sensible things I can make or work on myself.
26. Sometimes I can sit for long periods of time and work on puzzles or read or just think about life.

Source: Adapted by UCLA Career Planning Center from *Coming Alive From Nine to Five* by B. N. Michelozzi, Mayfield Publishing Company.

27. I have a great imagination.

28. It makes me feel good to take care of people.

29. I like to have people rely on me to get the job done.

30. I'm satisfied knowing that I've done an assignment carefully and completely.

31. I'd rather be on my own doing practical, hands-on activities.

32. I'm eager to read about any subject that arouses my curiosity.

33. I love to try creative new ideas.

34. If I have a problem with someone, I prefer to talk it out and resolve it.

35. To be successful, it's important to aim high.

36. I prefer being in a position where I don't have to take responsibility for decisions.

37. I don't enjoy spending a lot of time discussing things. What's right is right.

38. I need to analyze a problem pretty thoroughly before I act on it.

39. I like to rearrange my surroundings to make them unique and different.

40. When I feel down, I find a friend to talk to.

41. After I suggest a plan, I prefer to let others take care of the details.

42. I'm usually content where I am.

43. It's invigorating to do things outdoors.

44. I keep asking why.

45. I like my work to be an expression of my moods and feelings.

46. I like to find ways to help people care more for each other.

47. It's exciting to take part in important decisions.

48. I'm always glad to have someone else take charge.

49. I like my surroundings to be plain and practical.

50. I need to stay with a problem until I figure out an answer.

51. The beauty of nature touches something deep inside me.

52. Close relationships are important to me.

53. Promotion and advancement are important to me.

54. Efficiency, for me, means doing a set amount carefully each day.

55. A strong system of law and order is important to prevent chaos.

56. Thought-provoking books always broaden my perspective.

57. I look forward to seeing art shows, plays, and good films.

58. I haven't seen you for so long; I'd love to know how you're doing.

59. It's exciting to influence people.

60. When I say I'll do it, I follow through on every detail.

61. Good, hard physical work never hurt anyone.

62. I'd like to learn all there is to know about subjects that interest me.

63. I don't want to be like everyone else; I like to do things differently.

64. Tell me how I can help you.

65. I'm willing to take some risks to get ahead.

66. I like exact directions and clear rules when I start something new.

67. The first thing I look for in a car is a well-built engine.

68. Those people are intellectually stimulating.

69. When I'm creating, I tend to let everything else go.

70. I feel concerned that so many people in our society need help.

71. It's fun to get ideas across to people.

72. I hate it when they keep changing the system just when I get it down.

73. I usually know how to take care of things in an emergency.

74. Just reading about those new discoveries is exciting.

75. I like to create happenings.

76. I often go out of my way to pay attention to people who seem lonely and friendless.

77. I love to bargain.

78. I don't like to do things unless I'm sure they're approved.

79. Sports are important in building strong bodies.

80. I've always been curious about the way nature works.

81. It's fun to be in a mood to try or do something unusual.

82. I believe that people are basically good.

83. If I don't make it the first time, I usually bounce back with energy and enthusiasm.

84. I appreciate knowing exactly what people expect of me.

85. I like to take things apart to see if I can fix them.

86. Don't get excited. We can think it out and plan the right move logically.

87. It would be hard to imagine my life without beauty around me.

88. People often seem to tell me their problems.

89. I can usually connect with people who get me in touch with a network of resources.

90. I don't need much to be happy.

Name: ______________________ Date: ______________________

How to Find a Major

Scoring Your Answers

To score, circle the same numbers below that you circled on the exercise:

R	I	A	S	E	C
1	2	3	4	5	6
7	8	9	10	11	12
13	14	15	16	17	18
19	20	21	22	23	24
25	26	27	28	29	30
31	32	33	34	35	36
37	38	39	40	41	42
43	44	45	46	47	48
49	50	51	52	53	54
55	56	57	58	59	60
61	62	63	64	65	66
67	68	69	70	71	72
73	74	75	76	77	78
79	80	81	82	83	84
85	86	87	88	89	90

Now add up the number of circles in each column:

R 10 I 7 A 9 S 9 E 11 C 8 TOTALS

Which are your three highest scores:

1st E

2nd R

3rd S

■ Dimensional Analysis

Holland's Group	Characteristic Interests	Characteristic Personal Traits	Characteristic Occupations
Realistic (R)	Activities that involve the precise, ordered use of objects, tools, machines and animals and includes agricultural, electrical, manual, physical and mechanical things and activities. Example: Working on cars.	Present-Oriented Thing-Oriented (rather than people or data) Conforming Practical Shy	Engineering Skilled Trades Agricultural and Technical Occupations
Investigative (I)	Activities that involve the exploration and examination of physical, biological and cultural things to understand and control them: sometimes includes scientific and mathematical activities. Example: Reading fiction	Analytical and Abstract Rational Curious Intellectual Introverted	Scientific, Analytical and some Technical Occupations
Artistic (A)	Activities that involve the use of physical, verbal or human materials to create art forms or products; includes activities and things related to language, art, music, drama and writing Example: Listening to music	Creative Expressive Rely on Feelings Imagination Non-Conforming Idealistic	Musical Artistic Literary and Dramatic Occupations
Social (S)	Activities that involve interaction with other people for enjoyment or to inform, train, develop, cure and educate. Example: Entertaining guests	Sensitive to needs of others Friendly Outgoing Persuasive Tactful	Teaching Ministry Social Welfare and other "Helping People" Occupations
Enterprising (E)	Activities that involve interaction with other people to reach organizational goals or economic gain; leadership, interpersonal and persuasive activities included. Example: Working for a community action or political organization	Aggressive/ Assertive Self-Confident Ambitious Sociable Persuasive	Sales Supervisory and Leadership Occupations
Conventional (C)	Activities that involve the precise, ordered use of data, e.g., keeping records, filing materials, organizing numerical and written data, clerical, computational and business. Example: Working as a treasurer for a political campaign	Practical Conforming Efficient/Accurate Orderly Set in Ways	Accounting Computational Secretarial and Clerical Occupations

CHAPTER 12

Vocation
More than a Job,
More than a Career

Alan Weber (2000) interviewed business psychologists Timothy Butler and James Waldroop about differences between the words *job, career,* and *vocation*. Although people tend to use the three words interchangeably, the words do not share a common definition. A **job** has to do with specific tasks and responsibilities that someone is employed to carry out. The word *career* "comes originally from the Latin word for cart and later from the Middle French word for racetrack." A **career** is a line of work such as teacher, nurse, botanist, or author. But one's career may not be one's vocation. According to Butler and Waldroop, **vocation** is derived from the Latin *vocare* (to call) and describes what one does that brings meaning and purpose to one's life via work. Some callings are to do something while others are to be someone. Gregg Levoy in his book *Callings* (1997), recounts how the mythologist Joseph Campbell reminds us that we are continuously having experiences that hint at our calling. By listening to these hints and learning to recognize them, it is possible to choose the right vocation that can bring further meaning and purpose to life.

Vocational planning is a developmental process that involves self-exploration, career exploration, and occupational exploration. It can be an enjoyable, creative journey, but it does require purposeful planning to discover the kinds of opportunities needed to build life-skills for optimal growth. Zen masters inform us that every journey in life begins beneath our feet, even a 2,000-mile journey. Finding the right vocation is a journey that begins right beneath your feet. Choosing the right vocational path and identifying the college major and opportunities that can lead you to your calling are important steps in vocational planning, but not the only steps. The first step comes during the freshman phase of your college experience. This step's goal is to become more aware, through self-exploration, of your interests, values, skills, and aptitudes, and how your personality relates to career choice.

■ Self-exploration

Who are you? What do you want? If you know the answers to these two questions, and are willing to put forth the time and effort needed to answer your calling, you are off to a successful start. The definition of success is a personal one. For some students, success is synonymous with making a lot of money, owning a business, having a prestigious career, or being elected to public office. For other students, altruistic endeavors and relationships may define success. Success can also be a combination of all these values and many more. Being able to identify precisely what you want in life is not necessarily an easy task.

Marsha Sinetar (1987) writes about discovering the right livelihood. She believes that choosing the right livelihood is based on making conscious choices. Sinetar acknowledges that this, too, is a difficult task because "unfortunately, since we learn early to act on what others have to say, value, and respect, we often find ourselves a long way down the wrong road before realizing we did not actually choose our work." Where you are today has a lot to do with decisions you have made in the past. Decisions that you make now create new directions that will determine your future. When you are conscious of the choices you make, you are choosing to be responsible. You are choosing to accept the consequences of decisions that you make, and in doing so, you learn to make better decisions.

At different periods in life, people make vocational decisions based on different sets of motivations. According to Butler and Waldroop, the decisions you make in your twenties are related to creating opportunities for yourself. You are trying to enlarge your world to find all the channels for getting what you think you need and want. In their thirties, people tend to make decisions based on the realization that there is limited time available to accomplish everything, so decisions become more focused. As you become aware of your own mortality throughout your forties and fifties, the gap between your dreams and reality narrows as you search for meaning and purpose. People tend to become more conscious of the choices they are making.

Why wait until later, until your forties and fifties, to discover meaning and purpose? It sometimes takes courage to make clear vocational choices that are reflective of who you are and what you want. Being courageous is often worth the risks involved. Courageous actions can significantly lessen the amount of time required to create meaning and purpose in our lives. The more you know about yourself, the easier the task of finding meaning and purpose becomes. Knowing your values is an important piece of your vocational puzzle. Values are what ultimately guide our behavior and give us direction in life.

Values

Do you ever wonder why it is that you feel strongly about some issues, like abortion, the environment, or capital punishment, but not so strongly about other issues? The intensity of your feelings and thoughts on various issues is related to the strength of your values. Values are different from opinions and facts. **Values** are standards, reference points that guide your behavior, thoughts, and feelings. All your values together form your **value system**. Goals based on your value system will be stronger than ones that are not, and you will be more motivated to spend the necessary time and effort needed to reach them. If your career choice is firmly aligned with your values, you will be more enthusiastic and passionate about your career. Do you value competition? recognition? wealth? excitement? security? friends? volunteering? success? Where do these values come from? Did they choose you (inherited) or did you choose them (assimilated over a lifetime)? Your values may be similar to ones held by significant people in your life, but values adopted without engaging in critical thinking are not as strong as ones that have survived being examined and then accepted as your own.

Do values ever change? Yes, experiences can modify and change them. For example, someone who values material wealth, prestige, and power may when faced with a life threatening illness begin to value health, family and spirituality more. In college as you meet new people, have new experiences, and are exposed to different perspectives, your values will most likely be challenged.

Considering the following questions can help you identify your own set of personal values: What is the most exciting thing you have done? What do you value most about another person? Whom do you most admire? Answers to these questions may point to underlying values. Another way to identify values is to complete Exercises 1 and 2 at the end of this chapter.

Personality

When we talk about **personality**, we are referring to a set of motivations, beliefs, attitudes, traits, and response patterns that are consistent over time and distinguish one person from another. Each person is a unique composite of physical, biological, mental, emotional, and spiritual traits and potentials.

Personality factors influence vocational exploration. *Thinking types* prefer to systematically gather facts about interesting majors, weigh the pros and cons of each major, and then make an objective decision. *Feeling types* tend to make subjective decisions based on how they feel about particular majors. If they do not feel personally engaged in the curriculum of a particular major, they are apt to switch majors to find one they feel more in tune with. When it comes to acting on the decision about a major and investigating various careers, *judging types* tend to reach closure quickly and begin to investigate specific career options, whereas *perceiving types* may resist closure and hesitate to become focused on one particular career path because they see so many options.

How does personality affect career choice? It is much nicer to be in an environment that affirms and supports, rather than one in which you have to continually explain and defend yourself. When your personality traits match up with a career, you will tend to find more support for challenges that you undertake and greater understanding for failed attempts. Let us explore some personality attributes associated with careers.

Extroversion and Introversion. *Extroverts* tend to define themselves by how others recognize and respond to them, whereas *introverts* tend to be private and may not share what is significant and valuable about themselves with colleagues. In working situations extroverts prefer to be around people and seek opportunities to interact with others. Introverts need time and space to think through their thoughts carefully before answering a question or giving an opinion. A person with an extroverted personality generally prefers a job that offers a lot of variety activity and can become impatient with long, tedious tasks.

Intuition and Sensation.

Intuitive types in the workplace want to be appreciated for generating ideas and theories, whereas *sensing types* wants to be appreciated for all the details and facts they can bring to the work situation. People who rely on sensing prefer to use skills that they have already developed. They prefer work environments that have standardized procedures, and they do well in work that involves precision. Intuitive types are the opposite. They tend to dislike repetitive tasks and prefer careers that offer numerous opportunities to learn a variety of new skills.

Thinking and Feeling.

Feeling personality types like to work in harmonious environments, generally enjoy pleasing people, and are genuinely interested in the people they work with. *Thinking personality types* respond more to ideas than people at work and are good at analyzing situations. They tend to be firmer in their decisions and seek careers that encourage the use of logical reasoning.

Judging and Perceiving.

In a work situation, *judging types* are most productive when they have lists and plans to follow as well as the necessary resources (supplies, tools, and people) needed to begin work. *Perceiving types* are good at adapting to changes that arise at work and prefer to start projects rather than finish them. People who rely mostly on judging seek careers that require organization, whereas people who rely mostly on perceiving prefer work situations in which they can create their own schedule.

While no combination of preferences is inherently better than any other type, knowing your personality type can help you understand not only your behavior in a work environment but also those around you. Understanding how your values and personality influence your career choice is important knowledge to have when constructing a picture of your right livelihood, or calling. Next, let us connect some more dots and explore how interests influence vocational choices.

Interests

Most people are more likely to feel motivated to accomplish a task if they are interested in the task. Chances are good that if your interests are congruent with your occupational environment, you will achieve more job satisfaction. A student we know attended a large college for a year, intending to major in psychology. After his first semester, he started feeling apathetic about attending classes and studying. At the end of his second semester, he returned home and began thinking about what he "would like to be when he grew up." He realized that his major interests focused on food: cooking, creating new recipes, observing people cook, reading cookbooks, going to restaurants. He decided to become a chef. Now having successfully graduated from a culinary institute, he is working as a chef and enjoying the work even though the hours are long and the work is demanding. What changed? He is now motivated to work hard because he is doing what he likes! Your interests can be a good predictor of job satisfaction. Think of times in your life when you were deeply engaged in what you were doing. It is during these times that your interests are activated, and you feel a sense of satisfaction and completion in what you are doing. Can you identify your interests? Are you aware of which jobs match up to your interests?

The things that overwhelm one person in terms of challenge and supervision can stimulate and energize someone else. John Holland, a vocational psychologist, has proposed that our interests define our personality. He believes that different personalities cluster together in society, and that personalities can be differentiated from one another according to interests. Holland identifies six clusters of personality traits: realistic, investigative, artistic, social, enterprising, and conventional. According to Holland's vocational theory, career satisfaction and achievement are based on the degree of congruence between a person's interests and personality and his or her vocational environment (Holland, 1966). A popular career test based on Holland's theory of personality, which is found at most college counseling and career centers, is the Strong-Campbell Interest Inventory (SCII). It consists of 325 items concerning occupations, school subjects, activities, people, and characteristics. During the assessment you make decisions about likes and preferences. Results provide information about occupations you might wish to pursue based on your profile of interests.

■ Activity

Assessing Interests

Read over the descriptions of the six personality clusters developed by John Holland. Then answer the questions that follow.

R = Realistic. People who are classified as realistic deal with their work environment in an objective, concrete manner. They prefer working with tools and machines rather than people and ideas. Realistic people are often characterized as being practical. They often enjoy working outdoors. Occupations that are primarily realistic in nature include those in athletics, construction, technical fields, forestry, agriculture, and skilled trades.

I = Investigative. Investigative types can be described as analytical, logical, scholarly, creative, and independent. Occupations characterized as being investigative tend to be related to scientific activities. Investigative people tend to be less conventional and less practical than realistic types. People closely aligned with this cluster would usually prefer to work alone rather than with other people. They prefer jobs where they can investigate and engage in critical thinking and logical analysis. Some specific jobs within the investigative cluster are ecologist, biologist, college professor, mathematician, physician, and computer programmer.

A = Artistic. Artistic types describe themselves as being independent, artistically inclined, creative, and unconventional. They dislike rigid situations with rules and regulations that are enforced. Some artistic jobs include actor, journalist, musician, photographer, media specialist, and interior decorator.

S = Social. Others generally see people who score high in the social cluster as sociable, nurturing, helpful, and responsible. These people have a lot of concern for human welfare and tend to be more optimistic than pessimistic. Social people have good verbal skills and enjoy working with others in groups to solve problems. Jobs that involve these personality attributes include teacher, counselor, social worker, minister, travel agent, nurse, and recreational leader.

E = Enterprising. Enterprising individuals can be characterized as enthusiastic, assertive, and extroverted. They prefer occupations that involve sales or other situations where they are in a position of leading or persuading others. People who score high in this cluster are generally good at public speaking and interviewing. They prefer jobs in the fields of marketing, retail merchandising, health administration, real estate sales, law, television production, and politics.

C = Conventional. Conventional people tend to prefer jobs that are structured and predictable. They can be characterized as conscientious, neat, conservative, controlled, and persistent. They thrive on order and prefer systematic jobs such as banker, accountant, office manager, legal secretary, statistician, and dental assistant.

1. Which personality cluster fits you the best? _____

2. Rank the personality clusters based on how well each reflects your interests and personality traits, with 1 being the best fit.

    1. _____

    2. _____

    3. _____

    4. _____

    5. _____

    6. _____

Skills and Aptitudes

The ability to acquire a proficiency is called *aptitude*. Someone may have an aptitude to play a violin, but if that person is never given the opportunity to play, that skill may never be realized. Many students have the capacity to learn many things, but if the environment is not conducive to learning or students do not avail themselves of the opportunity, they may not learn. Do you have any aptitudes that you have not developed into skills? Skills are things you do well. Perhaps you are mechanically gifted, have good communication skills, are good at problem solving, or have a particular artistic skill like drawing, playing a musical instrument, or dancing. Some people have skills that are easily identifiable because they are observable. Others have skills that are harder to identify, like being able to analyze and synthesize information, mediate, and inspire others. Some people are better with data and information, and some are better with people. How quickly you learn and understand new information and engage in good critical thinking is based on skills.

When you have assessed your values, personality, interests, and skills, you have completed the first step in vocational exploration. Self-exploration will continue throughout your college experience (and life). As you become engaged in different activities and experiences, your beliefs, interests, values, skills, and even your personality may change. The picture that you create of yourself is likely to be revised along the journey. When you "connect all the dots," what picture do you have of yourself? Do you have a clear, accurate vision of what you want to do and who you are? Not only do you need a clear vision, but you also need a systematic plan on how to get there. Part of this plan is choosing the right major and the right career. The next stage of vocational exploration is career exploration.

■ Career Exploration

In addition to engaging in self-exploration, which should begin as a freshman, get curious about all the possible career options out there for you. Talk with parents, professors, parents of friends, and whoever else might provide you with information about careers. Become familiar with career services on campus. At your college counseling or career center you can find information about choosing a major and future career (e.g., information about jobs, career seminars, career planning courses). Be sure to attend career decision-making workshops (if offered), take some vocational tests, sign up for a class on choosing a major if one is available, sign up for internships, attend career fairs and seminars, go on informal interviews, and make a list of careers that interest you and review it often.

Based on what you know about your values, personality, interests, and skills and aptitudes, what career do you think is the best fit for you?

_____

_____

What major will help you get there? _____

During your sophomore year, you should continue to obtain information about careers, seek out volunteer opportunities and work experience, talk to people about their work, and check out memberships in different clubs, committees, and organizations that can provide you with opportunities to develop leadership skills and other life-skills. Visit your career center and read about careers, or go online and find information. Explore every career possibility you can. Consider taking an elective class in a major you are interested in. If you have not done so already, gather information about future employment and firm up your choice of a major. The following resources provide an enormous amount of information about careers and jobs.

Computer-Assisted Career Exploration Programs

SIGI Plus. This computer program is designed to help you identify your interests, skills, and values, find careers that match your personal preferences, and prepare for an occupation. There are eight sections from which to gather information related to careers, and you can use them in any order.

Discover. This computer program can also help you organize your interests and experiences into probable careers. There are nine sections that cover topics ranging from self-assessments and job characteristics to identifying training and finding financial planning.

State-Specific Career Information. Information relating to your state or the state where you will work after graduation can be used to match your interests and abilities with specific occupations. Current information is provided about occupations in different areas of the specific state, including working conditions, hiring requirements, and job outlook. For example, the Georgia Career Information Services (GCIS), which is updated every year, provides information about specific fields of study, financial aid, military careers, and other colleges throughout the United States.

Books

Guide for Occupational Exploration (GOE). In this book, put out by the U.S. Department of Labor, information is provided about interests, aptitudes, and adaptability for over 2,500 jobs. Jobs are clustered by major interest area. This is a good tool to use to analyze whether or not your interests and skills match up with specific jobs. Information about job preparation is also included.

Occupational Outlook Handbook (OOH). Published by the U.S. Department of Labor, Bureau of Labor Statistics, OOHInfo@bls.gov. This resource provides information on more than 300 jobs. Information is provided about training, qualifications, outlook, earnings, and working conditions. A good supplement to the Handbook is the *Occupational Outlook Quarterly*, published about every two years, which has important articles and information about aspects of career planning. For more information about these publications and others, you can contact the Bureau of Labor Statistics through its website at http://www.doL.gov.

Dictionary of Occupational Titles (DOT). This resource offers descriptions of about 20,000 jobs and is updated periodically. The Bureau of Labor Statistics also publishes this book. A good use for this book is to look at the job clusters to see related occupations. It may be that you think of a career and want to know about related professions (counselor, social worker, and psychologist). The DOT can help you discover various job options.

■ Occupational Exploration

Is there a perfect job out there for you? Without the right career guidance, finding the perfect job might be akin to finding a needle in a haystack. After all, most jobs are not advertised. In fact, only about 20% are advertised. There are plenty of jobs out there if you know how to find them and are able to convince an employer to hire you. According to Richard Bolles, author of *The 1997 What Color Is Your Parachute?*, mailing out resumes to employers at random, answering ads in professional journals and newspapers, and going to private employment agencies for help are the least *effective* ways to find a job.

As a junior, there are specific occupational exploration tasks that you can engage in to increase your likelihood of finding that perfect job. You will want to increase your work experiences, continue attending career fairs, develop a resume, develop career contacts, network, take on leadership roles in organizations to which you belong, and do some serious research about careers (including learning about entry-level positions). Other steps you can take are to participate in Cooperative Education Programs (co-ops) if possible, try to get jobs that are related to your major, do some mock interviews, and begin to gather information about graduate schools if you are planning to pursue a graduate degree. Check with your campus or counseling center to find the most comprehensive resources available to help you find the right job, or go online. You should be able to locate information concerning cooperative educational experiences, internships, student employment, mock interviews, interviews with recruiters, and a variety of other experiences. Executive, managerial, administrative, and other positions can be highly competitive. Different kinds of work experiences, including internships and specialized training, can help you secure a position.

Having a good resume is essential to getting a good job. Many career centers can help you write a resume (and show you how to create an online one), set up a credential file, and educate you on how to secure government employment. Many campus career centers have a variety of books, as well as people, to help you write your resume.

Resume

There are plenty of books on the market about resume and cover letter writing. Besides career centers and counseling centers, check with campus and off-campus bookstores as well as libraries for books on resume writing. The resume is a screening device intended to get you an interview. Remember, the receiver will probably invest very little time in looking over your resume; therefore, it must look great. Here are some general guidelines for developing a resume.

- Your resume needs to be well organized, neat, and easy to read. (No smudges!) Make sure your grammar, punctuation, and spelling are correct. Use a good-quality paper in either white or ivory and use a clear typeface and type size (10 to 14 point). Double-space above and below each heading.
- Learn how to format your resume to enhance specific information about yourself. The reader should be able to form a clear image of you and be motivated to meet you. When choosing a format for your resume, choose one that best suits your purposes. Become familiar with different formats. Know when it is best to use a chronological format (highlighting work history) and when to use a functional format. For example, if you have had little work history, you might want to focus on your skills using a functional resume format.
- Give identifying information at the top of your resume: name, address, and phone numbers where you can be reached. Be sure to get an answering machine or use voice mail to record messages if you are going to be away from your phone for long periods of time.
- Some people like to put an objective in their resume (e.g., "public relations position with a nonprofit agency"). If you include an objective, create it before you begin writing your resume. An objective can help you stay focused while developing your resume. Be sure that you support the objective throughout your resume.

■ List your education in reverse chronological order. Make sure you include the year, the type of degree (BA, BS), and name of the school you will graduate from. Include your overall grade point average if impressive, as well as professional affiliations and training seminars. Also include career-related experiences; the name and location of the company, the title of the position you held, and the month and year you started and ended employment. List work experiences from most recent to least recent. You may also want to include school and community-related activities, honors and transferable skills, achievements, and a statement that references will be furnished upon request. Make statements specific, using words that convey action (e.g., *organized, supervised, developed, implemented, generated,* and *eliminated*). Each sentence should convey information about you that you want the reader to notice. Do not put down anything that you cannot later substantiate in an interview.

Occupational exploration tasks during your senior year include reviewing and updating your resume, requesting letters of reference, completing course requirements, signing up for interviews, sending out resumes, setting up interviews, taking qualifying examinations for your profession (e.g., a teacher exam), and participating in campus recruiting efforts. If you have not done so already, register with your career center so you can access a variety of career services. Check their schedules to see what workshops and career fairs are being offered and when. Tell everyone you know that you are looking for a job and describe the type of job. This may also be the time to send out graduate school applications and begin buying a professional wardrobe. Let's assume you have made your contacts, networked through your career center, sent out your resume, and have been asked to interview for a position. There are some general interview guidelines that are important to know.

Job Interview

A job interview serves two purposes. It is a way for the prospective employer to decide if you are the person for the job, and it is a way for you to see if you want the job. This may be an opportunity for you to get farther down the path to attaining your goals. Campus career centers often work with recruiters to set up on-campus interviews, which are usually screening interviews, with students. Spend as much time preparing for your interview as you did writing your resume. Additionally, here is a list of tips to help you successfully navigate your way through an interview.

■ Dress neatly and appropriately.
■ Be punctual and communicate your appreciation for the opportunity to meet with whomever is interviewing you.
■ Job interviews generally start off with personal introductions and a bit of small talk. Do not forget to make good eye contact.
■ During the interview try to appear confident and relaxed. You will probably be asked to

  ■ Describe yourself (qualifications including strengths and weaknesses) and your professional goals.
  ■ Explain how your education and experience are related to the particular job that you are interviewing for. (Whoever is interviewing you is most likely assessing you to see if your goals match up with the organization.)
  ■ Explain why you are interested in working with the organization. Knowledge of the organization is vital. Do your homework before the interview. Research the nature of the organization, where it currently is, and where it is heading. It will demonstrate your interest in the position.
  ■ Explain why you are leaving your current job, if you are doing so.

- Ask questions. You can always ask about the organization's expectations for its employees as well as future challenges and directions.
- Communicate to the interviewer your skills and accomplishments. (Do not make outlandish claims. Dishonesty will not impress future employers.)
- Before you leave, ask when you can expect to hear from the interviewer again. After the interview, take time to make notes about the interview. Include in your notes people's names, ideas presented, further questions, and changes to make before the next interview. A few days after the interview, follow up with a note thanking the interviewer for the opportunity to meet with him or her and learn more about the organization. If you are interested in the position you interviewed for, say so, and state that you are looking forward to hearing from the interviewer should he or she have any further questions.

Employment Projections

Every year in the United States millions of new jobs are created. Although not everyone in this country attends college, 63% of the high school graduating class of 2000 was enrolled in a college or university, according to Bureau of Labor Statistics (BLS). Employment that generally requires a college degree or other post-secondary award is projected to grow faster than any other category of occupation. It is projected that the civilian work force in the United States will reach 158 million in 2010, an increase of 17 million from 2000. The overall job outlook for university graduates in the United States looks good, according to the BLS. The Bureau of Labor Statistics analyzes factors that influence economic trends in the United States (e.g., technology, foreign competition, demand for goods and services) to create projections about employment. The BLS projections for 2000–2010 were released in December 2001, but they were completed prior to the September 11 terrorist attacks. Although the lasting impact of this tragedy on the economy is unclear, projections for 2000–2010 include the following.

- Among the 10 occupations with the *largest job growth* are registered nurses, office clerks, food preparation and service workers, customer service representatives, retail salespersons, computer support specialists, cashiers, security guards, computer software engineers, and waiters and waitresses.
- The top ten industries with the *fastest wage and salary employment growth* are computer and data processing services, residential care, health services, cable and pay television services, personnel supply services, warehousing and storage, water and sanitation, miscellaneous business services, miscellaneous equipment rental and leasing, and management and public relations.
- The top ten occupations with the *fastest employment growth* are computer software engineers, computer support specialists, network and computer systems administrators, network systems and data communication analysts, desktop publishers, database administrators, personal and home care aides, computer system analysts, and medical assistants.

■ Closing Remarks

The earlier you begin the process of vocational exploration, the more successful you will be in finding the perfect job, the right livelihood, your calling, or the answer to what you want to be when you grow up. Table 1 summarizes some of the career-preparation activities that you can engage in throughout college. The right vocation is one that reflects your values, interests, personality, and skills. Marsh Sinetar writes about *vocational integration*, a term used to designate a person who is so completely congruent with and

Table 1. Your College Guide for Career Success	
FRESHMAN **Explore career areas** ◼ Visit career services. ◼ Meet with peer advisor for office tour. ◼ Talk with parents, friends, professors, and counselor about your career ideas. ◼ Complete career assessments and testing. ◼ Identify the following: —interests —skills and abilities —career related hobbies —personality style —career values ◼ Find out about *SIGI Plus*. ◼ Attend career decision-making workshop. ◼ Attend college majors fair. ◼ Declare intended major.	**SOPHOMORE** **Collect more information** ◼ Read more about careers. ◼ Conduct four or five informational interviews. ◼ Request a career mentor. ◼ Compare careers using *SIGI Plus*. ◼ List five career options for your intended major. ◼ Volunteer in the community to gain experience in your career field. ◼ Confirm your major. ◼ Join a student group related to your major. ◼ Select electives to increase marketability. ◼ Attend career fairs. ◼ Gather information on future job market. ◼ Explore experiential education options (co-ops, internships).
JUNIOR **Increase experience** ◼ Apply for a co-op or internship. ◼ Test career options through experience. ◼ Attend career fairs. ◼ Develop your resume. ◼ Become familiar with work settings/environments. ◼ Attend law/grad school recruitment day. ◼ Research grad schools through *SIGI Plus* graduate school selector. ◼ Check career services semester schedule for special career seminars and events. ◼ Develop career contacts through alumni mentor and career network night. ◼ Take a leadership role in a club or group. ◼ Apply to be a career services peer advisor.	**SENIOR** **Implement your plan** ◼ Register with career services for placement services. ◼ Check semester schedule of events. ◼ Attend workshops on —resume/cover letter writing —interviewing skills —resume critique ◼ Develop list of targeted employers. ◼ Practice your communication skills. ◼ Begin on-campus interviews. ◼ Send out grad school applications. ◼ Attend career fairs. ◼ Attend business etiquette dinner and etiquette of networking seminar. ◼ Network, network, network!

From *The Freshman Year* by Glenda A. Belote and Larry W. Lunsford. Copyright © 1998 by Florida International University. Reprinted by permission of Kendall/Hunt Publishing Company.

committed to his or her vocation that he or she has no doubts about whether or not to invest the energy required to get the job done. Some students feel that once they have chosen a major, that's it. In fact, many students change majors as their interests change, and as their values change. Remember that vocational exploration is a life-long process. Most people change careers several times, so throughout your life you will be making career decisions. Congratulate yourself for the steps you have already taken, and motivate yourself to take the necessary steps to continue on your career path. Plan for your future now.

■ References

Bolles, R. N. (1996). *The 1997 what color is your parachute?* Berkeley, CA: Ten Speed Press.

Employment Outlook, 2000–2010: A summary of BLS projections. (2001). Washington, DC: U.S. Department of Labor, Bureau of Labor Statistics, Government Printing Office.

Kendall/Hunt Publishing (1999). *First-year experience sourcebook.* Dubuque, IA: Author.

Levoy, Gregg. (1997). *Callings.* New York: Three Rivers Press.

Holland, J. L. (1966). *The psychology of vocational choice.* Waltham, MA: Blaisdell.

Sinetar, M. (1987). *Do what you love and the money will follow.* New York: Dell.

Webber, A. (2000, January). Is your job calling? *Fast Track*, pp. 13–16.

■ Exercise 1. Values Clarification

Look over the list of values below. Identify 15 values that are significant to you. Rank them from 1 to 15, with 1 being most important.

_____ Spiritual well-being

_____ Relationships

_____ Respect

_____ Empathy/compassion

_____ Sense of humor

_____ Autonomy

_____ Competition

_____ Security

_____ Wealth

_____ Good job

_____ Success and achievement

_____ Happiness

_____ Courage

_____ Strength

_____ Acceptance

_____ Appreciation of nature

_____ Adventure

_____ Learning/education

_____ Diversity

_____ Loyalty

_____ Freedom

_____ Intelligence

_____ Health

_____ Endurance

_____ Intimacy

_____ Creativity

_____ Love

_____ Challenges

_____ Altruism (helping others)

_____ Appreciation of beauty

_____ Recognition

_____ Ambition

_____ Pleasure and joy

Other

_____ a. _____

_____ b. _____

_____ c. _____

1. What are your top three values? _____ _____ _____

2. How are these values reflected in your life?

■ Exercise 2. Work Values

Work values are qualities about a job that are most significant and meaningful to you. Without them the job would not be satisfying. Identify 10 work values and rank them from 1 to 10.

_____ Great salary

_____ Recognition from others

_____ Security

_____ Fun

_____ Autonomy

_____ Variety

_____ Excitement

_____ Lots of leisure time

_____ Leadership role

_____ Helping others

_____ Prestige

_____ Creativity

_____ Improving society

_____ Influencing others

_____ Continuity

_____ Professional position

_____ Flexible work schedule

_____ Working outside

_____ Having an office

_____ Congenial workplace

_____ Competition

_____ Travel

_____ Affiliation

_____ Decision making

_____ Supervising others

_____ Work flexibility

_____ Public contact

_____ Working alone

Other

_____ a. _____

_____ b. _____

_____ c. _____

1. What are your top three work values? _____ _____ _____

2. Describe why each of these values is important to you.

3. Will your career choice satisfy these values? Explain.

■ Exercise 3. Greatest Achievements

Think about all the goals you have set for yourself thus far in your life and all of your achievements. List five achievements that you consider to be the most significant.

1. _____

2. _____

3. _____

4. _____

5. _____

Identify five *skills* that were used to reach your achievements.

_____

_____

_____

_____

_____

Identify five *values* that are reflected by your achievements.

_____

_____

_____

_____

_____

Identify five *interests* that are reflected by your achievements.

_____

_____

_____

_____

_____

Congratulations! You have completed the first step in vocational exploration: self-exploration. You have assessed and identified your values, personality, interests, and skills. Now look for patterns and themes among them all. What have you learned about yourself?

■ Exercise 4. Vocation

Career decisions are influenced by what people learn about themselves and various professions. Research indicates that having a specific career goal in mind is related to a student's academic performance at a college. Uncertainty about a major has been linked to poor performance and frequency of dropping out. Answer each question.

1. Review John Holland's six personality types: realistic, investigative, social, conventional, enterprising, and artistic, which are noted in the "Assessing Interests" activity found previously in this chapter. Discuss which type describes you best. Be sure to indicate traits or characteristics you have that make you believe this particular type fits you.

2. List occupations that match the type you selected above. Then explain why you think they match this type. Are there any careers you are interested in that do not exactly fit your personality type (e.g., your type is realistic, but you are interested in banking and accounting)? If the answer is yes, list these careers and indicate how you found out about the careers that do not fit your type (e.g., friend, family member, career assessment.) Finally, explain what attracts you to the careers that do not match your type.

■ Exercise 4. Vocation *(Continued)*

3. Select two careers that you are most interested in. Gather information about both careers using a career-exploration software program or printed source (e.g., *GOE, OOH, DOT*). The instructor of your course will specify whether he or she wants you to use a certain source.

    How might the information you gathered concerning these two occupations be used to move you closer to finding a career that will prove satisfying and rewarding? Refer to the list of work values in Exercise 2. When you respond, discuss the work values that are of importance to you.

CHAPTER 13
Skills to Enhance Communication and Relationships

Introduction

Our ability to succeed in life is often affected by our ability to get along with others. How we interact with family members, friends, co-workers, teachers, classmates, supervisors, and others in our environment can have a positive or negative impact on whether our needs are met or whether we are meeting the needs of others. For example, our relationship with a co-worker or supervisor can affect our satisfaction with our job, and can determine whether we are promoted, or even dismissed.

From *The Community College: A New Beginning* Third Edition by Linda S. Aguilar, Sandra J. Hopper, and Therese M. Kuzlik. Copyright © 2001 by Kendall/Hunt Publishing Company. Used with permission.

As you continue with your college education at a college/university, you may see changes in your interpersonal relationships. Some of your old friendships may weaken, especially with those who are away at different schools or with those who haven't continued their education. New supportive relationships may begin. Adjustments in family life may be required. This can be true if you are a traditional age student, gaining more independence from your parents, and it is certainly true for adult students whose families must make many adjustments when mom, dad, or spouse becomes a student again. Using effective communication skills will help you promote positive relationships with other people in your lives and can help you meet your physical, emotional, social, intellectual/educational, and economic needs.

This chapter focuses on the use of effective communication skills to maintain and build strong interpersonal relationships. You will explore the following:

■ Components of the communication process,
■ Aggressive, assertive and passive communication styles and how to distinguish among them,
■ Developing and using specific assertive communication techniques in interpersonal relationships.

Pretest: Assertiveness Self-Inventory

Take the Assertiveness Self-Inventory to determine your comfort level when behaving in an assertive manner. Review these situations and rate yourself using the following 4-point scale:

1 = I would be very comfortable in this situation.
2 = I would feel moderately comfortable in this situation.
3 = I would feel uncomfortable in this situation.
4 = I would feel very uncomfortable in this situation.

_____ Speaking up and asking questions in class or in a meeting with co-workers.

_____ Walking away without making a purchase after a clerk has spent a considerable amount of time showing you merchandise that isn't exactly what you wanted.

_____ Telling someone s/he is doing something that bothers you (smoking in your car, making sexist remarks, etc.).

_____ Beginning a conversation with a stranger.

_____ Returning defective merchandise and requesting a refund.

_____ Expressing friendship/affection/love to others.

_____ Requesting information from your doctor when your questions haven't been answered.

_____ Giving a classroom presentation or making a report to a committee or group to which you belong.

_____ Asking for the return of a borrowed item without feeling guilty or apologizing.

_____ Saying "No" or refusing to do a favor for a friend when you really don't feel like doing it.

_____ Requesting expected service in a store or restaurant when you haven't received it

_____ Going out with a group of friends when you are the only one without a date/partner.

_____ Admitting you made a mistake.

_____ Refusing to work overtime when it interferes with your classes or study time.

_____ Expressing anger directly and openly *without* verbally or physically attacking other people or property.

_____ Giving your opinion on a problem at work when asked for input by your boss.

_____ Disagreeing with others in a group when your opinion seems to be in the minority.

_____ Refusing a date with someone without making up excuses or lies.

Look at the items you marked with a 3 or 4. Is there a pattern of situations that make you uncomfortable? Do you have difficulty confronting others? Does having to say "no" bother you? Is it being alone or in the minority? When we practice using "I" messages later in the chapter, we'll let you return to practice some responses to situations that make you uncomfortable.

■ Communication—A Two-way Process

As human beings, our lives revolve around our interpersonal relationships with others in our environment—family members, friends, co-workers, teachers, classmates, sales clerks and service personnel, supervisors, and many others with whom we interact on a daily basis. We solve problems, purchase goods and services, socialize, and work with others by using communication skills. Communication is a **two-way process** involving a "sender" and a "receiver/listener." The *sender* expresses his/her feelings, ideas, or needs (known as the message) to a *receiver or listener*, who is expected to respond in some way (feedback) The process is interactive—we act as both the sender and the receiver/listener during the course of any conversation.

The sender's message is carried both **verbally** (words) and **nonverbally** (gestures, posture, facial expressions, appearance). The receiver/listener also responds (provides feedback) both verbally and nonverbally. This interchange completes the "communication loop," although both parties may change sender/receiver roles several times during their communication exchange.

The communication process begins at birth, when the newborn's cry communicates a need for attention and results in his/her being fed, diapered, or held. As the child grows and matures, the level of communication becomes more advanced as his/her language abilities develop. As adults, we are capable of developing deep, personal relationships based primarily upon our ability to communicate with one another.

We also use our interpersonal skills to handle problems and conflicts in our daily lives. Disagreements with friends, the division of household responsibilities, requesting help on a work project, resisting pressure from peers or parents, working on a committee, returning defective merchandise to the store, or solving differences with family members/partners, roommates/apartment-mates are all examples of situations which require the use of effective communication skills to solve the problem.

Unfortunately, many people never develop strong interpersonal skills and are thus unable to communicate effectively with others. Divorce lawyers see many couples whose relationships have fallen apart primarily due to their inability to effectively communicate with one another. Parents and children sometimes experience a "communication gap" when neither understands the other. At work, an employee may become isolated from co-workers or have a negative relationship with a supervisor due to an inability to "get along" with others. In the college environment, students may fail to achieve in classes that require group interaction for academic success. They may feel uncomfortable asking an instructor to explain something they didn't understand in the lecture or reading material, thereby decreasing their potential for success in the class.

It is apparent that developing effective communication skills can improve our relationships with others—at home, in the workplace, in social or business situations, in school, and in every day interactions with the general public. Remember that the communication process involves both the sender and the receiver (listener). If we hope to become effective communicators, we must develop specific skills in BOTH parts of the communication process.

The Receiver/Listener

Just as good note taking requires effective listening skills, the effective communicator must also practice effective listening techniques. Listening is NOT the same as hearing. Hearing is a passive, involuntary process in which our brain receives a signal (sound) from the external environment. **Listening** requires that we pay attention to the message received and respond in some way. Use the following strategies to become an *active listener*, fully involved in the communication process:

1. *Listen—don't talk.* Allow the sender to communicate his/her message without interruption. Concentrate on the message being sent rather than on trying to plan your response to the message.

2. *Use attending skills.* Generate an attitude of interest in what the speaker has to say by using and maintaining eye contact. Keep facial expressions attentive and lean forward slightly to show your attention to the speaker.

3. *Consider your response* before beginning to speak. Do NOT interrupt.

4. *Provide feedback* by first summarizing what you've heard. "Check out" your understanding of what was said before making your response. Responses such as, "In other words . . ." or, "If I understand you correctly . . ." allow you to clarify your understanding and keep communication going.

5. *Respond in a non-judgmental manner.* Respond to the sender's feelings as well as to his/her words. Be willing to acknowledge the speaker's views and his/her right to have them, even though they may differ from your own.

The Sender

When in the role of sender, use the following strategies to increase your communication effectiveness.

1. *Take responsibility for your ideas/feelings.* Use "I" messages to get your point across without blaming, criticizing, or making personal attacks upon your listener. "You" messages such as, "You make me crazy!" or, "You're always late!" make the receiver/listener defensive. Such messages almost certainly will be "tuned out." Instead, use "I" message responses such as, "I worry/get annoyed when you're late, and I haven't heard from you." This simple technique can prevent misunderstanding and promote open, honest communication.

2. *Be aware of your nonverbal messages.* Is your tone angry and/or your body language threatening? Are you avoiding eye contact? Is there a difference between what you are saying and how you are saying it? An apology can express the words "I'm sorry," but an angry facial expression or rude tone of voice will make the listener doubt your sincerity. If a classmate is trying to start a conversation or is asking for help, and you are repeatedly glancing at your watch, you've sent a nonverbal message that you aren't interested in what s/he has to say.

3. *Clarify what you want to say* in your own mind before beginning to speak. You can't expect others to understand you if you are not sure what it is you want to say.

4. *Be aware of the tone and quality of your voice.* Refusing your friend's request to borrow your car in a firm, decisive tone will make it clear that you are not going to change your mind.

5. *Be sensitive to issue appropriateness and timing.* Trying to arrange a study time with a classmate who just had an accident on the way to class or insisting on going out to dinner when your partner just completed a twelve-hour shift shows a lack of awareness of the listener's needs. More importantly, such actions reveal a lack of care and concern for the person him/herself.

6. *Avoid making demands* and using statements such as "you should," or "you have to." Comments such as these tend to cause resentment or anger in the listener.

■ Barriers to Communication

Even when people want to communicate, barriers may exist which can cause a breakdown in the communication process. These barriers are usually internal "blockers" which can prevent us from either sending or receiving a clean, undistorted message. Some common communication blocks are identified below:

1. *Preoccupation/Distractedness*—If you have something on your mind, you will not be able to listen effectively. Reading or doing something else while trying to listen, thinking about what else you need to do today, or worrying about a financial problem are just a few examples of ways in which your concentration can be lowered. Being unable to give the speaker your full attention can cause misunderstandings or a total breakdown in the communication attempt.

2. *Stereotyping*—Stereotypes are fixed ideas about people as part of a *group* rather than considering each person as an individual. Ethnic and gender differences account for many stereotypes, but other differences such as political, sexual, or religious preferences may also result in stereotyping. Persons with disabilities, people whose body size falls outside the socially accepted height/weight norms, and others who exhibit some difference are all targets for stereotypes.

   Some stereotypes may seem positive, such as categorizing women as "naturally nurturing and caring of others," or thinking "all Asian-Americans are good students." These assumptions, however, are generalizations that may be totally false when applied to individuals. Making false assumptions always interferes with clear, accurate communication. Stereotypes are also a form of discrimination, and, as such, inhibit the communication process.

3. *Emotional blocks*—Anger/defensiveness/grief—when either the sender or the receiver is attempting to communicate while angry or defensive, the communication attempt will most likely not be successful. An angry sender often communicates that anger through facial expressions and body language or through tone of voice, even though the words s/he is saying are not necessarily argumentative.

   An angry or defensive listener is likely to "tune out" much of the speaker's words or react in a hostile manner during the communication attempt. Grief, whether suffered by the sender or receiver, is also likely to cause a breakdown in the communication process. A parent who has lost a child, for example, may have very negative reactions during a classroom discussion or conversation about abortion.

4. *Past experience*—All of our past experiences also play a part in "filtering" our communication efforts with others. Students with previous negative experiences speaking in front of groups may resist their advisor's attempt to register them for Speech 101, even though they know the course is required for their degree. Spouses/girlfriends/boyfriends may bring up past difficulties or problems in the relationship whenever a new disagreement arises.

These kinds of barriers can make effective communication extremely difficult, and sometimes impossible. Try to eliminate any barriers you may bring to the process. If emotional blocks are the problem, it may be necessary to wait until you or the other party has had a chance to calm down before you attempt your conversation. If distraction is the culprit, ask the other person to give you a few moments of undivided attention. Don't destroy your friendship with someone you care about just to win an argument. Be aware that bad communication can damage relationships just as good communication can enhance them.

■ Communication Styles

Previously we have stressed the importance of interpersonal communication skills. As we examine the ways in which people communicate, we can see several distinct styles in action. The following scenario illustrates the difference between the passive, aggressive, and assertive communication styles.

> *Janet is taking a psychology class this semester that requires participation in a group project. The project will count for 1/3 of her final course grade. She is the group leader, and one of the four members (Tom) has missed several meetings and has not been completing his share of the work.*

The Passive Style

If Janet takes a passive communication approach, she will hint around about how soon the project deadline is coming up but not make a direct statement. She may say something like, "Tom, March 15th is just around the corner. I sure hope we can get it together by then." This approach shows a lack of acknowledgement of Janet's own feelings (concern over the grade and annoyance with Tom) and does not clearly communicate what she wants to happen. Tom may not get the hint or may not realize why Janet is concerned. Another passive approach would be to complain to the other group members, but say nothing to Tom. Either way, a behavior change on Tom's part is not likely to take place.

Passive communication is emotionally dishonest because you're denying your own needs and feelings. The passive communicator frequently allows others to manipulate or take advantage of him/her. This may result in feelings of anger, resentment, or depression. Passive communicators may have chronic ailments such as ulcers, stress, or high blood pressure because they internalize their conflicts with others instead of bringing them out and resolving them. Passive responses have the unconscious effect of absolving one of his/her actions rather than taking responsibility for them.

The Aggressive Style

An aggressive communication approach, on the other hand, would be if Janet confronted Tom in a demanding manner with comments like, "You're ruining all of our grades! How can you be so lazy and inconsiderate, or are you just too stupid to do the assignment? If you don't get it together, I'm going to tell the professor!" This approach does not respect Tom's feelings because Janet attacked without knowing why he hasn't completed the work as scheduled. It is also unlikely that Tom will respond positively and get the work done after this kind of attack.

Aggressive responses are inappropriately directed and frequently ignore the rights and feelings of others. Those who have been hurt or angered may, in turn, avoid or take revenge against the aggressive communicator. Aggressive behavior may, therefore, get short-term results, but in the long run will hurt your relationships with others. Think about the last time you were verbally attacked by someone. Did it make you care for that person and want to please him/her? In this chapter we are defining aggressive communication as demanding, selfish, hostile, confrontational and/or combative. Do not get this form of aggressiveness confused with the secondary definition of being aggressive which means working energetically, taking the initiative, being enterprising, or doing your best in a sporting event.

The Assertive Style

The assertive approach allows Janet to express her specific needs in a way that respects her classmate. She might say, "Tom, I'm worried that our group project is due next week and you haven't completed your part. I had mine ready yesterday as we agreed. My grade in this course is very important to me, and I would appreciate it if you completed your part by Wednesday so we can meet again on Friday for a final review. Thanks very much for your help."

Comparison of Passive, Assertive, and Aggressive Communication Styles			
	Passive	**Assertive**	**Aggressive**
Statements	Hints, uses indirect messages	Makes clear, concise statements	Speaks for self *and* others
Social Behavior	Denies own needs and feelings Lets others choose Puts self down Manipulates others into feeling guilty Absolves self of responsibility for own actions	Respects others Negotiates conflicts Chooses for self Accepts strengths and weaknesses or mistakes Feels good about self	Disregards the rights *and* needs of others Chooses for self and others Blocks communication May use verbal/physical abuse
Voice	Weak Quiet Child-like	Firm Strong	Loud Angry
Body Language	Poor eye contact Moves away, distances self from others Smiles are forced Uses few gestures	Uses good eye contact Relaxed—uses gestures Face matches mood Confident appearance	Moves into others' space Overreacts
Possible Consequences of Behavior	You feel hurt, angry, anxious Others feel guilty or superior Outcome—needs not met Others may take advantage of you.	You respect yourself Others respect your honesty Trust Outcome—needs may/may not get met Mutual respect	You feel lonely, angry, anxious Others feel hurt or defensive Outcome—may get needs met *at the time* Others may avoid you or seek revenge

This approach tells Tom specifically what Janet wants (his part finished by Wednesday) without attacking him, and it gives Janet a much better chance of meeting her needs (cooperation from Tom resulting in a good grade). Assertive behavior is emotionally honest because it requires us to "own" our thoughts, feelings, and opinions. On the other hand, it respects the rights of others and generally allows our needs to be met.

The chart on the previous page provides a comparison of passive, assertive, and aggressive communication styles. Examples of statements made, behavior exhibited, voice tone and body language used, and possible consequences of each behavior are identified for each style.

■ Defining Assertive Communication

What is assertive communication, and why does this approach result in more open communication and better interpersonal relationships? Assertive communication allows us to express our feelings, needs, opinions, or preferences in a direct and honest manner without threatening, harming, "putting down," or manipulating others. This communication style does NOT guarantee that our needs/wishes will always be met, but simply ensures that we have expressed those needs in an appropriate manner. In other words, the rights of both parties in the communication exchange have been acknowledged and protected.

Developing assertive communication behavior is a learned skill. We are not born being assertive communicators, and we do not generally behave in an assertive manner in all situations. We may, for example, be able to communicate in an assertive way when we are with friends, but be less able to use these skills when communicating with family members, college instructors, co-workers, or supervisors.

Our ability to practice assertive communication may also change depending upon the specific situation We may feel comfortable in expressing positive feelings—giving and receiving compliments, initiating conversations, and expressing affection/love. On the other hand, we may feel uncomfortable when we have to request help or make requests of others, when we want to express personal opinions, or when we feel annoyance or anger with others.

To increase our assertiveness levels, we need to consciously practice using assertive communication skills. One way to better our skills is to practice using the "I" message format described earlier in the chapter. **"I" messages:**

1. Identify the sender's feeling about the conflict/problem

2. Describe in a nonjudgmental way the specific action or behavior which took place

3. Focus on the effect or consequence that the action/behavior has on you.

The factual description of the behavior, rather than an attack on the person performing the action, reduces defensiveness in the listener and avoids judgmental evaluations by the sender/speaker. Compare the following responses in terms of their probable impact on the listener.

"You" Messages vs. "I" Messages

"You always interrupt me!"	"I feel upset when I'm interrupted because it seems like my ideas aren't important to you."
"You're lazy!"	"I feel annoyed when you don't do your share of the work because I have to do it or live in a mess.
"You never let me know what your plans are!"	"I am upset when I don't know your plans because I've kept time free for you."

"You" messages attack the other person. They put all the control or ownership of the situation on him/her. They are not likely to make the other person feel sorry about their offenses, which is what you really want. Instead, that person will probably attack back with insults or complaints about you. An argument will likely ensue or escalate, and your relationship with that person will suffer.

"I" messages, on the other hand, are designed to increase your communication and get cooperation from the other person. Although they may sound contrived at first, with practice, you will find this a more honest way of communicating with the people in your life. When you use "I messages," you take ownership of your emotions and actions. An "I" message may also include a statement about what you plan to do about the problem situation. This approach cannot guarantee a behavior change by the other person, but it lets you control your response to the situation. In the above "I" messages, for example, the statements might continue with the following intents:

"The next time you interrupt me when I'm talking, I'm going to just walk away."

"From now on, I won't be cleaning up after you. I will only do the chores I previously agreed to do. If you'd like to talk about a change in how we divide up the work, please let me know."

"I'll keep Friday evenings open until Wednesday. If I haven't heard from you by then, I'll make other plans."

Learning to communicate by using "I" messages requires practice. Go back to the Pre-test and look at some of the situations that make you feel uncomfortable. See if you can construct some "I" messages to use. The homework activity gives you another opportunity to practice writing assertive communication responses.

Assertiveness "Bill of Rights"

We've learned that our ability to be assertive varies with the situation itself and with the person with whom we're talking. A review of our "rights" will demonstrate how we can become more aware of ways in which we can increase our assertive communication skills.

1. You have the right to request help, assistance, or favors from others without feeling guilty.

2. You have the right to refuse requests from others without feeling guilty.

3. You have the right to be treated fairly as a person, to make your own decisions and to have those decisions respected by others.

4. You have the right to maintain privacy about issues that you feel are private.

5. You have the right to express your personal opinions and to expect others to listen to your opinions without being judgmental or making negative comments.

6. You have the right to express justified anger with others as long as you treat them with respect and express your feelings in a non-threatening way.

7. Finally, you have the right to make mistakes. Remember that becoming more assertive is a *learned skill*, and that your comfort level in using assertive responses will increase with practice.

Responsibilities in Assertive Communication

In addition to our "rights," we also have "responsibilities" as a part of the assertive communication process. These responsibilities include:

1. Having the responsibility to accept "NO" as a response to your requests for help, assistance, or a favor. Just as you have the right to refuse requests without feeling guilty, you have the responsibility to respond in a similar way when such responses are made to you.

2. Having the responsibility to treat others fairly and to make sure that your actions do not hurt or harm others.

3. Having the responsibility to treat others in a courteous manner just as you expect courteous behavior from others.

4. Having the responsibility to respect the privacy of others.

5. Having the responsibility to respect opinions that may differ from your own and to avoid trying to force your opinions on others.

6. Having the responsibility to take "ownership" of your feelings and to avoid blaming, accusing, or putting down others.

◼ Developing and Using Assertive Communication Skills

Dealing with Negative Feelings

College life is full of stress. It is inevitable that work demands, family commitments, study requirements, and the stress of personal relationships will sometimes result in anger, criticism, and/or complaints. It is important to recognize these feelings within ourselves and to learn to express justified anger or criticism in an appropriate way. Conversely, we should also team how to accept criticism or expressions of anger from others.

How do we express anger or criticize others in an "appropriate" way? The following common workplace scenario can be used to illustrate how criticism or anger can be legitimately expressed without causing injury to the listener.

John has been assigned responsibility for preparing a market analysis for a new client, but he failed to complete the report on time. Before leaving for the night, he tells his supervisor that he's sorry, but he just didn't get the report done. The supervisor, knowing that a client could be lost, decides to stay late himself to make sure it gets done. He is very angry with John but also recognizes that he should have checked the status of the report prior to the last day. How might the supervisor express his anger/criticism at John without being unjust?

FIRST—the supervisor should use an **"I" message** to take ownership of his feelings (anger). "I am angry . . ."

SECOND—the supervisor should describe the **action** or **behavior** that produced his anger, rather than throwing accusations at John. ". . . when I assign a task to you, and you don't complete it on time. . . ."

THIRD—the supervisor should identify what **effect** John's failure to complete the work has on him. ". . . **because** we might have lost this account if I had not stayed late and completed the work."

FOURTH—the supervisor should refuse to get involved in an argument or to let the situation push him into an aggressive response—threatening, using sarcasm, yelling, etc. It is better to walk away rather than to let a situation escalate beyond your control. At the same time, the supervisor should make clear what his/her expectations will be if a similar situation should occur in the future: ". . . I'd appreciate your letting me know in advance if you're having trouble in meeting the deadline on future assignments."

The above responses allow the supervisor to express his/her anger and frustration in a constructive way. The supervisor "vents," thus avoiding a build up in resentment, which might result in negative interactions with the employee in the future. The employee can accept the criticism because he was not humiliated or "put down" by the boss, and the communication link has been kept open to promote better working relationships in the future.

Keeping the focus on the **behavior** or **action** that caused a problem rather than on the person behind the behavior/action will help you to respond in an appropriate way whenever you need to express complaints/criticism/anger toward others. Whenever you are the recipient of a complaint/criticism, you will be more accepting of requested changes in behavior if you've been treated with respect. The criticism should be focused on your behavior or action rather than on you as a person.

Requesting Help/Service/Information from Others

How easy is it for you to ask others for help? If you left your night class and found that your car wouldn't start, who would you call—a friend, a family member, or an auto club service? Asking for "favors" or assistance from others may be relatively easy or very difficult depending upon the situation in which you find yourself.

Asking for a personal loan or for a favor which requires a serious time commitment from others will generally be more difficult than calling someone to give you a ride home from your night class. Our ease or "comfort level" in asking for help or assistance from others also varies with our relationship with our communication "partner."

We may be at ease in asking for help from friends or relatives but be hesitant to do so with work supervisors or with others who have some authority or control over us. How comfortable do you feel in speaking up in class and asking your college instructor to clarify lecture material that you don't understand? If you have special plans or if you've been scheduled to work when you should be in class, how easy is it for you to ask your boss for time off? Other examples could be asking a teacher to let you have a time extension for your research paper or asking your boss to rearrange your work schedule to accommodate your exams.

If your relationship with your boss, teacher, or other authority figure is positive, then requests such as these will obviously be easier to make. As you make a request for assistance or a favor, remember that the listener has the right to refuse your request. It is then your responsibility to accept that refusal without attempting to pressure or "guilt trip" the other party into changing his/her mind. Ultimately, you may have to make some tough choices if it comes to a showdown between work and college schedules.

Another area in which assertive communications skills are helpful is when we are requesting expected service from others. Returning an item which we decided not to keep, returning a well done steak when we ordered it medium rare, or returning our car to the mechanic who failed to solve the problem are all examples of ways in which we may request satisfactory service. Would you eat the meat that was not prepared as you ordered without comment or return it to the kitchen? Would you negotiate for adjustments on car repairs or accept unsatisfactory service?

As consumers, we are entitled to receive satisfactory services. Requests for appropriate compensation or service must, however, be made in a courteous manner rather than blaming or accusing the other party. Factually describing the event or problem that occurred will bring about better results than if you attack or blame the person who provided the service. In addition, making requests for changes or accommodations must be specific—"This steak is well done, and I ordered mine medium rare. Please return this to the kitchen and bring me one which is prepared as I requested." This approach makes your service needs clear without blaming the server.

Refusing Requests and Saying "NO"

We've already learned that appropriate assertive behavior includes the right to request help, assistance, or favors from others without feeling guilty. Others have the right to refuse to grant favors or to provide the help we've requested, and we also have the right to refuse such requests and say "No" to others.

Most people are able to ask others for help without feeling too uncomfortable. On the other hand, saying "No" positively and directly is very difficult for many people. Think about these situations:

■ Your friend's car is in the shop for a week, and she needs a ride to her 8:00 a.m. class. Your first class is at 11:00, and you hate getting up any earlier than absolutely necessary.

■ A friend who has previously borrowed money and not returned it wants to borrow $20 until next week when she gets paid.

How would you handle the above situations? Would you be able to say "No" if you were really uncomfortable in granting the request? Would you feel guilty if you did refuse the request? If you granted the request when you really didn't want to, would you be resentful?

Our right to say "No" to requests from others is a very important right. By denying requests with which we are uncomfortable, we are taking responsibility for our own feelings and actions. Thus, we can avoid being manipulated into situations in which we might be taken advantage of or in which we might feel uncomfortable.

Once you have decided to refuse a request, you need to refuse in a firm voice without making excuses. Don't get involved in allowing the other party to try to persuade you into changing your mind. Accept the fact that you have the right to refuse any request that makes you feel uncomfortable or which you just don't feel like granting, and make your intentions clear to the other party.

■ Summary

This chapter introduced us to the concept of assertive communication. We learned that communication is a two-way process that involves both a sender and a receiver/listener. Each of us plays the role of both sender and receiver in any conversation.

As a sender, we must take responsibility for our own ideas and feelings, be aware of the nonverbal messages which our body is sending, be clear about what we want to say before beginning to speak, avoid making evaluative judgments or demands, speak in a firm and clear voice, and be aware of issue appropriateness and timing as we speak to others.

As a receiver/listener, we must develop the skill of active listening. This requires that we allow the sender to speak without interruption, use attending skills to show our interest in what the speaker has to say, accept the sender's right to his/her views, consider our response before speaking, provide feedback to "check out" our understanding of what was said, and respond in a non-judgmental manner.

In addition, four barriers to communication were identified: preoccupation/distractedness, stereotyping, emotional blocks, and past experiences.

Passive, aggressive, and assertive communication styles and how to distinguish among them were also covered in this chapter. While the passive communicator attempts to avoid conflict and the aggressive communicator usually prefers to "attack," the assertive communicator's goal is to stand up for his/her rights and to express his/her true feelings. The assertive communicator gets what she/he wants more often than the passive communicator, but she/he is less likely to anger or antagonize others than the aggressive communicator.

Developing and using assertive communication skills to express anger/criticism, to request help or assistance from others, and to learn how to refuse requests and say "No" were also discussed. A specific skill that we can use to assist in our communication efforts is the "I" message. This message consists of stating our feelings about the event/situation (identified by a factual description of the behavior) because of the specific effect the behavior has on us.

Just as assertive communicators have certain rights, they also have certain responsibilities. We learned that our ability to be assertive varies with the situation and with the person to whom we're talking, and that learning to be an assertive communicator requires practice. The development and use of this skill will help us negotiate the conflicts and problems we experience in life. We will also be able to build strong interpersonal relationships that will help us meet our life goals.

■ Journal Assignment

Write an essay of one or more typed pages in response to one or both of the questions listed below.

1. Describe a situation in which you felt you didn't communicate your needs/feelings/opinion in an assertive manner. BE SPECIFIC. How did you feel about your response to this situation? What might you have said to express yourself more assertively? Use the "I" message approach when giving your response.

2. How has this chapter helped you to become more aware of how you communicate with others? What specific changes in your communication techniques would you like to make? Use the results of the Assertiveness Self-Inventory when giving your response.

■ In-class Practice Assignment

Discriminating Between Passive, Assertive, and Aggressive Communication Styles

DIRECTIONS: Read the situations listed below and decide whether each of the statements given is a passive, assertive, or aggressive response. Use the following codes to indicate your choice: A—Passive, B—Assertive, and C—Aggressive.

Situation 1: You're out with your friends and are trying to make a group decision on which movie to see. One person has just mentioned a movie you don't want to see. You say:

■ You always pick movies I don't like and just think about what you want to see. You're really selfish!

■ I don't care for movies with too much violence. How about one of those showing at the Plaza Theater?

■ Well, I don't know much about that movie. If that's what everyone else wants to see, I'll go along.

Situation 2: You and two friends car-pool to classes. One friend is not very dependable and has twice failed to call on her day to drive to let you know she wasn't going to class. The first time it happened, you finally called her and managed to get to class on time, but the second time, your spouse/roommate had made plans for the car, and you ended up without a ride. You're angry at your friend's lack of responsibility and say:

■ You are totally unreliable, and I refuse to be involved with you any longer. Drive yourself from now on!

■ Gee, Susan, do you think you could be sure and call me next time if you're not going to be able to drive?

■ Susan, I have a heavy schedule this semester and can't afford to miss any classes. Since you haven't been able to keep our ride arrangement, I prefer that you drive yourself for the rest of the semester.

■ Homework Activity

Practicing Assertive Communication Responses

After reading about assertive communication skills and learning to distinguish among communication styles, it is important to be able to practice using assertive communication responses. Read over the situations below and use "I" messages to write out your assertive communication responses. Remember that becoming skilled in any area requires practice!

Use the following guidelines in writing your responses:

- ■ **TAKE OWNERSHIP OF YOUR FEELINGS** by stating: I feel/I am (specify the emotion—angry, disappointed, hurt, sorry, annoyed, scared, frustrated, concerned, etc.)

- ■ **DESCRIBE THE SITUATION OR EVENT THAT TOOK PLACE** rather than making personal comments or blaming/attacking the other person. Be specific in your description and focus on one issue at a time.

- ■ **DESCRIBE THE EFFECT OF THE BEHAVIOR**—what are the consequences of the behavior upon you?

If you are requesting a behavior change from another person, be specific about the change you want to see.

If you are going to change your own behavior based upon the response made by another person, be prepared to follow through.

Use the following format in writing your responses:

I feel/I am _____ (specify emotion) _____ when _____ (describe behavior or event) _____

because _____ (describe effect upon you.) _____

Situation 1: One student in your history class often interrupts others who are talking and has now interrupted you. You say:

I feel/I am _____ when _____

_____

because _____ .

Situation 2: You've stopped by your instructor's office during his/her scheduled office hours for the second time, and she/he hasn't been there. When you next see your instructor, you say:

I feel/I am _____ when _____

_____

because _____ .

Situation 3: You did not understand your doctor's explanation for why she/he has ordered a battery of blood tests. You say:

I feel/I am _____ when _____

_____

because _____ .

Situation 4: A friend borrowed a CD/tape from you over two weeks ago and hasn't returned it. You say:

I feel/I am _____ when _____

_____

because _____ .

Situation 5: You and your best friend commute to classes together. You've been trying to save money, but s/he continually wants to stop off at fast-food restaurants before going home. You say:

I feel/I am _____ when _____

_____

because _____ .

Situation 6: Your roommate/partner/sibling/ has not completed his/her agreed-upon household responsibilities. You say:

I feel/I am _____ when _____

_____

because _____ .

CHAPTER 14
Citizenship and Leadership

College prepares you to earn a living. Ideally, it also prepares you for life. Whether in the workplace or as a citizen, leadership will be an enormous asset. You will face challenges that you cannot meet by yourself. You will need the assistance of others. You will have to lead.

The modern workplace is highly competitive, and leadership is a highly prized skill. The people who recruit college graduates to work for their organizations are on the lookout for can-do, results-oriented candidates. As you approach graduation in a few years and start interviewing for full-time employment, you will almost surely be asked about your leadership experiences: Did you hold an office in any organization? Did you chair any committees? Tell me about a time when you served on a committee which was responsible for an important project, and the work wasn't getting done. What did you do to help the committee accomplish its mission?

For most of our history as a nation, college was an option for only an elite few. Those privileged to attend were expected to be leaders. This obligation to serve society transcended professional success. College graduates were supposed to be civic leaders as well. Society still needs citizen leaders—individuals whose commitment to the common good is expressed through thoughtful, informed action. Our nation—and the entire world—requires statesmen and women, informed voters, social activists, and philanthropists at every level.

The 21st Century will pose enormous challenges: environmental, violence, public health, and economic inequities to list but a few. Because technology has made the world small, other people's problems are now our own. If urban youth are alienated and unemployed, their rage threatens us all. If the Mexican economy flounders, we get more illegal immigrants. If the Russian economy fails, we are faced with the prospect of a new regime that may be hostile toward the USA. Local pollution becomes international acid rain. Global warming affects the climate and shoreline of all nations.

John Donne wrote that "No man is an island." Ernest Hemingway reminded us that the bell tolls for each of us. So, why should you regard it as your obligation to make your school, your city, your country, and your world a better place? Because we sink or swim together. Citizenship is for the common good. Citizenship is also in your own interest.

Let us add that this is not an ideological position. It transcends liberal and conservative perspectives. Indeed this is one of the few principles upon which all our national leaders agree even though they may be divided as to just how to address the enormous challenges facing us. Conservative thinker William F. Buckley extolled the concept of voluntary national service in his recent book, *Gratitude: Reflections On What We Owe to Our Country*. President Clinton implemented a national service corps. So, whose job is it to be a better citizen? Yours and ours.

■ Leadership

In order to make a better world, we need better leaders. Citizenship requires leadership. So does professional success. If you can lead no one, your education is incomplete. True, you probably won't be President of the United States, a Four Star General, or the CEO of a major corporation. (But then, why not?) More likely, you will be a director, a teacher, or an entrepreneur. And you will almost certainly at some point chair a committee, head a project, propose an idea to neighbors or colleagues, or parent a child. Each and every one of these roles/activities requires you to lead. How do you do it, and can you learn the skills it takes?

The Components of Leadership

We believe there are at least six characteristics that make for successful leadership:

- ■ Vision: a sense of the future and its possibilities.
- ■ Ethics and integrity: a commitment to think carefully about the public good and our own values when we act.

- Service orientation: the habit of working for others.
- Communication skills: the ability to say and write what we mean, simply and powerfully as well as the ability and commitment to listen with understanding to the concerns of others.
- Self awareness: the ongoing realization of personal strengths and weaknesses, of knowledge of interests, values, temperament, aspirations, and abilities.
- Teamwork in diverse groups: skills to accomplish common goals by working with others who bring a variety of experiences to the task.

Let's take a brief look at each.

VISION. Before you can lead someone to the promised land, you must be able to see it yourself—even if you haven't been there yet. Indeed, the greatest leaders are able to create the future by vividly imagining it. John Kennedy envisioned a man on the moon. Stephen Jobs envisioned a world in which we all use personal computers. Mary Kay envisioned a network of small business women who were also saleswomen creating a business juggernaut. Why couldn't your vision be greater still?

While we encourage you to dream big, we also know that not every business prospers, nor is every dream realized. Nor is every vision about changing the world. Sometimes it's about changing a small part of it—seeing the successful child in the troubled youth you mentor, seeing a team that wins by playing together, picturing a residence hall in which students are a community of learners.

A vision is related to the goals that together will make the vision a reality, but a vision isn't a goal or even a collection of goals. A vision is a portrait of a future you wish to create. Although it comes from your imagination, it is something you can describe vividly. It is something that you can see and so you can describe it to others. A vision can sustain you in tough times. It can compel others to work together in the service of that vision. It can unite, motivate, and provide a common direction.

Where do visions come from? How do you become visionary? We believe you can become more visionary, but like everything else, you acquire vision only by paying your dues. First, you must understand yourself. You must know YOUR values, interests, abilities, and goals. You must create YOUR mission before you can create one that others will buy into. Second, you must know the world around you. You cannot create a new world (or even a small part of it) without first understanding the present one. You need to know the field or domain in which you would lead. You will also be well served to know something of the world beyond that field. True innovation often emerges from the synthesis of disparate ideas from seemingly unrelated fields. Ignorant, uninformed people are not likely to develop very useful, much less compelling visions.

Leaders face almost constant new challenges. They must come up with new strategies and techniques for coping with a world undergoing revolutionary change. While leaders must be grounded in solid, enduring values they must keep abreast of technical, scientific, and cultural changes. How can any business compete if it uses outdated information technology? How can medicine advance apart from genetic research? How can marketing executives sell new products if they don't know the mood of the public? Ted Turner, owner of a regional television station in Atlanta, read Alvin Toffler's *Future Shock* and envisioned an innovative way of communicating the news around the world. Eventually, his vision matured into a media empire revolving around CNN. In 1998, Turner was named man of the year by *Time Magazine.*

Probably the most important characteristic you can possess is an insatiable curiosity—a burning desire to learn. This desire must translate into action—reading, experimentation, involvement, reflection. You would be short-sighted to confuse going to college with acquiring an education. You would be a fool to pass up the education that's available to you while you're here. Moreover, right now is the time to cultivate the successful habits of the continuous, life-long learner. If you are not making quantum leaps in knowledge acquisition from here on out, you will be shortchanging yourself in the vision department and therefore in the domain of leadership.

Finally, the most compelling organizational visions resonate with constituents because the constituents had a role in developing the vision. Sometimes, this occurs indirectly because a leader knows her followers so well that she is able to incorporate their values and aspirations into a vision that resonates with the rank and file of the entire membership. On other occasions, leaders explicitly ask for input from members? What shall our strategy be? What should our organization look like a year from now?

ETHICS AND INTEGRITY. Before individuals will follow someone's lead, they must believe in that person. Leaders, therefore, must be true to their words. Their walk must match their talk. James Kouzes and Barry Posner, two of the most influential scholars of leadership today, argue that a leader's credibility with constituents is the absolute "sine qua non" of leadership. Why commit yourself to a cause to which the leader claims to be invested, but who behaves otherwise?

Ethics are important because leaders exert power. That power can be expended for good or evil. A dictator, such as Adolf Hitler, had many qualities that made him a powerful leader. He was able to mobilize large numbers of people to commit to a common cause. The cause to which he enlisted the German people, however, was based upon ethnocentrism. He led his people toward ignoble ends. His leadership caused death and suffering almost beyond imagining. While membership in the human race carries with it the responsibility to behave honorably, leaders must bear an even heavier responsibility. When they pursue the common good, society is enriched. When they do not, others will suffer.

Ethics are important because without them organizations cannot flourish. Customers do not want to buy from a company they don't trust. Customers won't come back to a store that sells faulty products. Organizations perceived to be unethical may not last very long. Members of an organization will form a culture that is based upon the practices of its leadership. If managers, directors, vice-presidents, and CEOs lie to their employees and fail to keep their promises, the employees soon start lying to management. As deceit and petty politics rise, morale and productivity plummet. This is true whether the organization is a giant multinational corporation, a local high school, or a college fraternity.

There is inevitably an ethical component to leadership. Think of great leaders, and you think of honorable men and women. This doesn't mean our greatest leaders were saints, but they are remembered as having a firm moral center. It's not enough to have good ideas and charisma. You must have a coherent set of values. Your actions must match your words. If people don't know where you stand, they will not want to back you. If people doubt your word, why in the world would they want to follow you?

SERVICE ORIENTATION. We usually think of charismatic leaders by virtue of their ability to deliver stirring public speeches. While inspirational speech-making is a useful leadership skill, research conducted by Jay Conger and Rabindra Kanungo reveals that constituents will commit to a leader's cause only when the leader is perceived as serving organizational ideals rather than merely self interest. Moreover, those leaders were regarded as more charismatic when they were perceived as serving the organization and its members.

Robert Greenleaf's name is synonymous with "servant leadership." He was profoundly influenced by reading Herman Hesse's *Journey to the East* in which the leader of the journey is initially mistaken by his fellow travelers as a "mere servant." Eventually, the travelers come to realize that this humble servant is the glue that holds the group together, maintains their safety, and keeps them headed in the right direction.

You can intimidate some people into following your lead, but people follow out of fear only so long as you have some power over them. Most of us do not typically have that sort of positional power over those whom we would influence. If you want to be an effective leader of a student organization, you will be effective because you are somehow able to connect with members who volunteer their time and energy. Even in the business world, the best managers and executives know that their best staff members are, in essence, volunteers. Top employees can always get good jobs somewhere else.

The best leaders motivate people to *want* to follow them. How do you get people to want to? Communicating a compelling vision certainly helps, but others won't even consider your vision unless they're convinced you have their well-being at heart. Think about some leader whom you would gladly follow through thick or thin. Chances are, you believe this person respects you, cares about you, desires your success. The best leaders exude concern for their colleagues and constituents.

You demonstrate concern for those whom you would lead by being considerate, by understanding them, and by encouraging them. While your first image of a leader might be some take-charge person giving an inspiring speech, you must learn to listen if you want others to listen to you. Good leaders are empathic: they can see things from the other person's perspective. The very best leaders understand others deeply, grasping what events mean to their followers. Because good leaders know their followers well, they know what resources are needed in order for the followers to complete their missions. Much of a good leader's energy is devoted to preserving the well-being and morale of every member of the organization and of securing the resources to enable members to do their jobs. A true leader, then, serves the organization and its members.

Servant leaders, then, are committed to their followers and to their organization's ideals. Ideas are cheap. Let us amend that. Ideas—even good ones—without the commitment and dedication to turn them into action are cheap. Many a lofty vision has died because the person who dreamed it did not invest the blood, sweat, and tears to make that vision a reality.

Think back on when someone wanted you to work for a cause. Did the captain ask you to sacrifice for the good of the team, but (s)he never passed the ball? Didn't make you very committed to the team, did it? Did the president of your organization ask you to work Saturday morning at the fund raiser, but (s)he slept in? Maybe next time you'll sleep in too. Leaders who aren't committed to serving their organization and its members soon have no one to lead.

Commitment starts in the heart. It is feeling passionately about something. Commitment, however, always boils down to action. It is standing up for your ideas. It is working long and hard without complaining to turn ideas into reality. So, how do you get committed? How do you kindle passion in your heart for something beyond yourself? How do you become a servant leader?

If nothing fires you up, we suspect you're avoiding life rather than living it. If you are a young adult just out of high school, you probably enjoy more freedom in your life than you have ever had or ever will have. You can spend your time playing computer games, watching TV, and taking naps. Or you can immerse yourself in academic and extracurricular life. You can join a professional society, start a small business, or work for Habitat for Humanity.

Sometimes, motivation fires you up to take action, but if nothing motivates you, we urge you to act anyway. Once you start thinking, doing, and serving, enthusiasm will follow. In a recent discussion on leadership, a number of fraternity and sorority officers revealed to me (Bill) what they thought most held their organizations back. Too many of the members didn't want to get involved, didn't want to assume responsibility for improving things, didn't want to stick their necks out. They were waiting for the other members to fix things. The following story, created by the prolific Anonymous, neatly captures this problem.

"Four people named Everybody, Somebody, Anybody, and Nobody met to accomplish an important task. Everybody was sure Somebody would do it. Anybody could have done it, but Nobody did it. Somebody got angry about that, because after all, wasn't it Everybody's job? Everybody thought that Anybody could do it, but Nobody realized that Everybody wouldn't do it. It ended up that Everybody blamed Somebody when Nobody did what Anybody could have done."

COMMUNICATION SKILLS. OK, you have a great idea—an idea that is positively visionary. It's almost certain that you will need help to make your vision a reality. How do you get others to buy into your vision? Throughout this book we've emphasized the importance of communication skills. In order to lead you must communicate your vision to the people whom you want to help you. Not only must you paint a clear picture, you must persuade others to make a commitment to work with you towards the realization of your vision.

This is partly a "public speaking" issue. Can you stand up in front of a group and speak confidently and sincerely? Can you do this before a handful, a dozen, a roomful, a thousand? Speaking effectively before a group may intimidate or even terrify you, but it is a VERY useful skill. Among the activities that most executives claim to like is speaking before large groups.

This doesn't mean that you have to be a declaimer of olympian proportions in order to be a leader. Some people are more persuasive one to one. If you saw the movie, *Malcolm X*, you may recall the lengthy conversations Malcolm had with the inmate instrumental in his conversion. The other inmate rarely raised his voice. Nor were his words flowery. But he spoke from the heart and convinced Malcolm to work for a much larger cause than himself.

In the business world, would be leaders are encouraged to master the art of the "parking lot speech." Everybody is busy, and the only time you have to sell your idea to a colleague may be in the minute or so when you meet in the parking lot on the way to or from the office. For students, the analog is the "walk to class speech." You run into somebody whose support you need, and you have just minutes together on your way to History class. Can you boil down your ideas so they are clear and simple, yet still persuasive before you reach the classroom?

If you are not sure of your persuasive abilities, work to improve them. Consider some of the following ways to improve this essential skill:

- Take a class in public speaking
- Attend an assertiveness workshop
- Participate in a sales seminar or workshop
- Volunteer to give a committee's report to the group-at-large
- Join an organization such as Toastmasters
- Run for office in an organization
- Try out for a part in a play

The written word is also an important tool for those who would lead. George Washington had Thomas Paine's words disseminated to every member of his army. These words helped to create a common understanding of why the revolutionary soldiers were fighting and increased their commitment to that cause. An executive with experience in both the public and private realm recently underscored to me the importance of writing clearly. Almost every day in the workaday world, you must write reports, memos, letters, summaries, and proposals. Your success hinges partly on how well you write. Moreover, if you write poorly, you leave a tainted track record. The only knowledge of your work that the CEO possesses might be your proposal. If it's laced with grammatical errors, misspelled words, and awkward phrasing, it is unlikely that your proposal will find favor. It is even less likely that your star will rise in the organization.

Communication is, of course, a two-way street. You must receive information from others as well as dispense it. Listening with sensitivity for the deeper meanings and emotions behind the words of others is vital for leaders. As one saying goes: humans have one mouth and two ears. This is nature's way of reminding us that we should spend twice as much time listening as speaking. Listening is crucial for leaders for a variety of reasons. Through active listening, a leader can learn about the concerns of the members of an organization. By listening attentively, a leader demonstrates concern for those members and thereby motivates them. By listening, a leader can get ideas which will influence the very direction an organization takes.

SELF AWARENESS. As a leader, your biggest resource is yourself. Does it not, therefore, make sense to know as much as possible about this resource—strengths and weaknesses, beliefs and values, skills and abilities. If you understand your weakness in public speaking, you can work on improving that skill. You can also delegate that responsibility to another member of your team who will better express your organization's perspective. I once had a very bright assistant who was blind to his inability to communicate in plain English to an unsophisticated audience. On several occasions, he mistakenly assumed he had persuaded his audience to buy his ideas when the only thing he had convinced them of was that he couldn't speak simply and clearly.

We urge you to cultivate a clearer self-understanding while you are in college. If self awareness is valuable for every person who will be educated, it is crucial for those who will lead. We suggest that psychological tests are one useful means of self-exploration. In fact, it is routine for individuals entering management training and leadership development programs to be given a battery of tests. Extensive feedback is provided to the trainee by a skilled clinician. Further feedback is provided by other trainees and trainers to corroborate the testing. It is commonplace for employees in many organizations to receive 360 degree feedback—feedback from bosses, colleagues, subordinates, and even customers. The purpose of all this feedback: to promote self-awareness.

Warren Bennis, in *On Becoming a Leader*, states that to "know thyself" is to understand clearly the differences between the way you define yourself and the way others define you. Leaders create change. Since not everyone likes change, those who interact with leaders may define them quite differently than would the leaders themselves. Some will assume a woman lacks the toughness to lead. Others will assume that a person of color possesses insufficient talent for leadership. There are countless ways that constituents can dismiss someone's leadership—too new to the organization, the wrong age, from the wrong part of the world, from the wrong social class. It is the leader's firm sense of self that will enable that person to perform in the face of such resistance.

It is not just that leaders know themselves, however; it is that they constantly try to improve themselves. Leaders use their self awareness as a springboard for recreating themselves. When they discover deficiencies, they work to overcome them. They read, they train, they study successful leaders, they seek out the experiences which will enable them to grow.

TEAMWORK IN DIVERSE GROUPS. Think back for a moment on some of your experiences as a member of a sports team, a member of a committee, or one of a team charged with completing a project. It is highly likely that you can recall some team member who was domineering, self-absorbed, inattentive, unfocused, argumentative, or irresponsible. Remember how frustrated you felt, how disheartening it was to have to cope with this character. You could have won the game, but Chris let everybody down because of poor practice habits. You could have had an outstanding organization which consistently got first-rate results, but Pat held the entire organization back because of a giant ego. Perhaps the group was able to compensate for the counter-productive member, but it made it harder for everyone else.

Managers and corporate recruiters are quite aware of the importance of teamwork. Business and management writers have covered many organizational success stories that were powered by effective teams. Katzenbach and Smith, in *The Wisdom of Teams*, cite a number of examples: Motorola was able to design and manufacture the world's leading cell phone. Ford became the most profitable American automobile company through teamwork. Teams are critical to 3M's ongoing success. The Desert Storm military victory over Iraq could not have been accomplished without the extraordinary teamwork it took to move 300,000 people, 100,000 vehicles, and 7,000,000 tons of equipment, fuel, and supplies. In Harlem, the first Little League in forty years was introduced through the efforts of a group of citizens working together. Glenn Parker surveyed fifty-one companies and reports in *Team Players and Teamwork* that effective teamwork consistently resulted in greater productivity, more effective use of resources, and better problem solving.

Student organizations are no different. Fraternities and sororities, sports clubs, and professional societies are less successful without teamwork. No officer wants to take on new members who impede group progress. Therefore, you must be a team player in order to succeed in today's world. Team skills are crucial for your professional success. They are also necessary for your success as a student and as a developing leader.

In *The Breakthrough Team Player*, Andrew DuBrin lists skills and attitudes that make for effective teamwork including:

- Assuming resonsibility for problems
- Willingness to commit to team goals
- Ability to see the big picture
- Belief in consensus
- Willingness to ask tough questions
- Helping team members do their jobs better
- Lending a hand during peak workloads
- Rarely turning down a co-worker request
- Openness to new ideas
- Recognizing the interests and achievements of others
- Active listening and information sharing
- Giving helpful criticism
- Receptiveness to helpful criticism
- Being a team player even when personally inconvenienced

In other words, the more fully human you are, the better a team player you will be, and the better a leader you will be. Needless to say, this is an ongoing life-long process of learning and development.

Not only must you collaborate, you will be called upon to collaborate effectively with people who are very different from yourself. In fact, much of the power of teamwork comes from combining the contributions of diverse talents and perspectives. The increasing complexity of today's business world requires such "alchemy." Better decisions are generally made by groups of diverse people. Moreover, in a global economy, you will be expected to work with people from all over the world.

Think of an outstanding football team. It is comprised of many talented athletes pulling together for a common cause. Perhaps the star is the quarterback. However talented that quarterback, the team would not be as effective if it were comprised of eleven outstanding quarterbacks. None would have the weight or strength to play on the line. They would probably not have the speed to play tailback, receiver, or in the defensive secondary. A successful sports team requires not just talent, but different kinds of talent. The same is true of a corporation. Scientists and engineers must be able to work together with accountants, managers, marketing specialists, and advertisers.

Most of us are more comfortable working with people like ourselves. Engineers like working with engineers and writers prefer the company of other literary types. Once you enter the workforce, however, you will be expected to collaborate with people whose skills and outlooks differ from your own. If accountants called all the shots, the company might never take any risks. If engineers called all the shots, aesthetics and design might suffer. If artists ruled, the new widgit might triumph aesthetically, but sink financially.

You must also be able to work with people whose race, religion, politics, and lifestyles are unfamiliar or, at any rate, different from your own. The American workforce of the future will be diverse. If you can't work with differences, your career will suffer.

Learning to Lead

We believe that learning to lead is imperative for every college student. Yet many students are notoriously indifferent to the leadership opportunities available to them. Leadership certainly requires careful reflection. Taking classes, attending speeches, and reading books about leadership can provide students with both insight and inspiration about their own capacity to lead. We believe, however, that leadership is a "contact sport." You learn by entering the fray. If you are not a member of an organization, if you never vote, if you avoid participating in the governance of your residence hall—your commitment to learning to lead is questionable.

In order to get a college degree, you are required to take an array of courses, including core course, courses in a major, and a smattering of electives. Chances are, you are NOT required to study leadership either in the classroom or through your involvement in campus activities. You will be cheating yourself, however, and jeopardizing your career if you do not resolve to improve as a leader. Today's apathetic student is tomorrow's indifferent citizen whose very inactivity amounts to fiddling while society burns.

While we urge you to cultivate your capacity to lead, do not make the error of confusing a position or an office with true leadership. While chairing a committee, presiding over an organization, and joining campus organizations all provide excellent leadership developmental opportunities, none of these inevitably guarantees excellence. That comes from practicing the six habits we identified at the top of this chapter. Leadership then is about serving others and operating ethically. It is about envisioning how to make things better and communicating that vision effectively. Leadership is about understanding yourself and collaborating with all kinds of people. These are six skills which are as important as anything you will ever learn, and no matter how committed you are to cultivating them, you will never master them. Like most things in life that matter, learning to lead is a life-long process. It's time to get started!

◼ Leadership Self Assessment

Vision

In order to be "visionary," you must first be well-informed. Today, that means being a continuous learner, both in school and on your own. How many of the following statements can you affirm?

_____ 1. I frequently read a daily newspaper.

_____ 2. I can name four political columnists of varying ideological points of view.

_____ 3. I frequently read a weekly news magazine.

_____ 4. I often watch a national news show on television.

_____ 5. I often read a business periodical (e.g., *Wall Street Journal, Fortune, Business Week,* etc.)

_____ 6. I follow the latest developments in science and technology.

_____ 7. I've been to a play within the past year.

_____ 8. I've seen a movie with subtitles within the past year.

_____ 9. I have read an unassigned work of literature within the past year.

_____ 10. I periodically read a professional or trade journal within my field of interest.

_____ 11. I attend meetings or conferences of a professional society.

_____ 12. I've learned some new computer skills within the past year.

_____ 13. I sometimes discuss my field of interest with others to find out more about it.

_____ 14. I have attended a serious concert/performance within the past year.

_____ 15. I occasionally watch television documentaries that cover history, science or current affairs.

_____ 16. I have eaten the food of at least six different countries within the past year.

_____ 17. I have friends and acquaintances of a variety of ethnic and religious backgrounds.

_____ 18. I can readily identify most countries on a world globe.

_____ 19. I understand some basic features of most major cultural groups throughout the world.

_____ 20. I have read a serious nonfiction book which was not assigned within the past year.

_____ 21. I know the basic tenets of each of the world's major religions.

What other actions do you take to indicate your commitment to continuous learning?

What do your responses reveal about your commitment to continuous learning? What do you need to do differently in the future?

■ Ethics and Integrity

Name an individual whom you judge to be high in integrity: _____

How long have you known this individual? _____

_____

How long did it take before you recognized the person's integrity?

_____

_____

What characterizes this person that spells integrity?

_____

_____

What actions does this person take that suggest integrity?

_____

_____

Can you identify a situation in which this person's integrity was tested?

_____

_____

How did (s)he handle the test?

_____

_____

Name an individual whom you judge to lack integrity: _____

How long have you known this individual? _____

How long did it take before you recognized the person lacked integrity?

_____

_____

What characterizes this person that spells weak integrity?

_____

_____

What actions does this person take that suggest weak integrity?

_____

_____

Can you identify a situation in which this person's integrity was tested?

_____

_____

How did (s)he handle the test?

_____

_____

In what related ways are you like the person with high integrity?

_____

_____

In what related ways are you like the person with weak integrity?

_____

_____

How will you increase your personal integrity?

_____

_____

■ Service Orientation

There are many ways you can serve others: through the political process, through philanthropic work, and through your demeanor in daily interactions. Check those items below which reflect YOUR personal behavior:

_____ 1. I'm registered to vote.

_____ 2. I vote in most elections.

_____ 3. I know who my congressman is.

_____ 4. I've worked in a political campaign.

_____ 5. I know the news well enough to be an informed voter.

_____ 6. I contribute money in support of my beliefs.

_____ 7. I contribute time in support of my beliefs.

_____ 8. I stay informed of the causes I'm committed to addressing.

_____ 9. I contribute money to the cause.

_____ 10. I contribute time and energy to the cause.

_____ 11. I'm a member of a group which serves the cause.

_____ 12. I avoid activities which harm the cause.

_____ 13. I compliment people when they succeed.

_____ 14. I congratulate people when they win an award.

_____ 15. I encourage people when they have setbacks.

_____ 16. I send notes or e-mail to encourage people.

_____ 17. I keep track of people's birthdays.

_____ 18. I send birthday cards to friends and acquaintances.

_____ 19. I give gifts or stage a surprise when a colleague achieves something big.

_____ 20. I work more for organizational goals than for personal glory.

Communication

_____ 1. I can be silent when others need to speak.

_____ 2. I can hear the feelings and meanings behind the words.

_____ 3. I can ask questions that encourage self-revelation.

_____ 4. I avoid criticizing other persons.

_____ 5. I convey my interest by eye contact and body language.

_____ 6. I ask questions in class.

_____ 7. I contribute to class discussions.

_____ 8. I offer my views during meetings.

_____ 9. If I disagree strongly during a meeting, I'll say so.

_____ 10. I can effectively report a committee's discussion back to the main group.

_____ 11. I can run a meeting effectively.

_____ 12. I know Robert's Rules of Order.

_____ 13. I can address a small group effectively.

_____ 14. I can hold a large group's attention when I speak.

_____ 15. I can make a strong case for my point of view.

If you're not satisfied with your persuasive skills, here are ten antidotes.

1. Prepare a meaningful question before class. Ask it during class.

2. Prepare a thoughtful observation before class. State it when appropriate during class.

3. Think about an issue likely to come up at your next meeting. Ask for the floor, and make your point.

4. Think about a perspective with which you're likely to disagree at the next meeting. Prepare a rejoinder. State your rejoinder at the next meeting.

5. Volunteer to speak for your committee.

6. Volunteer to run a committee meeting. Prepare an agenda, and stick to it.

7. Study Robert's Rules of Order.

8. Volunteer to speak before a small group on something that's important to you. Prepare thoroughly, and practice your speech.

9. Volunteer to speak before a large group on something that's important to you. Prepare thoroughly, and practice your speech.

10. Try to convince a friend or acquaintance to join you in some cause.

Self Awareness

It is difficult to assess yourself accurately. For example, answer the following question: Are you blind to your own faults? Even if you are, your blindness prevents you from knowing it. There are some habits that suggest an openness to self-examination that are worthy of cultivating, however. How many do you practice?

_____ 1. I read any critique of my work made by a professor and reflect on it.

_____ 2. I attempt to understand my personality survey scores in this class.

_____ 3. I solicit feedback from others about my performance.

_____ 4. I am willing to take some moderate risks in order to improve as a leader.

_____ 5. When others criticize me, I honestly try to weigh the validity of their remarks.

_____ 6. I compare my own skills to those discussed in this chapter.

_____ 7. When I read other leadership literature, I use the ideas to look at myself.

_____ 8. I can honestly identify some areas in which I need to improve myself.

_____ 9. I can honestly identify some areas of personal strength.

_____ 10. I use experiential activities in class and workshops to learn about myself.

Teamwork

_____ 1. I contribute my fair share on group projects.

_____ 2. When I disagree with other team members, I say so.

_____ 3. When forming a team, I try to select diverse talents.

_____ 4. I understand the stages of group development.

_____ 5. I understand how my personality best contributes to team performance.

Putting It All Together

Most of us will never head up a major corporation or hold a major political office. Nonetheless, we can exert leadership in many ways—by holding an office in a smaller organization, by speaking up at organizational meetings, by volunteering to handle a problem. Here are some ways you could stretch your leadership wings.

1. Identify an issue about which you have strong, unexpressed feelings in an organization to which you belong. Think about what you could say or do to strengthen the organization's stand on this issue. Craft a statement which you could make at a meeting. Imagine what it would be like to make the statement. What would the response of your fellow members be? Can you think of effective ways of responding to them? Pick an ally within the organization that you could share your views with. How does (s)he respond? Does (s)he have any suggestions for improvements? Are you accurately understanding the opposing point of view? Select a time when you will raise the issue and state your position. Go for it!

2. Identify a concern or a problem which you have. Then identify a person in authority who could address your concern. Think of a *reasonable* course of action which the authority could take to improve the situation. Make *sure* that the authority has the power to effect the change you recommend, that the action is cost-effective, that it will not cause undue damage elsewhere. Craft a recommendation you could make to the authority. Practice it with an ally. Make an appointment with the authority. When you meet, explain your concern, recommend your solution, and state your willingness to help implement the solution, if that's feasible.

3. Identify an office or position you would like to hold. It should be in an organization in whose goals you believe. Declare your intention to run for office. Or, if more appropriate, speak with current officers about your desire to assume a greater leadership role. If you run for office, secure the commitment of some friends who will help you. Get organized, plan a campaign, implement it. If the more likely route to power is through appointment, discuss your desire to serve on a particular committee or as a particular office holder. Explain why you think you can do the job. Ask for feedback and a commitment to be given the opportunity to lead.

4. Read some books and articles on leadership and citizenship.

5. Attend a leadership workshop.

6. Sign up for an academic class in leadership.

INDEX